KU-607-398

Contents

E-Business or Out of Business

Oracle's Roadmap for Profiting in the New Economy

Mark J. Barrenechea

McGraw-Hill

New York   Chicago   San Francisco   Lisbon   London   Madrid   Mexico City   Milan
New Delhi   San Juan   Seoul   Singapore   Sydney   Toronto

McGraw-Hill

*A Division of The **McGraw·Hill** Companies*

1 2 3 4 5 6 7 8 9 0   AGM/AGM   0 9 8 7 6 5 4 3 2 1

ISBN 0-07-137336-5

Printed and bound by Quebecor-World Martinsburg.

McGraw-Hill books are available at special quantity discounts to use as premiums and sales promotions, or for use in corporate training programs. For more information, please write to the Director of Special Sales, Professional Publishing, McGraw-Hill, Two Penn Plaza, New York, NY 10121-2298. Or contact your local bookstore.

This book is printed on recycled, acid-free paper containing a minimum of 50% recycled, de-inked fiber.

Foreword

In June of 1999, we announced that Oracle would become an e-business and, in doing so, would save $1 billion. We would use our own application software—the Oracle E-Business Suite—to put every aspect of our business on the Internet. The success of our move into the "new economy" would be measured by the standards of the old one.

That billion dollars in annual savings translates into a ten-point improvement in our operating margin. We've already exceeded that goal. In our spring quarter, Oracle's operating margin rose nearly 14 points, to more than 41 percent. For the full year, net income (without investment gains) increased 59 percent to more than $2 billion. Sales topped $10 billion. The stock was up 400 percent, and Oracle's market capitalization approached a quarter of a trillion dollars.

But not everything went up. While revenue climbed from $8.8 billion to $10.1 billion, headcount dropped from 45,000 to 41,000. Application sales rose 61 percent in the fourth quarter, yet quarterly expenses went down. We were selling more and spending less. And we were only halfway through our e-business transformation. How much faster could sales grow? How much more could we save? We'll find out this year, when we complete the process of becoming an e-business.

But what is an e-business anyway? The answer is all about the Internet and globalization.

An e-business uses a global network—the Internet—and a global database to integrate all aspects of doing business. Every business function—marketing, sales, supply-chain, manufacturing, customer service, accounting, human resources, everything—uses the same global network and the same global database. An e-business runs on one unified computer system. Everybody is connected, and all the information is in one place.

Oracle was the first software company to move its application products to the Internet. In fact, we started this process in 1995. The Internet systems we developed were a big improvement on the old client/server systems they replaced. Having all our customers, suppliers, and employees online made Oracle more responsive and efficient. But the huge productivity gains we were looking for were somehow eluding us. All our applications were on the Internet; everyone was connected. What was the problem?

Our information was scattered across hundreds of separate databases. That was the problem! Each one of our organizations—marketing, sales, service, etc.—had its own computer system, and each system had its own database. We had hundreds of databases around the world. Our data was so fragmented that it was difficult for people to find the information they needed to do their jobs.

Separate databases also made it hard to share information between organizations. And if groups can't share information, they don't cooperate. So marketing didn't cooperate with sales. Germany didn't cooperate with France. It was lack of shared information that was limiting cooperation between groups at Oracle—not cultural differences or flawed human nature. And lack of cooperation led to duplication of effort and inefficiency. To eliminate this inefficiency, we had to make information easier to find and easier to share. But how?

The solution was quite simple. If we put all our information in one place—a global database on the Internet—then our people would know where to look to find the information they needed. Although conceptually simple, this single unified database approach required fundamental changes to our application software; it turned out to be a massive engineering effort involving thousands of computer programmers. But, when we finished the Oracle E-Business Suite, it was the first and only set of applications to work with a single global database.

We also developed several new applications, so that the E-Business Suite would be complete. It now includes every application needed to run a business—marketing, sales, supply-chain, manufacturing, customer service, accounting, human resources—everything. It works in every country and in thirty major languages. It is the first and only complete set of business applications ever built.

Before Oracle released the E-Business Suite, customers had had to acquire application software from multiple vendors. They would scrutinize competitive offerings and choose the "best" application software for each business need: say Epiphany for marketing, Siebel for sales, BroadVision for the Web store, Clarify for service, Ariba for procurement, i2 for supply chain, SAP for manufacturing and accounting, and PeopleSoft for human resources. Unfortunately, these products had not been designed or built to work together.

After all, it's not the software vendors' responsibility to make their various products work together—it's the customer's. The process is called systems integration, and it consists of connecting the different vendors' applications in the hope that they'll work like a unified system. IBM vigorously promotes this multi-vendor systems-integration approach . . . and IBM employs 130,000 consultants to help make it work.

Systems integration is enormously complex, expensive, and time-consuming, and even so it has its limits. The biggest problem is that every vendor's applications are engineered to work with the vendor's own database schema. Systems integration cannot make different vendors' applications work with a single schema. So, if you choose five software vendors, you get five separate and distinct schemas. And that's if you operate in only one country. If you operate globally, the data-fragmentation problem multiplies.

Of course, it would be much easier if all your applications were designed and built to work together. Then no systems integration would be necessary. Information would be easy to find and share, because it would be in one global database.

Choosing between a unified suite of applications and a multivendor approach is not simply a matter of software strategy— it's not just about how well your applications work together. It's about how well your organizations work together. Sharing information is key to eliminating duplication of effort, to achieving specialization and economies of scale, to standardizing business processes and implementing best practices. Sharing information among employees, distribution partners, and customers has helped Oracle save more than a billion dollars—already.

Today, everyone is excited about the prospect of saving more. But, when we first began to move our business processes to the Internet and our information into a global database, we encountered a lot of resistance. Most Oracle managers wanted to proceed cautiously. But I felt that we had to move fast or we were going to miss the biggest opportunity in the history of business. It took a while for me to understand that changing technology was the easy part of becoming an e-business. Persuading people to change the way they worked—that was the hard part.

Before you can change, you have to admit you have a problem, you have to understand your problem, and you have to communicate the problem clearly so that everyone understands why the change is needed. In our case, the problem was clear: our data was so fragmented that people couldn't find the information they needed to do their jobs. Because Oracle is the world leader in information-management technology, this was especially embarrassing. But it was also intriguing: If we were having trouble with our internal computer systems—and we're supposed to be experts—how well were other companies doing?

I talk with CEOs almost every day. Virtually none of them has access to all the information that they need, even though all of them are spending a fortune on information technology (IT). If we could solve our internal problems, we would be ideally positioned to help our customers understand and solve their problems. And solving our problems would not only help us save money, it would demonstrate that we really were experts—not just in technology, but in using technology to run a business efficiently.

Back to the problems. All of Oracle's information was in databases, of course, but there were too many of them. We had hundreds of large server computers managing hundreds of separate databases. For example, Oracle had six separate customer databases—marketing, Web store, telesales, field sales, accounting, and services. And that was just in the United States.

Around the world, we had more than 100 customer databases. France had six customer databases; so did Japan and Brazil. Virtually every country we did business in had multiple customer databases. Scattering our customer information across more than 100 separate databases might have been our worst data-fragmentation problem, but it wasn't our only one. We had 140 product and pricing databases, 70 separate human-resources databases, and 97 e-mail databases. The list went on and on.

Every country had its own data center filled with computer hardware. Every data center had its own IT staff maintaining separate systems for marketing, sales, service, etc. We were paying top dollar to maintain hundreds of separate computer systems and hundreds of separate databases around the world. The more we spent, the worse it got. Every time we added a new computer system and database, our information became more fragmented. The more databases we had, the harder it was to get information about our business.

And we had another problem. Because every organization within Oracle had its own computer system, every organization could invent its own business processes, then tailor its computer systems to automate those processes. Marketing in France invented its own marketing processes and tailored its marketing computer system to suit. Germany did the same. So did the UK, and so on. Every country invented its own business processes for marketing, sales, service—everything—and operated the way it deemed best. Everything was non-standard. The duplication of effort was appalling.

To solve our problems, the only thing we really had to do was to move our business processes to the Internet and our information to a global database. But we wanted to do more than just solve old problems—however big they were. We wanted to use the Internet to pursue new opportunities. To do that, we would have to globalize not only our computer systems but our whole business. That meant changing the way we were organized and managed. The Internet global network and global database were simply technologies that had made globalization possible.

Oracle has always been organized by geography. The business is divided into four regions: North America, Europe, Asia-Pacific, and Latin America. A senior executive with a regional headquarters staff managed each region. Each country had a general manager as well as teams of people doing marketing, sales, service, accounting, legal, etc. Every regional headquarters and every country had its own computer systems to support its activities.

These distributed computer systems, along with divided management responsibility, conspired to create our duplication-of-effort problems. For example, we had a marketing group at corporate headquarters; we had another at European headquarters; we had a marketing team in every country. Every country manager would invent the marketing strategy that he or she felt was best. So every country had different marketing policies, processes, and programs.

Take a simple matter like pricing. For a long time, I headed a group at Oracle headquarters that set global prices for our products—or so

I thought. In actuality, my pricing decisions were first reviewed by the marketing group at corporate headquarters, then by the marketing group at European headquarters, and then by every other country's marketing team. Any price could be changed several times—sometimes up, sometimes down—before it got to the customer. Some countries would decide not to sell a given product at all.

In effect, Oracle was a feudal operation run by a group of autonomous general managers. We could set global prices and other global policies at corporate headquarters, but it was difficult to monitor or enforce them. For years, our general managers had set their own prices, invented their own policies and procedures, and run their own computer systems. As long as they delivered adequate profit, we had left them alone to run their businesses.

This loose federation of independent organizations had worked reasonably well for a long time. But, in an era of increasing globalization, it was breaking down. Our customers wanted us to offer the same prices, products, and services around the world. And we wanted to eliminate duplication of effort. Instead of doing everything 150 times, we wanted to set a price once, develop a marketing program once, develop a business process once. We needed to globalize the business.

The very first organizational change we made was to globalize IT. We decided to move all the IT people from the country and regional headquarters to a new global organization. Our general managers fiercely resisted this change. They were not enthusiastic about relying on corporate headquarters for their essential automation systems. They were used to feeling self-sufficient. How could we persuade them to support our globalization program?

We changed their compensation plans. Our general managers have always been paid a bonus based on how much they increased sales and profits. If they wanted to go on running their own IT departments, they had to pay for them out of their budgets, thus lowering their profit margins and their annual bonuses. Or they could use our new global IT systems for "free"—we would not charge them for global services. Resistance weakened, but it didn't disappear. Our general managers just didn't trust a corporate headquarters organization to deliver all the computer systems that they needed to run their businesses. Global IT first had to prove itself.

It did so with its very first project—global e-mail. When Global IT started the project, Oracle had 97 client/server e-mail systems running on 97 large server computers scattered all over the world. Every country had its own e-mail system and its own team of people to manage it. Global IT replaced all 97 of the old e-mail systems with a single Internet e-mail system running exclusively on two computers in our global data center in California. (For safety, we have copies of all our data, plus standby computers, in our backup data center in Colorado.)

The global e-mail project was a stunning success. We had used the Internet and our own database technology to link everyone in the company to a unified e-mail system. The new system cost one-tenth as much as all the systems it replaced. It's faster, more reliable, and more secure than the old in-country e-mail systems. It supports all local languages. It's much easier to use. And it's "free" to the country managers.

Our global e-mail system now saves Oracle more than $30 million a year. By making it work, the new Global IT organization had proven itself, so we no longer had to push for people to transfer from the countries to Global IT. The country managers loved the idea of computer systems that simply worked—especially when they didn't have to pay for them!

As we completed the globalization of IT, we gained huge economies of scale—not only in labor, but also in purchasing computer equipment and network services. The best example of this was our newly upgraded global network. Though it cost less than our old network, the new network proved to be much faster and more reliable. And it was exactly what we needed for the next phase of our e-business transformation.

Global e-mail had been relatively quick and easy, and its benefits were immediately visible to everyone in the company. We had proved that this Internet thing actually works and saves money. But now the cheap thrills were over. The next computer systems to go global on the Internet were to be marketing and sales.

We decided to globalize not just the marketing computer systems but the marketing organization as well. We left the marketing people in their countries, but they now reported to a global marketing executive—not to country or regional managers. Today, only sales and associated consulting services still report to our country managers, and even these activities are automated and monitored by our new global computer systems. Oracle has abandoned the model of distributed general management: management specialization was part of our globalization process.

The marketing changes were no exception to the basic compact with the country managers. If the managers chose to keep their marketing people and marketing computer systems, they would pay for them. But marketing services—people and systems—provided by the global organization were "free." By this time, trust in corporate headquarters and confidence in Internet technology had grown dramatically. Soon, most of Oracle's marketing people around the world had moved voluntarily to the global marketing organization.

Benefits were immediate. Because the Internet had enabled us to implement a single worldwide marketing program, country organizations stopped designing their own. Because prices set at headquarters were instantly visible to customers all over the globe, countries stopped doing their own pricing. Costs dropped as duplication of effort was eliminated. There were no more delays; no more duplication of effort; no more bureaucracy; no more ignoring policy.

However, Global Marketing's finest accomplishments focused on using the Internet to extend the reach of our marketing programs. For example, generating leads via e-mail costs one-thousandth as much as using conventional direct mail, and we get a better response rate—even in Fiji. It works all over the world. Today, we spend less to generate more and better-qualified leads. And e-mail is environmentally more friendly than direct mail, even if you recycle paper.

Global Marketing moved our product seminars onto the Internet. Internet seminars cost about $2 per attendee, while a hotel seminar costs 100 times that. Internet seminars are better attended because they consume less time for everyone involved—prospects, customer references, and product experts alike. Now our top product experts and our top customer references meet regularly with large numbers of prospects from all over the world, and it takes only an hour out of their day. Most people don't miss traveling to hotel seminars. And nobody misses the food!

We moved all of our product demonstrations to the Internet. Now we demonstrate our software products at our Internet seminars and on our Web store. Anyone can simply click a button to see how our latest products work. If they like what they see, they can buy it or get more information with just one more click. Internet product demonstrations and our Web store delivered big productivity gains to our sales force. But that was just the beginning.

Our new Internet sales system has automated and regularized our entire sales process. When prospects come to our Web site, we collect information about them and then immediately route them to the latest information about the products and services that interest them. In a day or two, the system automatically follows up with additional information by e-mail, and optionally by regular mail. And it keeps the salesperson informed through every step of the process.

Ideally, we make the sale at our Web store without assistance from a salesperson. This minimizes Oracle's costs and conserves sales staff time. And there's no dissension, because we pay the salesperson the same commission regardless of how we sell—through the Web store, on the telephone, or face to face.

The new system enforces a uniform step-by-step process for selling our products. Because the sales process is global, it is the same all over the world. The system tracks every lead through every stage of the process, from capture to the close. This gives us a highly accurate view of sales activity, so we can forecast the quarter much more reliably than ever before.

And our sales force is becoming even more productive, because the Internet enables it to share leads with distribution partners. We are now sharing leads with a major computer manufacturer and a large consulting firm. Their sales teams collaborate with ours throughout the sales process. This makes our Internet sales system a sales-force multiplier—our one sales force has just become many.

And our many service organizations are becoming one—on the global Internet. Our customer support organization, 6,000 strong, had been divided into several geographic groups. Each group had its own computer systems and its own support database. Sound familiar? Last year, customer support submitted a plan for more hiring and lower margins. The plan was quashed. Instead, we used the Internet to improve customer service and satisfaction without hiring any additional people.

First, we moved all of our service information onto our Web site. That gave our customers immediate self-service access to most of the information they needed. Now we are moving all of our customer-support people to a single global system on the Internet. When we complete that process, later in 2000, we will be able to organize our thousands of support staff by product expertise, rather than by geography. That means that the most qualified person will work on every customer problem, no matter where in the world the problem occurs. We will track problems around the clock and around the globe. Our support people will be more productive and our customers more satisfied.

In 1999, education was our worst-performing organization. Education submitted a budget with margins targeted at a dismal 13 percent. I thought that education was capable of margins of 50 percent, but to achieve those margins, they would have to move aggressively to the Internet. They would have to market and sell classes on the Internet, register students on the Internet, and teach classes on the Internet. Education is now doing all of this, and more. In fiscal 2000 their margins hit 40 percent. When we complete our e-business transformation, they'll be at 50 percent.

I could go on and on. There are many more examples of improvement at Oracle, but virtually every one springs from the same strategy. We standardized our business processes and moved them to the Internet. We consolidated all our separate databases into a single global database. We unified all our separate computer systems by using the E-Business Suite.

Shared information enabled people to communicate more clearly and to work together more effectively as a team. Because our newly unified computer systems were interdependent, groups using those systems came to depend on one another. With interdependency came cooperation, specialization, and economies of scale. When we globalized our business, our operational inefficiencies began to melt away. It was amazing.

The introduction of Internet technology led us to globalization, which, in turn, gave rise to even more profound changes at Oracle—changes in the culture and values of the company and its management. Oracle had been a company made up of many independent business groups, managed by self-reliant generalists who valued their autonomy. It has become a company of interdependent business groups, managed by specialists who value their knowledge and excel at teamwork.

As a result, it's more fun to work at Oracle these days. There's less management conflict, because decisions are based on up-to-date, shared information. Facts, not force of personality, rule the day. The more we know, the more rational our decisions.

Mark's book takes the Oracle experience as a springboard for an overview of e-business today, and of how companies need to exploit the Internet to remain competitive or to evolve into world-beaters. There is no enterprise, great or small, that cannot transform itself and advance its interests by acclimatizing itself to the new global environment. *E-Business or Out of Business* sets forth the business practices and the resources needed to maximize the commercial value of the World Wide Web.

Larry Ellison
Founder and CEO
Oracle Corporation

Preface

Before the Internet, the level of competition in business was such that few CEOs would have wished it higher. But the advent of the Internet raises the bar another notch. Some pre-Internet companies that have survived into the Internet era now confront competitors that sprung into existence in order to exploit the new medium; other pre-Internet companies have established a Web presence to realize the savings it promises or to avoid losing business to traditional competitors and now must grapple with the challenge of reconciling the new channel with their traditional modes of business. Building an electronic business is not easy, whether it means converting an established company or constructing a new one from scratch.

Three messages relating to the Internet are crucial for business-people:

- The Internet means immense change.

- Immense change means enormous opportunity.

- Enormous opportunity means a feeding frenzy.

As with piranhas, whenever a tasty morsel appears in the waters of the Web somebody will take a chunk out of it at once and the predators late to the feast will find only pink water. E-business or out of business!

In 2000, any enterprise fully enabled for the Web meets many criteria; Web-enabled enterprises

- Conduct business globally from one or a few data centers

- Maintain a small but efficient IT staff

- Add products or services, as appropriate, overnight

- Empower their customers to serve themselves

- Command high customer loyalty
- Achieve low average cost of customer acquisition
- Process an average order for a few dollars or less
- Handle an average customer interaction for pennies
- Delight their customers, shareholders, partners, suppliers, and employees

This is not a simple prescription. In part, however, simplification is the key to filling it. Scrutinize and simplify existing business processes to avoid the inefficiencies that would result from jury-rigging them for the new, more flexible environment. Concentrate on labor-intensive business practices as the natural targets for cost cutting. For instance, are you setting up an Internet storefront? Then focus on order management and fulfillment. Look for ways to use electronic applications to replace banks of workers who traditionally have checked orders for accuracy or reviewed customer credit data; implement systems that check physical levels of documentation and then initiate printing or electronic fulfillment, when needed, instead of allowing stocks to run out. Enterprises that do not seize such opportunities will fail to realize the gains that the Internet offers, and they will not scale to business volumes that would otherwise prove well within reach.

Becoming an electronic business means transforming your company, or creating it along new lines, so that the existence of the Internet conditions every point of interaction: call centers, field professionals, business partners, retail stores. It means enabling full collaboration among the enterprise, its employees, its partners, and its customers. The successful outcome of this process we call, today, e-business; tomorrow we shall call it business.

Readers must understand that electronic commerce will continue for some time to be an area of enormous volatility. In draft, this book included a final chapter framed as a conclusion, but e-commerce has not attained even the end of the beginning, so that chapter has been redesigned as a gateway. To quote Tennyson's *Ulysses*:

> I am a part of all that I have met;
> Yet all experience is an arch wherethro'
> Gleams that untravell'd world whose margin fades
> For ever and for ever when I move.

As with life, so with the Internet.

One facet—perhaps the most volatile of all—is the prices set on Internet companies by investors. I have tried to bring share prices, market capitalizations, and other price-related information up to August 31, 2000.

Acknowledgments

Thanks to Mark Jarvis for my title, and to Brad Scott for the MoSCoW Principle. Thanks also to David Book, Holger Mueller, Max Schireson, and Carl Theobald for reviewing the book for concerns of content, style, and accuracy—and making many helpful suggestions.

For material on the Web's impact on marketing and on partner relationship management, I am indebted to Juliette Sultan.

Sincere thanks to Carolyn Balkenhol for moderating executive discussions of business issues. And plaudits to Oracle's sirens of e-business, Lisa Arthur, Karen Houston, and Judith Sim!

Special Acknowledgements

It is customary at this point to distribute credit for all the book's merits to one's coworkers, contributors, editors, and other suspects, and to reserve blame for all its defects to oneself. In this case, however, I must forego any blame, having solemnly promised David Norton the bragging rights for all shortcomings. But, *seriously*: David read and edited every page, and he pushed back vigorously against ideas not within the book's reasonable scope. His dedication is inspiring; and, though overuse has cheapened the phrase, it is true that this book would not exist but for his work.

Thanks finally to Chung-hang Mak for enduring support and encouragement.

1

Changing the World

"It's hard to make predictions—especially about the future."
ALLAN LAMPORT, MAYOR OF
TORONTO, 1952–1954

"It's hard to make predictions—especially about the future."
ROBERT STORM PETERSEN, DANISH
WRITER

"It's very difficult to make accurate predictions, especially about the future."
NIELS BOHR, NOBEL PHYSICIST

It's hard to make predictions, especially about the future.
UNKNOWN

As the great American philosopher, Yogi Berra, once said, "It is hard to make predictions, especially about the future."

1

These citations come from the Internet—where else?—and they suggest that it can be hard to make predictions even about the past. (Though, to be fair, a majority of the references found on the Internet favor Mr. Berra.)

Whoever uttered these immortal words was correct. Yet this book ventures one double-barreled prediction: that the Internet will come to be recognized (if it is not already) as a revolution in the history of technology and as the culmination of the history of business.

This book does not propose "the end of business history," to paraphrase Francis Fukuyama. But it does take the view that future advances in technology and in business will enhance and reinforce—not replace or supersede—the Internet.

Benefits of the Internet

Already the online community has witnessed the rise and decline of several technologies and business models inspired by the advent of the World Wide Web: e-mail, chat, push technology, content distribution, dot-coms, business-to-consumer, business-to-business, wireless Web access, and business exchanges. Each was hyped nearly beyond plausibility, yet had to beat an embarrassed retreat as reality reasserted its claim on our attention. Paris and Milan have never been more fashion-conscious than is the world of Internet commerce.

Yet, as each wave of enthusiasm subsides in turn, its subject is revealed as one essential strand in a complex fabric of services that will transform our lives profoundly. The essential themes of this transformation are three:

- Empowerment of the individual
- Enhancement of business efficiency
- Enhancement of market efficiency

As in a Beethoven string trio, each theme interacts with, overlaps with, and reinforces the others.

For Individuals

The Web empowers individuals to communicate with each other very rapidly and at zero marginal cost. (So seductive is this new ability that people use Web sites to post pictures of themselves and of their homes; some on the extrovert fringe have mounted webcams in their homes, inviting the world into their daily lives.) The Web gives people quick access to a vast range of information and entertainment. It enables them, as prospective consumers, to search out the most favorable business terms from among a broad range of competitive suppliers. It allows them, as customers, to place orders instantaneously, bypassing the risk that some indifferent clerk will record their orders erroneously. And it enables them, as users of products and services, to seek help rapidly when they need it, whether by referring to relevant problem and maintenance information, by logging their concerns with the suppliers, or by selecting and notifying the most promising repair services. Also, as users, they can contribute to and take advantage of rating mechanisms that will help them make purchasing decisions; at the same time, such mechanisms will discourage the production, or drive down the prices, of services and goods of inferior quality.

The Internet will bring its benefits first to citizens of more advanced countries and to those who can afford devices that give them access to the Web. For this reason, its early effect will be to further enrich the rich and to further privilege the privileged. But the Internet is spreading its filaments around the world, and the devices that connect to it are growing less and less expensive. (I have seen children in Bali writing HTML.) It is easy to imagine how the poor and the underprivileged will come to benefit by it—farmers could access weather forecasts that would help them to plan their crops, and scattered people with a common interest could organize (like the Falun Gong) to take action or to express a political opinion.

It seems probable that Web access will one day be almost universal, and that day may not be far off. The chart below shows that users of the Net are multiplying far more rapidly than did those of radio, TV, or cable. Near-universal Web access will tend to level the playing field for all human beings, and it may well do more to transfigure the lives of the poor than it can ever do for the rest of us.

For Businesses

Review the list of benefits that the Web confers on individuals and you will see that virtually all of them accrue to businesses as well. Probably businesses will have less use for entertainment; but they

NO CHICKEN AND EGG THING...
THE INTERNET IS A MASS MEDIUM

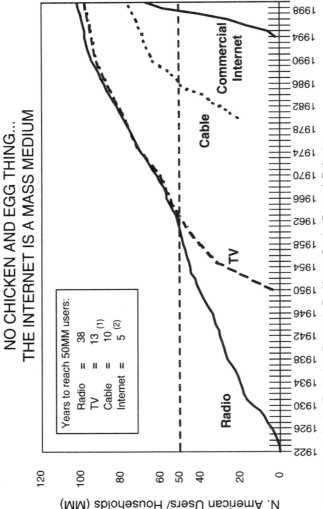

N. American Users/ Households (MM)

Years to reach 50MM users:

Radio	=	38
TV	=	13 (1)
Cable	=	10 (2)
Internet	=	5 (2)

Radio

Commercial Internet

Cable

TV

Source: Morgan Stanley Technology Research. E = Morgan Stanley Research Estimate.
Notes: (1) We use the launch of HBO in 1976 as our estimate for the beginning of cable as an entertainment/advertising medium. Though cable technology was developed in the late 1940's, its initial use was primarily for the improvement of reception in remote areas. It was not until HBO began to distribute its pay-TV movie service via satellite in 1976 that the medium became a distinct content and advertising alternative to broadcast television.
(2) Morgan Stanley Research Estimate.

MORGAN STANLEY DEAN WITTER

certainly need the abilities to communicate, to locate and exploit information, to secure favorable business terms, to place orders efficiently, and to summon rapid assistance from their suppliers. Yet the benefits for businesses range far beyond these. Confining ourselves at first to the external relationships of businesses, we note that they can use the Internet to distribute information to consumers and to other businesses, to solicit and collect feedback as to their products and services, and to interact with their business partners. Also, obviously, they can use the Net to represent themselves directly to customers and to transact business without intermediaries.

But the Internet's implications for the internal workings of businesses are just as significant. Communications and information access and dispersal are as important for the internal workings of companies as for their public relations. But the Internet's outstanding service to smaller businesses is that it suddenly extends their marketing reach around the world. For the enterprise that is already multinational, the outstanding service provided by the Internet is to enable it to consolidate its business information, allowing potentially enormous reductions in the expenses previously required to maintain multiple IT sites and staffs—and potentially enormous gains in the ability to marshal and interpret business data in order to shape the company's strategy and tactics.

An important subset of this business information consists of data that enable the company to distinguish among its customers and to personalize its relations with each of them. Such data derive from purchases made by the customer but include customer profile data—which the company can now empower its customers to maintain. This empowerment promises to correct and extend such data at the same time as it relieves the company of data-entry and data-verification expenses. At the same time, it puts more power in the hands of the customers, and holds out the prospect of marketing efforts more relevant to their personal concerns, making it less likely to waste their time.

The greatly increased scope for direct interaction between suppliers of goods and services and their customers can vastly reduce paperwork, reducing the average cost to complete business processes. Internet-mediated automation, for example, will cut the cost of processing an order by up to 90 percent. At the same time, the progressive elimination of paperwork will largely eliminate a fertile source of processing errors. And in doing so, it will benefit the customer as well as the business.

Reductions in paperwork, like cuts in IT expenses, are expressions of an ability that the Web has made newly pervasive: for companies to minimize the human labor required for any business function, to identify the minimum level, and to staff to that level. Positions will be eliminated, but our experience so far suggests that the economy will be able to redirect effectively the human resources that are released in this way.

The Internet further confers on the Web-enabled business the ability to present a single uniform face, and interface, to all its customers and stakeholders around the world, and to refine or update that presentation instantaneously and simultaneously worldwide. No longer do businesses need to distribute upgrades to multiple data centers, to undergo the tribulations and uncertainties of multiple installations, or to withdraw their systems from customer service while those installations are being carried out.

For Markets

The constituents of markets are simply the businesses and individuals that make them up. Customs and laws may deeply influence their forms and functions, but to the extent that any government takes part in a market, it does so, in the broad sense, as one more business.

But the health and efficiency of a market will not reliably coincide with the interests of any one of its participants. Indeed, when a market functions predictably to the advantage of any single participant, its doing so is a symptom of a serious commercial malady; the effect will usually be to drive away other participants, to discourage investment and innovation, and to promote social inequity.

The central function of a market is to present to a would-be buyer the lowest price at which somebody is willing to sell, and to a would-be seller the highest price at which somebody is willing to buy. The Internet promotes this function in many ways: It accommodates more potential sellers and buyers than any physical marketplace can bring together, partly by bringing participants together, virtually, from around the globe. What's more, each participant is, or can be, represented by a Web site that never sleeps, ensuring that the associated offer to buy or to sell is in effect 168 hours per week.

The near future holds for us an example of such an Internet-based marketplace: the global stock exchange. Only technicalities separate us from a system on which all major stocks can be traded at any time from any place in the world. Such stocks will no longer have opening or closing prices, though the market may observe a convention whereby a single opening/closing price is the price effective at midnight GMT. Stock XYZ will be subject to long swells of enthusiasm or disdain that run all the way around the world, some many times.

Market examples already in operation include, notably, a large number of business-to-business exchanges. Some, like eBay, are horizontal, accommodating trading in virtually anything legal. Others are vertical, like Covisint, the emerging exchange for the auto industry. But they all share a characteristic feature: each replaces point-to-point commerce with an electronic hub. In the most familiar commercial model, one buyer negotiates with one seller. With the exchange model, every participating buyer can interact with and choose among a large number of sellers, and vice versa; but all buyers and sellers are implicitly competing with others for one side of every transaction of interest to them. It is for exactly this reason that ways in which the Internet enhances a market may work to the detriment of any single market participant.

No one can foresee the full impact of the Internet on the markets that it is creating. But, to the extent that competition in these markets is fair and free, one consequence to be expected is that sellers' margins will be driven relentlessly down. Many services and products are already offered across the Web for no charge at all or at steep discounts, though consumers often have to provide personal information or to endure bombardment by ads in return.

This trend will ultimately benefit consumers—unless, of course, so many companies are actually forced out of business that the survivors can manipulate the markets to their own advantage. The risk of cartels, monopolies, and monopsonies cannot be taken lightly. Indeed, the FTC expressed concern as to the formation of Covisint, though it eventually (on Sept. 11, 2000) approved the exchange. Participants in the exchange have said that they welcome the involvement of other car manufacturers. Nevertheless, Covisint could be plausibly construed as a joint effort by Ford, GM, and DaimlerChrysler to control the biggest electronic marketplace in their industry, perhaps with the intent of charging competitors for access or of denying it to them altogether.

The FTC's concern ratifies the central role of the Internet in the future of big business. That the Net will empower and transform the businesses that use it is beyond question, but its exact impact on virtual marketplaces will depend on the level, and the intelligence, of governmental supervision.

Winners and Losers

The Internet is a momentous advance for human civilization, but like previous momentous advances, it will not work to the benefit of everybody. Even companies that respond rapidly to its challenges and opportunities may find themselves relatively disadvantaged in some cases, if only because some of their competitors have been luckier or more skillful. And people who lack access to the Net, though they may continue to lead their lives much as before, will miss out on opportunities that "Netizens" are positioned to exploit.

Among the losing businesses are hundreds, if not thousands, of Internet enterprises that have already come and gone. Among today's survivors are many more that are probably doomed in the long run, whether because they chose businesses that the Internet could not effectively enhance or because they didn't know how to take advantage of such enhancements as the Net made possible. Examples are Pets.com, PlanetRx.com, and Webvan.

Understandably, much of the illustrative material in this book is based on developments at Oracle Corporation. Oracle has been a major beneficiary of the Internet, and it owes its success to the foresight of Larry Ellison, who was in touch as early as 1994 with major implications of the *Information Superhighway*, as it was then called. Ellison hitched the fortunes of his corporation to the Internet, reconfiguring Oracle's products and business practices to take full advantage of the new medium. His insight has been a major force in driving the company's market capitalization from $8 billion in early 1994 to a recent high of $260 billion.

Forerunners

I have introduced the Internet as a milestone in the evolution of technology and in that of business. But readers will want to form their own opinions, and the next few sections help that process by placing the Internet in the contexts of the evolution of technology and of the evolution of business.

Although both of these evolutions could be treated by discussing certain historical figures and their contributions, I decline to do so for two reasons. First, that approach would make it awkward to deal with innovations that cannot be tied to a single person. Second, that approach does injustice to our understanding of both technology and business as pursuits in which any decisive achievement grows out of work done by others in earlier generations or at roughly the same time. For the most part, human progress is more fruitfully viewed as a collaborative enterprise.

Nevertheless, before I move beyond the great-man approach, I offer the reader some guidance in the form of a table of personal contributions. Darwin appears because his ideas are central to an understanding of business in general, not to one of the Internet in particular. The PC and the Internet router are both absent, because each, as we now know it, is the composite brainchild of so many parents. As for the Internet developments shown, I advise some caution: I gathered the bulk of the information concerning the developments from the Internet, which, like many other autobiographers, is unreliable, often vague, and given to self-dramatization. Notes appear following the table.

Technology

A broad survey of the development of technology would have to cover many subjects. No two readers would agree exactly as to the importance of any one of those subjects—and no one reader would ascribe exactly the same importance to any two of those subjects. Which has been most important for humanity: the domestication of the horse, the breeding by which it became big enough for armored men to ride, the invention of the stirrup that made it an effective military instrument, or its replacement by the one-horsepower steam engine? Broadly speaking, these are all technological developments, with huge implications for work, transportation, communication, warfare, and automation. But which development was the most significant could keep the philosophers splitting hairs for decades.

Personal Contributions Leading toward the Current Internet

Date	Person	Contribution(s)	Note
1448	Johannes Gutenberg	Invents movable-type printing press	
c. 1500	Leonardo da Vinci	Designs analog mechanical calculator	
c. 1600	William Gilbert	Conducts early researches into electricity and magnetism	
1623	Wilhelm Schickard	Invents analog calculator that adds and subtracts six-digit numbers	
1674	Gottfried Leibniz	Invents "stepped reckoner": first analog calculator to multiply as well as add and subtract	
c. 1779	Charles-Augustin de Coulomb	Pioneers electrical theory	
c. 1800	Alessandro Volta	Develops first electric battery	
1801	Joseph-Marie Jacquard	Introduces punched cards for control of machinery (weaving looms)	
1808	Pellegrino Turri	Invents typewriter	
1820	Hans Christian Oersted	Discovers relationship between electricity and magnetism	
1822	Charles Babbage	Develops concept of *Difference Engine*, a *digital* mechanical calculator, to be driven by steam, like a locomotive, and about the same size	
1827	Georg Simon Ohm	Discovers basic law of electric current flow	
c. 1827	André-Marie Ampère	Develops electromagnetic theory	
1831	Michael Faraday and Joseph Henry	Each independently discovers electromagnetic induction	
1833	Charles Babbage	Develops concept of *Analytical Engine*, a programmable calculator	
1835	Samuel F. B. Morse	Invents telegraph	
1842	Ada Byron, Lady Lovelace	Works with Babbage; proposes first computer program, introduces concepts of looping and conditional branching	
c. 1854	George Boole	Develops Boolean algebra, which is essential to computer logic	
c. 1855	Wilhelm Weber	Conducts fundamental work in electrodynamics	
1859	Charles Darwin	Publishes *On the Origin of Species by Means of Natural Selection*	
1865	James Clerk Maxwell	Develops theory of electromagnetic waves	
1876	Alexander Graham Bell	Patents telephone	
1884	Herman Hollerith	Patents punched-card tabulator	

10

1886	Heinrich Rudolf Hertz	Experimentally confirms electromagnetic waves
1914	Theodore Vail	As president of AT&T, oversees building of first coast-to-coast telephone system
1927	Vannevar Bush	Invents electricity-driven analog "Differential Analyser"; the second version (1935) weighed 100 tons
1929	Bell Labs	Develops coaxial cable
1935-1950	Alan Turing	Develops concepts of programmable computers and of artificial intelligence
1936-1941	Konrad Zuse	Develops first binary digital computer, first fully functional program-controlled electromechanical digital computer
1939	George Stibitz	Invents first modern digital computer
1943	Tommy Flowers	Leads team in North London that builds Colossus, the first programmable electronic computer, to break Nazi codes
1943	Howard Aiken	Constructs first widely known electromagnetic programmable calculator
1945	Vannevar Bush	Introduces concept of hypertext
1945	John von Neumann	Describes computer with memory-stored program
1945	J. Presper Eckert and Gene Mauchly	Coinventors of ENIAC (Electronic Numerical Integrator And Calculator), first nonsecret programmable electronic computer; covers 1,000 square feet; consumes 160 kilowatts
1947	John Bardeen and Walter Brattain	Coinventors of the first (point-contact) transistor
1948	William Shockley	Invents improved "sandwich" transistor
1948	Norbert Wiener	Publishes *Cybernetics*, which discusses communication and control in machines and nature
1954	J. H. Felker	Builds TRADIC, the first *transistorized digital* computer, at Bell Labs; measures 3 cubic feet; consumes less than 100 watts
1955	William Shockley	Founds Shockley Semiconductor, giving birth to Silicon Valley (1971, the phrase "Silicon Valley" first appears in print)
1958	Jack Kilby	Invents the integrated circuit
1959	Bob Noyce	Invents improved integrated circuit
1960	Benjamin Curley	Develops first minicomputer, the PDP-1, at Digital Equipment Corporation

Personal Contributions Leading toward the Current Internet

Date	Person	Contribution(s)	Note
1962	J. C. R. Licklider	As first head of ARPA computer research program, introduces *Galactic Network* concept	
1962	Leonard Kleinrock	Develops queuing theory in communications networks	2
1964	Paul Baran	Publishes *On Distributed Communications*, packet-switching theory (developed at RAND Corporation)	3
1963/1965	Doug Engelbart	Invents the mouse, windowing—and many other user-interface-related concepts—at Stanford Research Institute	
1968	Bob Noyce and Gordon Moore	Cofounders of Intel (*Integrated Electronics*) Corporation	
1968	Bob Taylor	As director of Information Processing Techniques Office at NASA, develops with Larry Roberts the idea of a network to link existing computers—motive, to save money on mainframes	
1969	Leonard Kleinrock	Presides at birth (at UCLA) of ARPANet	
1970	E. F. Codd	Introduces concept of relational database	
1970	Robert Maurer, Donald Keck, and Peter Schultz	Coinventors, at Corning, of optical fiber	
1971	Ted Hoff	Invents microprocessor (at Intel)	
1972	Bob Metcalfe	Invents Ethernet	
1973/74	Robert E. Kahn and Vinton Cerf	Codevelopers of Transmission Control Protocol/Internet Protocol (TCP/IP)	2 4
1989/1991	Tim Berners-Lee	Develops HTML, HTTP, World Wide Web, first WWW browser, first WWW server, and concept of URL; browser rendered commercial (as Mosaic) by Marc Andreessen and Eric Bina at NCSA	
1990/1991	James Gosling, Patrick Naughton, and Mike Sheridan	Begin work at Sun Microsystems leading to Java; helped by Bill Joy	5

Note	Item	URL
1	Bush's article introducing the concept of hypertext	http://www.w3.org/History/1945/vbush/
2	A (presumably authoritative) history of the Internet, written by Kahn, Kleinrock, and others	http://www.isoc.org/internet-history/brief.html
3	A useful guide to publications by Baran and others	http://www.rand.org/publications/RM/baran.list.html
4	Cerf's own (also presumably authoritative) account of Internet history	http://www.fnet.fr/history/VintonCerf.html
5	"The Java Saga," from *Wired*, Dec. 1995	http://www.wired.com/wired/archive/3.12/java.saga.htm

Even the branches of technology that seem to have withered cannot be dismissed without ambivalence, for the evidence conveys strongly that they occupied the outstanding minds of earlier ages. For example, Roger Bacon searched in vain for the philosophers' stone, and later ages dismissed alchemy as a wild goose chase after that logical impossibility, the transmutation of elements. Now we take transmutation for granted, and we understand it by a theory that can be traced back to Democritus in the fifth century B.C.E.

Ptolemy's second-century theory of the celestial spheres led to fantastic elaborations of cycles and epicycles, all in increasingly metaphysical attempts to save the perfection of the heavens. However, by the time of Johann Kepler, the work of Copernicus and Tycho Brahe had shattered the Ptolemaic theory. When Kepler set out to make sense of Tycho's data, he argued instead for perfection of another kind—by which the orbits of the planets would be related, through the five Platonic solids, in another set of ever-widening spheres. Kepler struggled desperately to fit the data to his own theory. His intellectual heroism consists in the fact that when he could not reconcile the two, he gave his allegiance to the data, discarded the theory, and worked out his three great laws of planetary motion.

Those laws proved accurate; but they could not be explained until Newton developed the calculus. Having done so, Newton then turned his attention to alchemy, which he worked at for many years. He viewed astronomy as one science and alchemy as another, lacking the scope for scientific hindsight that he, perhaps more than any other, left to posterity.

What are the lessons of these stories? That a theory may be interred as hopelessly obsolete and yet rise from the grave to command scientific consensus. That the truth may prevail in spite—and perhaps because—of a theory that proves to be logically irrelevant. That even the greatest minds are captive to their times and cannot reliably distinguish the "important" from the "trivial".

Unimportant Technology

Consequently, when we speak of unimportant technology we must be prepared to eat our words. But it is no challenge, in recalling some of the boldest headlines of the past, to find examples in which the promise of the technology, once seemingly a river of unlimited potential, has run dry in the sands of trivial applications. In theory, a technology might be justified by applications—military, for instance—that have nothing to do with its commercial value. In fact, the great technological disappointments of history have flopped because they have proven hopelessly uncommercial.

Lighter-than-Air Craft

One example is provided by lighter-than-air craft, which got off the ground—to enormous enthusiasm—with the Montgolfier brothers in eighteenth-century Paris. The hot air that they used was soon replaced by hydrogen, despite its dangerous flammability; and the discovery of helium in 1868 meant nothing for lighter-than-air craft until about 1920, when a method for extracting it in quantity from natural gas was finally developed.

Meanwhile, Count von Zeppelin had developed at Friedrichshafen the enormous dirigibles that bore his name. They were used to bomb London during the First World War. But the age of hydrogen-borne airships ended forever when the *Hindenburg* went down in a sheet of flame on May 6, 1937.

By then the U.S. Navy had for many years funded helium-borne airships, built mostly by the Goodyear-Zeppelin Corporation. These, too, were gradually shown to be impractical by fatal accidents resulting from storms. The Navy's last great airship, the *Macon*, was knocked out of the sky by high winds in 1935; it was never to fly again, and the Navy's use of airships gradually dwindled to a full stop in 1962.

Balloons remain a popular form of recreation; the *Goodyear Blimp* and many others continue their careers as advertising vehicles; and the armed forces periodically reconsider the attractions of lighter-than-air craft for aerial surveillance. They retain their prodigious power of excitement, and they may yet—some day—demonstrate proportional value for commercial transport.[1] In the meantime, they remain one of the great disappointments in the history of technology.

The Apollo Program

The moon landing of 1969 provides another example. What symbolism! What exhilaration! But the Apollo Program died a slow and disregarded death, and the last three decades have shown that funding for manned space flight beyond earth orbit cannot be justified by any commercial or military potential that we can detect. Proposals to spend hundreds of billions—perhaps trillions—of dollars to fly men to Mars have aroused little enthusiasm except among experts paid to divert themselves with such pipe dreams. The costs of an orbiting space station, of the space shuttles, of an aerospace plane—even of the Concorde—probably can never be justified except as providing overpaid employment for crowds of theorists, soldiers, and engineers that might otherwise address their attention to more sinister schemes.

Technology that Changed the World—But Not Business

The great disappointments in the history of technology have been commercial failures. But the converse is not true. Three of the greatest technological innovations of early man had little or no direct connection with business.

The first of these was fire. Mastery of fire provided early man with three essentials: heat, light, and protection. Without it, the Ice Ages would have wiped out humanity in what we now call the temperate zones. Fire also was, and continues to be, important in agriculture. Yet it is not a thing to be sold or traded, even in its manifestation as the archetypal medium for converting fuel into energy.

The second innovation—or perhaps the first, chronologically—was tools. These could be sold or traded, but that was not their primary purpose, which was to lighten the burden of the everyday tasks that confronted early humanity, and to make it easier to kill human beings and other animals.

The third innovation was agriculture. This made possible explosive increases of settled populations and led directly to large-scale social organizations. It also figured in the earliest development of surveying and geometry. Both plants and animals were domesticated and bred, with consequences that transformed hunting and warfare. However, agriculture had no obvious bearing on business except that it vastly increased the store of things of value that could be sold or traded.

Technology that Changed the World—AND Business

In contrast to the innovations cited in the previous section, all of the greatest technological developments of the last 10,000 years have proven, over the ages, to be far more important for business than anybody could once have imagined. These innovations include:

- *Metallurgy*, which began about 7000 B.C.E. In the Age of Bronze (starting about 3000 B.C.E.) metallurgy built up the great hierarchical empires of the ancient world—the Hittites, Mycenae, and the Egyptian New Kingdom. When these collapsed, about 1200 B.C.E., the advent of the Iron Age may have been a contributory cause. More recently, iron and steel made possible the swords and guns with which Europeans made themselves the masters of the world.

- *Money*—which, if we define it as a medium of exchange consisting of fungible units, probably dates to about 5000 B.C.E.—figures preeminently as an instrument of business, but has become almost indispensable for innovation itself.

- The *wheel*, which originated about 3000 B.C.E. It transformed (most obviously) transportation and business, but also had tremendous implications for warfare and presumably figured as the ancestor of the gear, thus underpinning vast breadths of technology.

- *Writing*, which made it possible to record knowledge permanently. Though it is intrinsically a technology of communication, it has served from the earliest days as an instrument of business—for laundry lists, tax bills, grain tallies, and so on.

- *Timekeeping* began with the development of calendars, which were crucial to the plans of farmers. Early attempts to subdivide the day used sundials and clepsydras (water clocks), but the first serious mechanical clocks appeared only in the early days of the Renaissance, which they helped to invigorate. By dividing the day into equal units, the clock imposed a new conceptual framework, advancing social coordination and improving efficiency.

- *The Industrial Revolution*, a concept so broad that we scarcely know where to draw its boundaries. But its essence consists in the replacement by machines of human and other animals as sources of energy, in the resulting restructuring of the conditions of labor, and in the rapid spread of urbanization. (So defined, the Industrial Revolution continues into the twenty-first century, and it will never conclude until machine labor has replaced the manual labor on which billions of people still survive.)

- *Computers,* which are progressively relieving us of mental drudgery as the machines of the Industrial Revolution have relieved (many of) us of physical drudgery.

This list could be extended forever, and every reader may note the absence of some favorite milestone: electricity, the telephone, television, nuclear power, the laser. Note, however, that all the items on this list share one property: *enormous commercial importance.*

Business

Business must be distinguished from other conventional methods of redistributing goods: war, theft, taxation, and charity. Charity (if we define it to include transfers of goods from parents to their young) is, of course, well known among other animal species, and is clearly an essential behavior of humanity. Many would make the same two claims for war and theft.

Business is not an essential human activity. Humanity did not begin to barter on any significant scale until about 10,000 years ago, when it inched across some low, but crucial, threshold of sophistication.[2]

The next portion of this chapter briefly presents the development of business, relating it as appropriate to computers and the Internet. The sections are arranged in rough chronological order, but each major development, once begun, has persisted throughout history in one form or another; as successive developments become important they gradually intermesh, and their effects gather cumulative force.

Barter

Barter presumably began as exchanges within a family or a tribe, but the next logical step was exchanges over distances. Distance has always been an impediment to barter; but it is also a main reason *for* barter, because the goods that are plentiful in your locality are often worth less to you than those that are rare where you are but plentiful somewhere else.

By 8000 B.C.E., materials including flint and obsidian were being traded in Europe over distances as great as 200 km. Standard weights and measures originated—is this a coincidence?—at about the same time. The European trade in amber[3] began about 3500 B.C.E. Because amber was relatively common in northern Europe, its

inhabitants were willing to trade it for the materials and technology of the Bronze Age, which had begun earlier in southern Europe. (Articles made with Baltic amber were found in the tomb of Tutankhamen, who died in 1327 B.C.E.)

Such distances were covered at first on foot. Long journeys might last months or years, and many such journeys were never completed, because they were not safe. Caches of amber have been discovered along the amber trade routes, suggesting that their carriers were often alarmed, and sometimes killed, by bandits.

By comparison with the exchange of goods for money, barter has advantages and disadvantages, which are summarized below in the section "Money." The Internet can facilitate barter, but not very much.

Metallurgy

Starting about 7000 B.C.E., metallurgy (like agriculture) increased the store of valuable things that could be traded. Its importance for warfare was demonstrated dramatically by the Spanish conquests of the Aztec and Inca empires in the New World in the sixteenth century. But its impact on commerce has been much more gradual, with innovations of various kinds—for transport, for agriculture, for coinage, for construction—spread out over thousands of years.

Metallurgy was, of course, essential to the construction of the first large-scale telegraph and telephone networks, the forebears of the Internet. The copper wire used for those networks is gradually being replaced by optical fiber.

Money

Money, in the broadest sense, is just a medium of exchange. However, it must have certain attributes: it must be common enough to serve as a convenient medium, yet uncommon enough to retain recognized value; that value must persist over time (unlike the value of a banana); and its usefulness is related to how widely that value is recognized. Also, for flexibility, the smallest monetary unit in circulation must be either divisible or of small worth.

Among the earliest things to be used as money were cowrie shells; one species is even named the money cowrie (or *Cyprea moneta*, after the Roman goddess of wealth). Cowries have been found in tombs of predynastic Egypt (c. 5000 B.C.E.) and of Shang-Dynasty China (c. 1500 B.C.E.). Small, ornamental, and hard to counterfeit, they were used as currency throughout the Old World and were known, valued, and traded in the New World. (Money cowries are available through the Internet for $9.50 a gallon.)

Other things used as currency have left fossil traces in the language: salt in the word *salary* (from Latin *sal*) and cattle in the words *peculiar* and *pecuniary* (from Latin *pecus*). Coins were introduced about 700 B.C.E., in western Anatolia; paper currency made its debut in China about 900 A.D. The origins of checking are unclear, but it first became important in early sixteenth-century Holland.

Money promotes trade by serving as a fairly stable standard of reference and by allowing the values of guns and of butter to be measured on a single scale. For people who had no goods that a trader might be interested in, the possession of money meant that dealing with the trader was still an option. Money was usually very compact; small volumes of money could be transported in one direction to be exchanged for large volumes of goods. Historically, money has usually been ornamental and could be hoarded or worn as personal decoration when it was not needed—or until it was needed—for trade.

Money thus plays out its three classical roles as a unit of account, as a medium of exchange, and as a store of wealth. Especially in the first two of these roles, money is indispensable to the efficient operation of economies and governments. Russia's partial reversion to a barter economy is simultaneously a result of the degradation of the ruble and a contributory cause of loss of faith in the central government, which only with great difficulty can tax barter transactions. This difficulty cuts the flow of cash to the government, which then defaults on its cash obligations.[4]

From our point of view, in the context provided by the Internet, the crucial fact is that money consists of fungible units. For this reason, it is instantaneously and automatically transferable via the Web, eliminating all work required to effect one side of any Web transaction. In some cases, where money is transferred to pay for an item that is downloadable, or where one currency is used to buy another, all transport costs associated with the transaction effectively disappear.

Progress in Transport

Donkeys were domesticated about 5000 B.C.E., and after some time began to be put to work in caravans. About 3000 B.C.E., oxen and horses began to be used to draw sledges; these soon acquired wheels, which were invented near the Black Sea at about the same time. Llamas were domesticated 500 to 1,000 years later in South America, and camels about 1500 B.C.E. in the Middle East. Use of the camel allowed the traversal of the Silk Road starting about 200 B.C.E. Beasts of burden made possible new trading routes and heavier loads; they probably did little either to reduce the time needed to traverse those routes or to make them safer. Nevertheless, they could be regarded as saving time, because they allowed the transportation, during one transit, of goods that would otherwise have required multiple journeys.

The importance of wheeled vehicles grew with the passage of the centuries. Their value was much enhanced by the Roman construction, over five centuries beginning about 200 B.C.E., of a network of roughly 50,000 miles of roads stretching from Mesopotamia to northern Britain. During and after the Roman Empire, these roads were crucial for communication as well as for transport, and large portions continue in use today. The Roman roads were, in effect, the first internet.

Meanwhile, over millennia, shipping evolved from tree trunks on which a few men could stay afloat to sailing ships, the sail having been invented by the Egyptians around 3,500 B.C.E. By Roman times, sailing ships could carry cargoes typically of 100 to 200 tons and in some cases substantially more; for this reason, shipping—in the Mediterranean, the Middle East, and the China Sea—came to dominate long-distance transport. But the voyages of sailing ships, dependent on the winds, were notoriously long and unpredictable, while oared commercial galleys were more reliable but required slave labor. The bandits that beset trade routes on land were replaced by pirates at sea, and to this danger were added the hazards of storms. Tens of thousands of commercial vessels have gone to the bottom of the Mediterranean.

Writing

The next great business revolution was the development of writing, which took place in the Middle East, but perhaps in as many as three places independently: Harappa, in what is now Pakistan; Sumer, in what is now Iraq; and Egypt. Cuneiform and hieroglyphs incised on clay tablets made possible the first databases, and the earliest records deciphered (carbon-dated to about 3250 B.C.E.) have to do with

Egyptian tax payments made in oil and linen. Other early tablets record alphabets and syllabaries—instructions in how to write, or what we would now call database maintenance.

The permanent records made possible by writing allowed the transmission across distance of complex messages; checks on the probity of traders entrusted with known amounts of goods (that is, checks that nothing went astray in transmission); and comparisons of current prices of commodities with prices from earlier years, whether those commodities were measured in units or by weight. Permanent records made possible crude credit systems, whereby (for instance) taxes paid during a fat year could compensate for taxes forgiven during a lean year; and crude systems of social security, by which issues of grain to starving peasants could be made balanced and equitable (as implied by the story of Joseph in *Genesis* 41). Each of these applications is explicitly implemented in modern computer systems, allowing the application to be handled with greater precision and reliability.

Writing also provided the basis for complex calculations; but its impact on the affairs of humankind is incalculable.

Numerical Advances

Complex calculations required not only a system of notation but the invention of zero as a placeholder, something for which there was no equivalent in Roman numerals. In fact, zero seems to have been invented several times, but the time that counts for Western civilization was during the fifth century A.D., in India. From India the concept passed to Cambodia, then to China, and then to Arabia, where the Arabic word (as we transliterate it) was *sifr*; from this derive our words *cipher* and *zero*.

Zero was ushered into Europe in 1202 by Leonardo Fibonacci of Pisa (c. 1170 to c. 1250), the most renowned mathematician of his time. Fibonacci had found the zero in the works of the eighth-century Persian scholar al-Khwarizmi, whose name is the source of our word *algorithm*. Zero was represented by the Arabs as a dot; when European scribes asked about this they were told that it meant "empty" and were instructed to draw an empty hole, thus: 0.

Space does not allow me to show that zero is crucial to modern mathematics. (I remind skeptical readers that 0 and 1 are the *only* numerals required for the work of present-day computers, and I invite them to try using Roman numerals to multiply 1999 by 2000.) Instead, I move on to the next essential advance in the business of numbers: double-entry bookkeeping.

This practice, the invention of which is credited to Benedetto Cotrugli of Dubrovnik, was popularized by Luca Pacioli of fifteenth-century Venice, and it does honor to Venice as the Renaissance center of world trade. For the importance of double-entry accounting, and for the way it depends on and draws together many of the developments I have treated above, I refer the reader to a fascinating history of accounting, with illustrations, published on the Internet by the Association of Chartered Accountants in the United States at this URL: http://www.acaus.org/history/hs_anc.html.

The principal contribution to business of double-entry accounting was to make accounting more reliable and thus to promote trust and credit. Eventually, credit led to credit cards, now a major factor in business-to-consumer commerce over the Web.

Printing

Johannes Gutenberg is credited with the invention of printing (about 1450 A.D.) in the West, but his work brought together several technologies that were first developed in China: the printing press, movable type, ink, and paper. (Paper is named for the Egyptian papyrus, but the Chinese worked out the first efficient process for paper manufacture.) These were never effectively united in the Orient, probably because the number of ideographs for which type blocks would have been needed was overwhelming.

If the direct influences of printing on the Internet are very limited—one can cite at least the development of a vast range of fonts—this is largely because the indirect influences are innumerable.[5] Historians generally view printing as urgently promoting the Renaissance, the Reformation, and the Scientific Revolution, in large part by enabling the progressive accumulation of knowledge. The Renaissance, as we define it, began before Gutenberg; but, as a rebirth of humanism, it was scarcely distinguishable from earlier abortive revivals "until the printing press 'fixed' it and helped spread it north of the Alps."[6]

Printing is the one technological development that most parallels the Internet. Both enable new modes of communication: we can say, somewhat loosely, that printing enabled one-to-many communication and that the Internet enables many-to-many communication.

Each technology, writes James Dewar,[5] "enables important changes in how we preserve, update and disseminate knowledge; how we retrieve knowledge; the ownership of knowledge; and how we acquire knowledge." It may be disproportionate to expect the Internet to bring about social changes as great as those that sprang from printing, although Dewar stresses the importance and general desirability of the unintended consequences of printing, and argues on this basis against regulation of the Internet. If the impact of the Internet proves less revolutionary, that is likely to be because we (at least in the countries of the European tradition) are no longer emerging from the Dark Ages.

The Industrial Revolution

The Industrial Revolution began about 1760, with the mechanization of weaving. James Watt invented his steam engine soon thereafter, in 1769. Together, the two inventions led to the rapid rise of the factory system. Broadly construed, the Industrial Revolution continues today, and it embraces a vast range of developments that are crucial forebears of modern business, some of them related directly to the Internet. Notable among these developments are:

- Electricity, without which we might be relying today on steam-driven computers
- Interchangeable parts, the assembly line, and mass production
- Railroads, automobiles, and airplanes, which have greatly advanced the delivery of physical goods
- The telegraph and telephone, and the international networks to which they gave rise; these reduced, effectively to zero, the time required to communicate over long distances, or—in terms specific to business—the time required to complete one side of a transaction

Our view of the Industrial Revolution as an ongoing phenomenon means that it embraces not only the Information Age, as James Dewar defines it in his article cited in footnote 5, but the Internet Age as well. How developments of these respective ages are displacing manual labor is exemplified, for the Information Age, by the spreadsheet, and, for the Internet Age, by the fact that you no longer need to visit the grocery store. These two ages are not synonymous,

but the Internet *is* putting an exclamation mark after the growing accessibility of information.

Computers

As we have seen, work leading to modern computers dates back to Leonardo da Vinci, if not beyond. In practical terms, however, the era of computers begins with World War II. The Industrial Revolution finds its logical successor in the Computer Era: the Industrial Revolution saw the gradual replacement, for physical labor, of human beings (and other animals) by machines; in the Computer Era, machines are gradually replacing human beings for mental labor as well. Computers may be thought of also as extending the Industrial Revolution, because we use them to improve the precision and reliability of our control over other machines.

The impact of computers extends far beyond the Internet, which is "only" one major development that, in their first 60 years, computers have made possible. Aspects of the computer revolution that empower the Internet are so many and so extensive that we cannot do justice to them here. But it may help to point out a few of those aspects.

- Computer programming, enabling machines to perform automatically, enables Web sites to represent their sponsors 24 hours a day.

- The speed of computers enables the Internet to handle fantastic volumes of messages.

- Codes developed for computers made it possible to use bits to represent texts, pictures, and sounds, without which Web sites would scarcely command our attention.

- The same codes also enabled bits to represent money; this led to electronic funds transfer (EFT), which is indispensable to commerce on the Internet.

- The calculating power of computers makes possible public-key cryptography, which secures consumer privacy on the Web by its use of integers too large to be factored by normal processes, whether human *or* machine. (DES [the Data Encryption Standard] uses keys ranging up to 2^{56}, or 72,057,594,037,927,936; by using DES, computers can easily encipher and—given the key—decipher messages. But to decipher a DES-encoded message without the key, by brute force, the computer may have to test each of the 72 quadrillion possible keys.)

The Internet

Since the advent of the computer, there has been only one development—the Internet—that augurs such revolutionary changes for business. In conceptual terms, the development of the Internet is a climactic step in the simplification and acceleration of communications. The Internet changes everything.[7]

Client/server applications distribute complexity onto every user's desktop PC, then fragment information into little database servers everywhere. Internet applications centralize complexity onto a few professionally managed servers, consolidate data into a few global databases, and distribute information via a global network.

Taking the historical perspective, we can see the Internet as a construct evolving from and bringing together many of the milestones in the development of business: simple exchange of goods, metallurgy, money, writing, calculation, the zero, credit, printing, electricity, international networks, and the computer. Electronic business unites all these business technologies and yokes them (when necessary) to delivery systems for fulfillment, all sheltered by modern governments enacting and enforcing laws to protect the interests of all parties to every transaction. This great and complex organism is the culmination of business as we know it.

2

The Internet Changes Everything

"It is not the strongest species that
survive, nor the most intelligent, but
the ones most responsive to change."
CHARLES DARWIN

The End of the PC Era

PCs have been with us for a quarter of a century, though some would say that the PC Era did not begin until the introduction of the IBM PC in 1981. Whenever it began, the era was confirmed on December 7, 1992, when Microsoft definitively passed IBM to attain the highest market capitalization among all the world's computer companies. For the most part, Microsoft retained this position until it was surpassed by Cisco on April 3, 2000 (although there were interruptions during which it was displaced by Motorola and/or Intel). The PC Era attained a quantitative summit on November 23, 1998, when (after a brief game of leapfrog) Microsoft definitively superseded GE to become *numero uno* worldwide in market capitalization.

The practices that elevated Microsoft to that height were soon to cast it down again. The war clouds of the federal antitrust suit were gathering in late 1999, and by November the leapfrogging had resumed, with Microsoft and GE joined this time by Cisco. This period ended at 5 p.m. (EST) on April 3, 2000, when Judge Thomas Penfield Jackson released his finding that Microsoft had violated the Sherman Antitrust Act. In two days, the company shed one-sixth of its market

Market Caps (at end of month)

Cisco ——— GE ——— IBM ——— Intel ——— Microsoft ——— Motorola

value; as it sank, other high-tech stocks were sucked into the vortex, and GE was left comfortably atop the world once more. By April 24, Microsoft was down $214 billion, and GE's market cap was higher by 55 percent. (Between December 30, 1999 and December 15, 2000, Microsoft's market cap declined by $365 billion. That missing piece would have been the world's second biggest software company.)

Microsoft had been caught and dragged down in a net of its own weaving; but the Internet had played a crucial part in the fall of the Redmond titan. The company's fierce effort to conquer Netscape in the Battle of the Browsers—Microsoft's principal Internet initiative— had led Jim Barksdale to complain to the Department of Justice (DoJ), prompting the filing of the DoJ antitrust suit in May 1998. And the outcome of the Browser Battle proved to be a Pyrrhic victory in more ways than one; the struggle had also blinded Microsoft to the full spectrum of opportunities that the Internet had to offer. Having dreamt of conquering the world, Gates awoke to find that the world was much bigger than he had ever imagined.

Cisco was drawn into the maelstrom of April 3, 2000, but lost "only" 9.5 percent of its market cap—much less than Microsoft. The result: On the same day that GE regained its world preeminence, Cisco dethroned Microsoft as the most valuable computer company. Networking had conquered the PC.

For the foreseeable future, IBM will remain the world leader in mainframe computing, Microsoft in PC software, and Cisco in networking. But the stage is now set for a new world power to emerge, a company that can produce a comprehensive and compelling suite of e-business applications and that can use that suite as a surfboard to ride the monster wave of the Internet.

Centralize Complexity, Distribute Service

A major theme in the evolution of computing has been the centralization of complexity and control. Consider some of the professionally managed networks with which we deal every day:

- Gasoline
- Radio
- Telephone
- Television
- Utilities: electricity, gas, sewerage, water

Although each of these systems involves great complexity, we nevertheless take them for granted. Why? Because, to the highest reasonable degree, the complexity has been distanced from the user. To be sure, automobile engines and television sets remain complex devices, but—with allowances for their effective functioning—they have been simplified and commodified to a very high degree, and the most important result has been their ever-increasing reliability and ease of use.

Consider television. The concept underlying television technology can be stated in a few words, but the technology itself is fantastically elaborate. And, beyond the technology, television as a social construct incorporates recording and live broadcast studios; programming and scheduling; negotiations and contracts for intellectual property rights; advertising campaigns with ad splicing based on viewer demographics; standards for transmission (sometimes including encryption); satellites, cable, land lines, and towers enabling transmission; and complex billing systems involving a majority of viewers. What contribution is required from the viewer? Plug it in, press a button: it works! The complexity is in the network.

As the computer network matures, it will follow—fast!—the tracks laid down by older networks. Microsoft likes to tout Windows 2000 as the most complex engineering project ever undertaken by man. And so it may be: a Manhattan Project for our time. But who wants the atomic bomb sitting underneath his or her desk—or any other product of monstrous complexity and dubious stability? Imagine an *electric* system that could not improve your service without your purchasing a $500 upgrade—a system that might crash time and time again, and, to be debugged, might require a highly trained technician to visit your basement!

From such a system, in which your PC is trapped, the Internet offers emancipation to the whole world. In effect, the home PC will become simply one more appliance, connecting to the Internet as your taps connect to the municipal water system, your radio to the airwaves, your phone to the telephone network, and your refrigerator to the electric grid.

Compare surfing the Web to channel surfing. Again, the technology underlying the experience is of awesome complexity. And, beyond the technology, every Web site is the end result of content creation and development, sometimes very extensive. In addition, every Web site relies on a production environment and may be supported by staging and testing servers, performance labs, and databases scaling into the gigabytes. Then the connection of the viewer to the site relies on complex networks, traffic patterns, and routing over multiple Internet routers, the networks themselves owned by multiple partners. Again, there are elaborate standards for transmission and complex billing arrangements, and now we find centralized ad servers for personalized content. Yet, again, the only requirement of the viewer is normally a few clicks—sometimes only one—of the mouse. On those occasions when the viewer must type in an entire URL, we recognize this as the price of having an effectively unlimited set of destinations—a feature which television has yet to offer us.

The prescription for success is to centralize complexity and distribute service.

How We Got Here

The advent of the Internet inaugurates the third generation of computing.

The first generation was mainframe computing, in which complexity was centralized in powerful but very costly mainframes that were under IT control. Relatively hard to program, mainframe computers were associated with low-speed local networks of unintelligent terminals and a command interface hostile to users. Centralization of complexity was a virtue of first-generation installations, but it was outweighed by the very high price of computing power, by the deplorable user interface, and by the scarcity of extended networks.

Service depended entirely on the mainframe, but operating-system reliability was much lower than what we now experience. At first, distribution of service beyond the mainframe site depended on slow modems and unreliable telephone lines. Later, these obstacles were eliminated in some cases by installation of local controllers subordinate to the mainframe, but the introduction of such machines added a level of complexity and did not fully free users from their mainframe dependencies.

IBM dominated the first generation, and is still the leader in mainframe computing. When PCs arrived, the company naturally saw them as a threat and portrayed them as agents of chaos; it failed to perceive the awesome potential they also held. The result was that IBM failed to extend its dominance to embrace that potential.

The arrival of the PC led to massive decentralization and to an attendant loss of control by IT teams, but it also brought about a gradual displacement of the terminals that had provided the principal user interface to mainframe computers. In doing so, the PC made possible the development—for corporations—of client/server computing, which, in turn, supported the distribution of processing across multiple machines, usually with each regarded as principally a client or a server. The client/server period brought increased local-area network (LAN) speeds and the introduction of reliable (but low-speed) wide-area networks (WANs).

To some degree, this development restored control to IT personnel. It was also associated with much-reduced costs and with a greatly improved user interface. However, the exploitation of the computing power of client PCs became associated with daunting expenses for software licenses and for maintenance. These were aggravated by growing shortages of personnel for technical support and for database administration, which drove associated salaries to unprecedented heights.

Through its heavy influence on developing standards, Microsoft was able to dominate the PC generation, and it is still the leader on the desktop, with the most-used operating systems and applications suite. When the Internet began to flourish, Microsoft naturally saw it as a threat to its empire and went into denial. When it regained consciousness, the rapid but narrow response it mounted extended its domination, illegally, to the browser market, but this was only lapping at the shore of the new world created by the Web.

The Internet defines the Computer Age's third generation—the Internet Age. Now, for any given application, complexity and control can be concentrated within one or a few machines (for example, at Amazon, eBay, E*TRADE, and Yahoo!). Additionally, a skeleton client that needs little processing ability other than a browser has replaced the obese client PC that typified the second generation. PC processing power is much less essential, and the machine itself now figures more importantly as a data-storage device and in support of the user interface and other input/output (I/O). This minimizes the need for technical support at user sites, while the centralization of databases reduces the need for database administrators (DBAs). Meanwhile, the Internet Age brings with it wide-area networks and extranets that are characterized by low cost, high speed, and high reliability.

With regard to centralization of complexity and control, the third generation looks like a return to the first. But there are crucial distinctions. The current centralization is achieved by virtue of global networking, whereas each of the early mainframes was isolated. The often mammoth application backlogs of the mainframe era have shrunk to minor proportions, if only because the competitive pace set by the Internet is so fierce.

The Internet constitutes the last great change in computing architecture. Of course, it will become faster, cheaper, more reliable, more ubiquitous, and accessible by a wider range of devices. But the architecture will remain *the same*. The impulse toward centralization that it promotes will prove to be a permanent feature of the computing landscape, and it is partly because this centralization so facilitates management that the rate of change has become so dazzling.

Impact of the Internet

Within the universe of business, there are four broad areas in which the impact of the Internet is irresistible:

- Complexity, formerly distributed, becomes centralized.
- IT support, formerly distributed at local and regional levels, becomes centralized.
- Transactions, formerly merely exchanges of money for products or services, become sources of business intelligence.
- Service, formerly provided by others, is now often performable by users.

Here I introduce a motif that appears repeatedly in this book: the crucial importance of Internet-based applications and services. These will pave the way toward a future in which individual, business, and market efficiencies have advanced far beyond what we can foresee.

Consider the implications for a corporation that makes a service application available to its customers over the Internet.

Single instance. Ideally, the enterprise can implement a single instance of each application. To take an example to which we will return again and again—Amazon.com implements a single instance that Amazon has found adequate as an interface through which all of its customers can deal with the company—or *almost* adequate: some poking around on the Amazon site reveals an 800 number for customer service, and Amazon undertakes to send a postal address to customers who want to pay by check or money order. But the site is designed to be as self-sufficient as possible, and it presumably handles the overwhelming majority of all interactions.

Many enterprises, operating in more complex environments, will face a traditional decision: whether it makes more sense to offer a single product which, however, must be very complex to handle all the enterprise's business responsibilities, or to offer multiple products, each of which can be significantly simplified because it includes, beyond some common functionality, only what is needed to support one relatively specialized customer set. In either case, the product(s) once developed can be implemented over the Web, though multiple products will usually be accorded multiple sites.

Overnight extensions to functionality. The instance implosion will make it possible to update the product in a fraction of a second, even if it exists in multiple instances. On the other hand, the updating of multiple instances can be staggered if doing so serves a recognized purpose. Updating can easily be scheduled for a time when it will least disturb the product's users.

Global functionality. Whether the enterprise uses an Internet site to implement one product or more than one, each product can be accessed and exploited from any point on the globe.

The one catch here is that, to be cost-effective globally, a Web-enabled product may need to be multilingual. In most cases, such a requirement will probably entail the implementation of multiple instances of the product. In cases in which it is considered sufficient to use only a few languages, each screen might carry instructions in each language used; or the application might display most of its screens in a language that the customer has chosen from an introductory screen.

Greater freedom in development siting. Just as a product implemented on the Web can be accessed from anywhere, so a new Web product can be implemented from anywhere. A team working in Iceland can do everything that needs to be done—or, if it's more convenient for the enterprise, the work can be divided equally among Bangalore, Silicon Valley, and Slovenia.

Flexibility of access. The proliferation of intelligent devices providing access to the Web means that almost everybody in the developed world can easily plug in to the Internet using any one—or more—of a range of machines (PCs, ATMs, NCs, phones, palm devices) in any of a variety of venues (homes, airports, malls, cars, trains, airplanes).

Centralization of complexity. The enterprise can now exercise much more detailed and responsive control over the product, because every production instance now remains in the hands of the developers.

Integration of information. Business analysis becomes a much less daunting assignment when the universe of relevant data can be assembled, in real time, at one point. For global corporations, this ability has become a reality with the advent of the Internet, which can link electronically all databases and all sources of input.

Suppose that a global corporation wants to count its employees. In the days before the Internet, the corporation might have had to direct distinct queries to each of 60 or 100 databases, one or more for each country in which it conducted operations; collect the results by phone or by mail; add the numbers, perhaps using a pocket calculator; and thus arrive at a total that was probably out of date before it was known. Now, using the Internet, the same company can execute all updates to—and all queries against—a single centralized database. (This will usually be mirrored by a backup database in a different physical location.) The new model not only facilitates company-internal queries, it also enables the use of business-intelligence methods that, by comparison with the old days, are astonishingly easy and blindingly fast.

Self-service. The Web is accelerating us toward a world in which services for which we used to have to depend on—and wait for—other people are going to be services that we can perform for ourselves, at our own convenience. You can now use the Web at any time of day or night to check your account information, pay your bills, read book reviews (and buy a book if you like its reviews), review movie listings, buy a car, or book a trip.

Great user interface. The gradual spread of emerging conventions for Internet browsers and for Web sites, together with users' rapidly accumulating experience of the Web, means that sites will grow ever easier to use. Competition among sites will encourage experimentation with innovative techniques and tools for design, but it will deal promptly—and harshly—with innovations that users find confusing, slow, annoying, or hostile.

Minimal installation of software at user sites. Java implementations will lead increasingly to a model in which software—whether rented, leased, or owned by the customer—is executed over the Internet. Installation and maintenance costs at customer sites will be slashed to the bone.

No training manual. For computerized applications, at least, the world is moving away from paper documentation, and this trend has been greatly accelerated by the advent of the World Wide Web. Most applications are still sold on CD-ROMs that include documentation files, but the Web will work in three ways to eliminate such files:

- It will require one—at most—instance of the documentation.
- It will make it feasible to keep that instance—like the product itself (see above)—literally up to date.
- As with user interfaces (UIs), the fanning out of conventions for the use of Internet-enabled applications will confine the documentation effort to the production of online help and/or will much reduce the need for any documentation at all. Who has seen the user manual for Amazon.com, eBay, or Yahoo!?

How to Get from Here to There

The Coming Revolution

The Industrial Revolution was (has been?) a time of unprecedented business opportunities—opportunities for the proliferation and sophistication of technology throughout society. In part it prefigures the Age of the Internet, in which the great business opportunities are in integrating and simplifying the systems that had grown hideously complex during the reign of client/server architecture, in part because of that architecture. The challenge now is for companies to re-create themselves through the use of applications and application suites that press constantly for simplification; through the development of global price books and catalogs; through the ability to administer products centrally while they sell, deliver, and service them globally, with the highest attainable degree of efficiency.

The Case of Oracle

The majority of American businesses today are brick-and-mortar companies that are morphing into Web-enabled enterprises. This is happening both inside and outside the firewall. The Web is extending and facilitating the ways in which those companies interact with their employees, while changing the face that each such company presents to its customers, adding to customer abilities and removing obstacles to customer satisfaction. Companies that spring into existence as "pure Internet plays," as Amazon did, must clear a long series of hurdles, but those hurdles are fewer and lower than the ones that await companies trying to transition from brick-and-mortar to brick-and-click. This section focuses on companies confronting the great e-transformation, and it presents Oracle as a prime example of a client/server business scrambling onto the Internet.

Oracle, which conducts business in nearly every country on the globe, had more than 100 operations centers in 58 countries. Oracle headquarters would set guidelines for these centers, to promote standardization of accounting and hiring practices, job titles, price books, product catalogs, and so on; and each center would be measured on its margins, its performance, etc. Yet each center was to some extent autonomous, building its own IT team and deploying its own systems for financials, HR, marketing, order management, sales, and service.

This much might be true of any multinational corporation. In Oracle's case, multiplication and local autonomy spread also to the databases and applications that Oracle not only markets but uses internally. In many cases, the applications, especially, were not suitable to local needs; that is, some of the operations centers could not or would not use an application without making local changes to it. Among them, the centers were running more than 140 customized applications, and some centers were using third-party products as well. The results: dozens of IT teams; local bespoke systems; decentralized business practices; thousands of local servers[8]; enormous labor pools performing redundant tasks; enormous expenses; data fragmentation; prohibitive business complexity; regional fiefdoms; and, in short, loss of control of the business.

In retrospect, it looks crazy, but it took Larry Ellison's direct involvement for all the craziness to be generally recognized. When, in response to his request, the HR development team gave him their top-of-the-line demo, they focused excitedly on the number of keystrokes required to create a record for a new employee—only five, they enthused, beating the PeopleSoft application's nine by a factor of almost two!

Larry interrupted the demo, asking the team to show him how many employees Oracle had and how their skills distribution mapped to the company's product revenues and service requests. The team never got as far as the second question; they couldn't answer the first. Not only had Oracle fragmented its IT expertise and its systems, it had scattered its data across the face of the earth. The world's leading database company didn't know how many people it employed.

Though the situation was grim, Oracle at least recognized the problem and understood what had to be done to solve it. Ellison began by restructuring Oracle so that development and IT became a single organization in the sense that the development group was now involved in the definition and understanding of the business processes to be implemented; for any company that (like Oracle) wants to use its own software, this means further that the development group must take final responsibility for deploying the software and validating its operational use. Hundreds of application-support people were moved into development, with the ratio of support staff to employee total dropping from 1:25 to 1:50, and expected to drop to 1:75.

Ellison set the following corporate goals:

- To integrate the automation of all business functions: marketing, sales, service, the eStore, call centers, field professionals, HR, financials, and procurement

- To minimize the number of corporate e-mail servers, to access any of which an Oracle employee would need only a browser

- To make all Oracle UIs look familiar, as do those of Amazon or Yahoo!

- To reduce training requirements for end users to zero—or close

- To run Oracle on uncustomized out-of-the-box Oracle applications

- To deploy Oracle products internally at the moment they become available

- To simplify and globalize all business practices

- To extend the boundaries of self-service to embrace even the difficult tasks

- To drive manual labor and clerical tasks out of the corporation

- To bring worldwide corporate data together within a minimum number of data centers and production databases (The company now maintains three IT operations centers—in Redwood Shores, the United Kingdom, and Singapore.)

Readers will see that, at a higher level, these goals coalesce into one:

- To develop one applications suite that uses the Internet and corporate intranets to automate, integrate, and rationalize all business processes at Oracle (and, within reason, everywhere else)

Ellison predicted in mid-1999 that, in pursuing this goal, Oracle would realize savings of $1 billion over the next 18 months. In mid-March 2000, Oracle's quarterly results showed that he had underestimated the impact of the changes he was championing. In the intervening nine months, Oracle had already saved more than $1 billion and had raised its operating margin from 19.6 percent to 31.4 percent. The company's head count had dropped by 4 percent, increased efficiency enabling Oracle to refrain from hiring replacements for employees lost through normal attrition.

By deploying an electronic store, collaborative selling tools, and other applications for self-service buying and selling, Oracle had enabled sales reps and prospects to demo together, price together, and buy together, while eliminating the need for cross-country flights in support of on-site sales pitches. The online Oracle Store mandated uniform pricing and standardization of contracts worldwide—the company's "let's make a deal" days were gone forever. These changes, together with the Internet-enabled consolidation of corporate IT into a locally managed, but globally effective, staff, unyoked Oracle's revenues from its cost of sales, enabling the top line to spring forward and to yank the bottom line along with it.

These were the two keys to reforming the sales process at Oracle:

- Coordinate all sales channels—Web, field staff, call centers, and partners—on a global basis
- Maximize, within reason, the automation of the process

This meant providing and promoting electronic channels to the Oracle customer set; directing business that requires a human response to the least expensive and most scalable channel, the call center[9]; and reducing the field sales force accordingly, but not beyond the point of diminishing returns.

Oracle's operating margin continues to rise toward 40 percent, and the company is well-advanced toward its second billion dollars of savings. Still further savings will be achieved by the automation of Oracle customer care. The current cost to Oracle of an average customer call is $300; yet 30 percent of these calls originate with concerns that are either (if not both!) easy to address through automation or simply trivial, such as address changes, inquiries relating to contracts and service levels, contract renewals, and the like. Conservatively, Oracle support organizations can recognize savings of $400 to $500 million by automating their support for these concerns. (Some Oracle executives think that Oracle can achieve $4 billion in savings and an operating margin of 50 percent by the middle of 2002. But the company has not formally taken this position.)

In the short run, the pursuit of these goals has resulted in several monumental achievements for the company:

- The delivery of Oracle Applications Release 11*i* (the first suite of e-business enterprise applications)
- The consolidation onto 158 machines at Oracle headquarters of operations previously running on thousands of servers scattered around the world, and the storage of all company data in three databases, each accessible across the Web
- The consolidation of corporate e-mail services from 97 servers and 120 databases onto 4 servers and into 4 databases worldwide
- The benefit for Oracle of more than $1 billion in savings

Further, the company came to understand that virtually all businesses relying on client/server configurations were effectively out of control, and that, as a lever to reestablish control, the Internet presented an immense business opportunity for Oracle to reinvent itself and in doing so, to help its customer enterprises to reinvent themselves.

Milestones

Oracle's experience provides guidance along the road from here (client/server) to there (e-business).

Think Revolution, not Evolution

Evolution is about brown spots turning into black spots over millennia; whales still have their leg bones. The e-transformation is about transmuting your business overnight. (Chapters 3 and 4 deal with business practices that have changed forever.) The world is no longer moving at geologic speed or even at client/server speed; it is moving at Internet velocity. The era of Andersen Consulting's 3-year $100-million contracts for system implementation is gone forever.

Becoming an e-business means "tomorrow the world." Many companies will not make the cut; those that do will have been reinvented, and their leaders will find that they can understand and control their businesses again. This is an opportunity not to be missed.

The Senior Executive Must Own this Transformation

Many CEOs, COOs, and presidents are far removed from the details of their businesses for two major reasons. First, the executives themselves need to be upgraded, which often means modernized; and second, their business systems are too complex to be understood. I'll be tactful and address only the second reason.

It's true—most business systems *are* too complex. Let CEOs define their own home pages, their key performance indicators, and the information that they want to see every day—global leads, global new orders, global sales forecast, global new customers, stock quotations, and so on. Their business systems must be redesigned and reconfigured to generate this display on an Internet browser; it must look familiar and must require no training. The reconfiguration is a success at the top level when the CEO feels compelled to access this home page every day—or many times per day.

This is the napkin test—it starts at the top of the organization and drives change downward. Top executives will still need to build a collaborative approach, to appeal to all lines of business within their organizations. The systems they need to evolve comprise people, processes, and products—three forces that collide, and *must* collide, in the boardroom, where they must also be reconciled. Executives will need to hold regular meetings to review progress toward corporate goals, and those meetings will need to focus on actual product screens, not on PowerPoint presentations.

Disentangle Complexity

Client/server systems impose a business model of enormous complexity. The costs of divisional or national fragmentation of systems and IT groups are too huge to overlook, but they shrivel by comparison with the costs of data fragmentation and of the wild proliferation of localized business practices that not even the shrewdest chief executive could understand.

Take an easy question: what is the company's global sales forecast? Client/server systems cannot answer this question promptly or cost-effectively. CEOs would fall to their knees and weep if they could use their browsers to view a chart showing global sales forecast, global lead and order positions, cost-effectiveness of marketing automation, and global marketing expenditures and return on investment (ROI)— *not* client/server fragmented data, but up-to-the-minute, accurate, global information.

As companies undergo this e-transformation, they will uncover pockets of twentieth-century tradition: here a business practice optimized for local IT control, there a large labor pool doing the same things (perhaps in different ways) as another pool somewhere else. To shake off these remnants, the enterprise must ask questions at every turn, driving toward high automation, slashing clerical staff, accelerating self-service, and eliminating all redundant tasks.

Single Customer Reality

The brass ring for every business has always been to achieve a single global master record for each customer, eliminating duplications and contradictions and providing a focus for all the company's information about that customer. This goal has never been generally met. Client/server systems, in particular, obstructed it by promoting the duplication of customer data across servers. The Internet has brought for the first time the goal of a *single customer reality* within the grasp of those companies inclined to reach for it.

Oracle's situation in the client/server era exemplifies just how unreachable this goal was in the past. With servers functioning all over the globe and with no reliable way of tying them together, Oracle was operating roughly 58 contract and support systems, 58 order-entry and financial systems, 58 sales-management systems, and 150 local marketing systems. This meant that, for Oracle, the face presented by another global corporation—say General Electric—had as many as 300 profiles, with many internal contradictions and no rational procedure for their resolution. This is the familiar story of the blind men and the elephant.

But what else could the company do? Oracle France needed information on GE's French operations, didn't care much about GE's

German operations, and wanted to control its own records. Likewise for Oracle Germany. But the two autonomous sets of records allowed for inconsistencies—say about GE's presence in the Saar—to creep in, and perhaps the only way to avoid such inconsistencies was for each of Oracle's national presences to deny itself all information that had to come to it across national borders. To do so, however, would not have helped them to conduct business effectively.

The Internet, at a blow, destroys this need for national autonomy. Oracle offices all over the world now have the potential to access any single Oracle server, which means that any such server can host a single comprehensive set of single comprehensive customer records. The task for Oracle, and for any other company emancipated by the Internet from client/server bonds, is to construct such a set—so that the company can begin to interact with each customer in consistent and effective ways and to accumulate further customer information systematically, reconciling it with the data it already has.

What are the steps in this procedure? The company must:

- Identify the data it needs for each customer and throw away the rest; having no data is preferable to having invalid data.

- Scrub the data, imposing common formats and reconciling inconsistencies.

- Create a provisional database to house the emerging data collection.

- Populate the database created, merging and de-duplicating input data streams. De-duplication can be complex, because each record in a set of customer records is typically linked to many subordinate data: bill-to and ship-to addresses, accounting information, sales history, contracts, opportunities, service requests. Merging two or more data streams means merging all subordinate data as well.

- Standardize on a timely and trusted external source of corporate information, such as Dun & Bradstreet, Hoover's, or Experian. Outsourcing maintenance of standard corporate data is very cost-effective and promotes consistency across companies and industries.

A single integrated record-set for each customer confers prodigious advantages on the corporation that possesses it:

- It brings together—so that it can be viewed together—all corporate information about the customer: revenues, credit status, service levels, installed base of products and services, outstanding sales opportunities and quotes, and so on.

- It empowers every employee of the corporation to relate to the customer in terms consistent with the corporate view of the customer reality, and with the customer reality.

- It provides a consistent basis for prioritizing customer concerns, making it possible for automated systems (e.g., call-center queuing and routing systems) to immediately direct issues raised by the most valued customers to the corporation's most knowledgeable and effective workers. Without such a basis, multimillion-dollar customers all too often get parked in service queues behind customers who may have licensed only a few thousand dollars' worth of software.

Customers are *not* interchangeable. Every company needs to be able to distinguish among them, not in order to provide inferior service to the less important but to provide excellent service, reliably, to the more important.

Tear Down the Fiefdoms

Divisional or national staffs and lines of business entrench themselves and their leaders, whose positions within the corporate hierarchy are rationalized on the basis of the fiefdoms they command. The conversion from traditional to electronic business, if it is not to miscarry, must break down these fiefdoms, then harmonize their constituents within the framework of the electronic enterprise.

At Oracle, the initiative to consolidate corporate information in as few data centers and databases as business requirements would allow was opposed by a number of managing directors who foresaw that closing down local or country-specific data centers would mean ceding control to corporate headquarters. Those who refused to support the consolidation effort are no longer with the company. In such circumstances, it is necessary to turn away from the corporate organization charts and to look for those—employees or not—who have the inclination, the skills, and the flexibility to lead the company's people toward the company's goals.

Toe the MoSCoW Line

The MoSCoW Principle is simple: it divides your wish list into "Must haves", "Should haves, "Could haves", and "Would haves." Why? Because the electronic business needs an operational infrastructure that moves at Internet speeds—with a rapid succession of narrowly defined and measurable deliverables, achieving incremental and predictable improvements.

Remember, Internet-enabled systems do not require client-side software upgrades or large-scale training efforts; a development team can take a globally centralized application and, literally over the weekend, add a "new tab" and the features and functions to support it. Concentrate on initiatives that promise healthy ROI or that build confidence with internal users; get these operational and reliable. Focus on the "Must haves." Often, by the time these are operational, some features or functions that used to be contenders—or some gate-crashers—will have risen to "Must have" status; if not, move on to the "Should haves."

Above all, define a pathway to the envisioned goals; demonstrate that progress can be made along that pathway; and build a development machine that, month after month, can reliably deliver new functionality.

Screen Your Business Practices

This may be the most difficult milestone to get past. Most businesses struggling to escape from the client/server world will find themselves encumbered with any number of business practices that have outlived their century. For example, many companies still have prices and discount structures that vary from one country to another. Does this make sense? Why not enable every customer to go to the company Web site and find a single global price—or a price targeted to that specific customer? A second example: For collateral and documentation, why do you need printed materials, possibly stockpiled in warehouses, for which the customer is to be invoiced, and with complex roles for compensation? Online services can now personalize every item of collateral or documentation and print it on demand.

Bills of material (BOMs) provide a case in point. Client/server systems did not support the metalinguistic application of complex rules for pricing, promotion, and product configuration. These rules, specifying such things as size-color-and-style matching and two-for-one pricing, became institutionalized for major corporations in extremely large and complex BOMs. Oracle, for instance—a company with only dozens of products—had a bill of materials with 15,000 line items.

The temptation when confronted with such complexities is to back away, simply replacing the existing client/server interface with something suitable for e-business. But the key to success is to dismantle the complexities and to rebuild them into much simpler structures, easier to understand and to deal with. For Oracle, this commandment meant defining a new corporate BOM, the iBOM—which emerged, with 200 line items, simple and complete.

A second such initiative at Oracle has been to standardize on a small number of languages in which the company will conduct business. Although Oracle does business in some 60 countries around the world, and although it produces versions of its products in as many as 28 distinct languages, it recently determined to do its contractual business in only 8 languages: Chinese, English, French, German, Italian, Japanese, Korean, and Spanish. Only in these languages will the company bring forth ads, budgeting, collateral, stores, Web sites, online services, and support. This rationalization is dictated by the demands of "Internet Time," to which Oracle must march if its new products and services are to be introduced at a competitive pace.

The point is that it is all too easy to erect an Internet superstructure on top of the company's current business practices or to implement those practices on the Web without attention to the underlying business logic. Any company that is migrating to the Internet needs to scrutinize its ways of doing business and to rethink or jettison every way that makes no sense in the new economy.

Among the most important business practices to implement are these:

- Consolidate all data for each customer into a single, comprehensive customer record.

- Simplify and globalize price sheets, bills of materials, and the product catalog.

- Drive sales to the Web.

- Automate contract authoring, license sales, and service renewals.

- For global corporations, resolve to conduct business in six to nine languages—not in dozens.

Prepare to Sustain Casualties

Along the road from traditional to electronic business, there will be teams that fall by the wayside: teams that do not glimpse the vision; teams that are naysayers; and teams that used to be productive but that cannot adapt to the new environment. Teams of crabs.

The fashion, when you go crabbing, is to throw your crabs into a bucket in the middle of the fishing boat; but, oddly, nobody bothers to put a lid on the bucket, even though the crabs develop a foul temper and will claw, pinch, and bite. Why no lid? Because the crabs are conformists: If one crab is inspired to climb the side of the bucket, the other crabs grab at it and pull it back down into the crowd at the bottom. What's the result? Nobody breaks out.

People are like crabs, more or less. Everybody knows ways to do lots of things and will often turn, by preference, to a way that works pretty reliably. But the point of the Internet is to break the mold. So, the migration is full of challenges:

- To keep the conformist crabs from dragging the soldier-of-fortune crabs back down.

- To channel the conservative impulses of the conformists in such ways that the soldiers of fortune tend to struggle constructively toward the goal of e-transformation, not away from it.

- To channel the innovative impulses of the adventurous crabs in such ways that the conformists are inspired to follow them when they see them headed in a promising direction.

The E-Foundation

Regaining control of your business requires a willingness to rebuild it from the ground up. If its current basis is the client/server paradigm, then there is no guarantee that the business processes now in place are cost-effectively replicable to the Internet environment. They must be treated with skepticism.

A secure foundation for the future includes one, and only one, master record for each customer; it includes a global price list and global bills of material; and it includes simplified contracting processes to ensure that negotiations, renewals, and postsale service can all be conducted efficiently. Such a foundation will ensure a sound internal understanding of the business and will make possible its healthy growth.

Existing business systems must be pruned or uprooted if they do not help you to focus on the principal e-targets. If necessary, you can build ladders from your client/server systems to your Internet applications, but once the new systems are fully functional you must be able and willing to pull those ladders up behind you and let the old systems—and the business practices they institutionalized—atrophy and die.

The Top Seven E-Targets

Here are the top seven targets for companies undergoing e-transformation. They head the agenda because every global business needs these results, and because each represents a quintessential e-business practice. Chapters 3 and 4 address more broadly the ways that Web-enablement changes business practices, but I highlight these seven here specifically as measures of progress on the road from traditional to electronic business.

- Global sales forecast
- Global lead position
- Global order position
- Global inventory position
- Global marketing expenditure
- Global contracts
- Collaborative sales automation for suppliers, partners, customers, and employees

Global Sales Forecast

Can you state your exact global sales forecast, up to the minute, covering all geographies, all lines of business, all products, all services, all customers, all partners? And including all licenses, product renewals, support contracts, Web-based sales, call-center telebusiness, direct business, mail catalogs, and business through partners and other channels? Can the forecast reflect management judgments as well as the estimates of the sales reps? Can you review opportunity data and identify which opportunities your sales organizations are committing to? Can you see multiple views of that information—one by manager and one by salesperson?

Global Lead Position

How many new leads did you get today? Where did they come from? How do they group by geography, by product, by line of business? Which leads went to partners? How many are sitting idle and aging?

Suppose your business issues a press release to introduce a new product and to direct readers to the URL for a "landing pad" on your Web site where they can find further information. Suppose you've started to run a new TV commercial, or you've sent out a large set of e-mail proposals, or you've initiated a new call-center campaign. You can measure the cost-effectiveness of any of these efforts only if you can assess how many leads are being generated, and in response to which promotion. Without a centralized e-business application that can monitor leads globally, that information will be very difficult to collect and to analyze.

Global Order Position

What orders are in and booked—up to the minute? . . . from campaigns through leads through opportunities, to a global sales forecast and a global order position. . . .

Understanding this position thoroughly depends on a detailed analysis. You need to know how many orders are generated through your Web site, through your call center(s), through your partners, and through your retail sites. You also need to know how much business has been quoted, how much quoted but not signed, how much signed but not booked, and how much booked but not processed because of some constraint, e.g., a shortage of materials or of inventory.

Finally, each of these figures needs to be broken down by language, by currency, and by country. Orders can be vitiated by an ineffective translation of an ad, or by pricing that responds too slowly to currency fluctuations; orders can also be enhanced by factors that nobody has foreseen. The locations in which orders originate are important because of fulfillment issues. Executives need the ability to stay in close touch with these numbers and to react to them rapidly.

Global Inventory Position

Manufacturing executives must be able to access detailed information as to what products exist, in which location(s), in what configurations, and in what condition, for sale or service. A part or parts needed may be available in multiple locations, raising issues as to the least expensive part(s) and path(s) available to meet the need (e.g., for the repair and/or sale of a jet engine). A full understanding of the global inventory position is the foundation of a rapid response to an available-to-promise inquiry.

The holy grail for every company is to maintain inventory at zero— not positive, meaning that goods are sitting idle on a shelf, but not negative, meaning that a customer is asking for what the company can't provide. Like the Holy Grail, zero inventory is not a realistic goal. As the Internet provides visibility into more and more links in the supply chain, however, it will enable the typical e-business to carry a much leaner inventory and to cut expenses associated with it.

Global Marketing Expenditure

Can you state your exact global marketing expenditure, and identify what proportion of that expenditure converts to booked orders? Can you interrupt or modify campaigns in real time—for instance, by adding more outbound call-center agents to campaigns that are disclosing unexpected opportunities? Can you measure the success of any campaign by region, by product, by channel? Can you identify what leads and opportunities were generated, what interaction channels were most used by consumers, in consequence of the marketing expenditure?

There are many valid objectives for marketing campaigns: to create awareness; to create demand for products or for training; to generate leads; to promote the electronic sales process. Ideally, the marketing executive can measure the effectiveness of a campaign according to any or all such criteria—and then can tweak some knobs to increase or decrease spending on the campaign or on a target segment, or just to terminate the campaign entirely.

This level of control is made possible by an e-business suite that comprises business-intelligence systems (BIS) applications for gathering the information required and marketing applications that enable detailed real-time control of the campaign.

Global Contracts

Although service contracts are typically a major source of revenue for companies that offer them, their administration is often haphazard.

Many service organizations have little understanding of how to map products sold to products to be serviced; their contracts are often poorly organized, and the result is debilitating leakage of license and service revenues. Indeed, for many such organizations the difficulty of staying in touch with which contracts need to be renewed means that the renewal process itself cannot be cost-effective.

Soon such organizations will find it essential to implement global systems that enable automatic renewal of contracts and leases. Once more, the watchword is "evolve or die."

Collaborative Sales Automation

Can every constituent among your "business partners"—customers, telesales and field employees, partners, and suppliers—participate in your selling cycles? Do you have an integrated automation solution for your telesales and field-sales agents? Can customers place orders and negotiate terms directly? Can sales representatives review these terms and approve them? Can they co-browse with prospects on your Web site and guide them through the process of selection and ordering? Can your partners get leads and manage sales cycles with your sales teams or with sales teams from your suppliers?

Answering these questions—hitting these seven targets—is what being an e-business is all about.

3

E-Business or Out of Business

Eternal Verities

For my purposes, the "eternal verities" are those aspects of business that are *less* changed by the Internet than the others. The leading example is the importance of focusing on the customer—or, more broadly, on the "trading partners" of the enterprise: customers, employees, suppliers, and business partners.

Historically, focus on the customer has varied in importance depending on the industry, typically being less important in product industries than in service industries. Variations of this kind will persist. Nevertheless, the Internet promotes this importance across the board by making it easier for Web-enabled companies to collect information about their customers and thus to sharpen their customer focus. Companies that do not exploit this ability, or that fail to organize and to use their customer information effectively, will lose ground to their competitors.

Further, the Web will stress more heavily the importance of retaining customers. Though companies have long recognized that it is generally much less costly to retain a customer than to acquire a new one, this fact gathers new vigor as customer profiling catches on. For starters, it's much easier—and less expensive—to collect useful information about your customers than to collect useful information about the rest of the population. Additionally, if you can't figure out how to use increased customer information to retain current customers, what's the point of acquiring new ones? To watch as they gradually slip away?

Recognizing the new opportunities provided by the Internet, the forward-looking enterprise will capitalize on them roughly as follows:

- It will assess carefully what information it needs to maintain for each customer. Most companies will probably want to record, in addition to standard name-and-address data, information as to revenue generated by the customer, customer complaints and concerns, date and nature of latest transaction, how the customer came to the company, and many other items that will vary by industry. In gathering this information, the company will consider and respond constructively to the risk that its asking for or using one or more data items might be viewed by customers as invading their privacy.

- The enterprise will design or modify a standard customer profile as a receptacle for that information, reserving a field in the profile for miscellaneous notes related to the current customer and other fields for future use.

- It will maintain the profile record in a single place, with a single backup record, and will work to bring together and reconcile all information about customer X that has previously been scattered across the organization.

- It will design its Web site to encourage viewers to submit information for which the enterprise has a legitimate need. In most cases, the enterprise can allow the customer to actually maintain a major portion of his or her profile.

- It will exploit customer information, with vigor and sensitivity, to customize and personalize its product and service offerings, whether those offerings use the Internet or a more traditional medium.

The Internet: Key Advantages
Cost-Effectivity

The Internet is astonishingly cost-effective, for four main reasons.

First, moving paperwork online speeds communications and reduces material and administrative expenses. The savings to be realized here are difficult to quantify, but consider these points:

- Potentially, every telephone call or business letter that would have been sent in a given business situation is replaceable, with a net saving, by an e-letter.

- E-communications can be addressed, at zero marginal cost, to multiple recipients in cases in which physical memos would have had to travel to such recipients serially (for instance, because of a physical attachment). Remember buck slips?

- Because it is inexpensive and easy to use, e-mail is often sent in instances when no phone call or business letter would have been sent, promoting the spread of useful information and conducing to intelligent business management.

- Information can be posted once for all to see—or to be seen only by those authorized. When it must be corrected or updated, changes to one source have the effect of placing a fresh copy in the hands of every viewer.

- Online records can be converted automatically into permanent records.

Second, transaction costs plummet. A business enabled for the Internet can generally communicate directly with any or all of its customers, and vice versa, at zero marginal cost. A customer can place an order instantaneously and usually with very little work; the order can be propagated automatically to the company's shipping and billing departments; it can also be recorded for analysis that will help the company to deal with the customer, and with its entire customer population, in ways designed to promote customer satisfaction and corporate profit.

Too many companies have only vague ideas as to how much it costs them to handle an order. Ray Lane, former president of Oracle Corporation, estimated that processing an order, pre-Internet, cost $100 on average, but only $10 when using the Internet—and that the average cost of processing a payment declines in proportion, from about $10 to less than $1. Lane quoted figures from Xerox Corporate Strategic Services to the effect that purchase-order processing at Xerox has fallen, on average, from $150 to $25, after implementation of Oracle Internet Procurement; and he cited an Internet-enabled procurement system installed at Boeing Corporation for a cumulative cost of $10,000,000, from which Boeing projects savings of hundreds of millions per year.

These numbers are breathtaking. Government data, which for two decades or more reflected no visible productivity gain from corporate use of computers, have since 1996 begun to reflect gains that would be incredible if it were not for the rapid rise of the Internet.

Other online interactions hold startling potential for savings. Remember what it used to be like to call a governmental public-service number? If the average American spent 15 minutes per year waiting for one or another public servant to answer the phone, then the savings in moving all interactions online would approach 70,000,000 hours, or roughly 1,000 working lifetimes—per year.

I note, parenthetically, that the ability of the Web user to place an order or to fill out a form automatically means that the company or agency accepting the input no longer risks getting it wrong. That risk, and the associated liability, are now reserved to the user, which is one advantage for the recipient; a second advantage is that disputes as to who made any mistake are now eliminated. (This does not apply to mistakes in shipping; but, at least, orders coming in to shipping can now be guaranteed valid.) Xerox Corporate Strategic Services reports that order accuracy has risen from under 50 percent to over 99 percent.

Third, capital expenses and expenses for business processes and human resources are sharply reduced. Consolidation of servers and databases will eliminate or defer substantial capital expenditures; it will also render superfluous many personnel for technical support and for database administration. Employers will redirect such people to tasks that continue to be vital or will reduce their numbers through attrition. Business processes will be simplified and redundancies eliminated.

Fourth, improved availability of more comprehensive information enables it to be used more effectively to manage the business. Setting aside those Internet sites that are intended as auction houses, the Internet greatly facilitates searches, by consumers or companies, for the most desirable product at the lowest price, or for the highest bid for a product or service offered. Re-intermediation has sprung up as sites catering to specific industries centralize offers of, and bids for, products and services. (The Gartner Group has projected that market-maker sites will number 10,000 by the end of 1999 and 100,000 by 2001!)

More broadly, the Internet enables access to a universe of information that may be of great business value even when it has no immediate bearing on transactions. Business decisions may be enhanced by a more detailed understanding of stock-price fluctuations, by access to up-to-the-minute data on commodities prices, by limited but easily available information on competitors' business plans and capabilities, and so—at great length—on.

Compelling Customer Experience

The customer's experience of doing business on the Web was touched on earlier. The user interface is evolving, and this means changes that customers will sometimes dislike. But the process is truly an evolution: new approaches to design will be tried, as well as new bells and whistles. The less popular bells and whistles will die away. Innovations will increasingly be confined to marginal variations on two well-developed standards—one for browsers, largely derived from graphical user interface (GUI) standards associated with Microsoft, and one (as yet much more tentative) for site content. So many readily accessible sites are contending for attention that none can long afford to annoy its viewers.

This convergence on user-friendly standards for the UI will be promoted further by the fact that many of the Web-enabled applications needed to implement e-business solutions are already available off the shelf. For many companies, the cost-effective approach to electronic business will exploit packaged—and proven—software or online services.

A second compelling aspect of the online experience is that the customer is now empowered to do so much more. Self-service, at the customer's convenience, is now possible across a wide range of sites. Web-enabled techniques such as co-browsing and URL sharing make possible the gentle introduction of PC illiterates and technophobes to the delights and resources of the Internet.

A growing number of sites are enabling configuration of the user interface to the customer's personal needs and preferences. The customer can choose what information is to be presented, in what order or arrangement, using which colors, and so on. Users will come to take a proprietary interest in company sites because those sites have allowed them to express their individualities.

Finally, new technologies are being developed constantly to enable customers to do things with the Web that were formerly impossible.

These include streaming audio, streaming video, Net telephony, instant messaging, co-browsing and other collaborative technologies for sales and service, and the videophone (we've been waiting for decades to get this from the telephone company). Intelligent Web agents will follow, as will virtual reality, and who knows what thereafter. Think how this record of innovation and self-transformation compares with that of any other medium of communication.

Permanence

The Internet is here to stay. Not only has it been around for thirty years, it has been accumulating more popularity with every year, and it is now far too massive to be dislodged. There will be an Internet2, and a Next Generation Internet, but neither is intended as a separate network. To the extent that these come to "replace" the Internet, they will do as the skin is said to—once every seven years, cell by cell, mostly imperceptibly, and with backward compatibility. The result will be that the network will extend its accessibility to a greater variety of devices, and that it will grow faster, more reliable, and (even) less expensive.

This permanence distinguishes the Internet from a variety of elements familiar in the current high-tech environment, but most obviously from client/server computing configurations; and the distinction confers on the Internet a huge competitive advantage. Applications that can be made to work on the Internet may be rendered obsolete for any of a variety of reasons, but inherent shortcomings of the platform will not be one.

Aqueducts built by the Romans, including one begun by the Emperor Hadrian and completed in 140 A.D., are still in use, having survived the Dark Ages. Short of an utter collapse of civilization, the Internet will still be interconnecting the world at the beginning of the fifth millennium . . . and far beyond.

The Internet: Business Processes Affected

The influence of the Web will transform all business processes, effecting pervasive reconfigurations of resource pools of labor and

One company enabling e-marketing is MatchLogic, since 1998 an independent subsidiary of Excite. MatchLogic software uses viewer profiling and sophisticated effectiveness metrics to help marketers plan, implement, manage, and evaluate online advertising campaigns. It also strengthens those campaigns by arming them with targeted ads that exploit rich media to achieve consumer interaction rates of 12 percent to 15 percent, in contrast to rates of 1 percent and downward for traditional static banner ads.

Change of Marketing Focus

The Internet enables or enhances the automation of many marketing activities: customer surveys, interaction personalization, content management, collection of purchase and interest data, lead generation, and sharing of leads with business partners. Even when ethical constraints keep it from identifying you, Web-enabled software can automatically recognize you; it can determine which sites you have visited and how much time you spent at them. More fundamentally, the Internet powerfully accelerates a business revolution that had already begun to transform the traditional relationship between American corporate enterprise and its customers, shifting the focus of commerce away from products and toward services and information.

- **Channels have grown more diverse.** While traditional marketing channels continue to be important, they have been progressively augmented by the exploding use of call centers, and now by mass acceptance of the Web. Now, more than ever, companies must work to understand which channels encourage the customer interactions they are seeking and which enable the most cost-effective delivery of marketing communications.

- **Times to market are telescoping.** Technological advances and heightened competition are fostering constant innovation and accelerating product life cycles.

- **Loyalty is key.** In the new business environment, with its greater volatility and intensified competition, the key to market leadership for sustained growth and profitability is building relationships with customers to maximize their loyalty over the long-term.

- **Interactions are more complex.** Refinements to collection of customer information have made it possible for companies to segment their customer sets much more precisely. Together with computer-enabled advances in the flexibility of manufacturing processes, this development has enabled companies to recognize and respond to markets that are smaller, more tightly defined, and more volatile. Doing so has endowed customers with more choice and more information.

This growth in complexity is fast overwhelming traditional marketing approaches. Under pressure to jettison one-size-fits-all strategies for marketing and sales, companies are increasingly recognizing the need to understand their customers, the dynamics of their markets, and the details of how given target segments respond to selected marketing and sales initiatives.

Collaboration

In the client/server world, collaboration meant having a call-center supervisor monitor a call. Although there are situations in which such collaboration is adequate, the term means much more in the e-business environment; here it means your employees, your customers, your suppliers, your business partners, working together in real time. It can take the form of presentations by employees to other employees or to customers; of three-way phone calls involving employees, customers, and suppliers; or of Web-mediated sharing of information through chat, whiteboarding, URL-sharing, and/or co-browsing.

Consider a challenge that Oracle has traditionally faced: that of delivering training—provided by numerous trainers—to thousands of employees, customers, and business partners in dozens of cities and countries worldwide. Until recently, such training cost Oracle $900 per student per class. But the Internet enabled the company to set up its E-Business Network, a medium through which it now offers up to 40 free, interactive eSeminars per month—at a cost of $10 per student per class.

While this great reduction in expense benefits everybody involved, it is perhaps less impressive than the flexibility that springs from the new medium. Instead of absenting themselves from their usual work responsibilities for days or weeks at a time, employees and customers can now slot their training in what was formerly "disposable" time. If the student has some time early in the morning, during lunch, late in the evening, or between calls—time that might otherwise be dissipated on low-priority tasks—that time can now be used to get needed training in a subject that the student or the student's manager has selected.

Web Tone

The dial tone tells you that your telephone is working. Someday we may have an exact equivalent for the Internet; until then, *Web tone* means that you are assured of a reliable connection to a given URL.

Web tone is the basis of online collaboration. In client/server days, Oracle would demo its products to a prospect by bringing the needed hardware and a team of consultants to the prospect's site. Such an effort, multiplied by thousands of opportunities per quarter, translated into enormous expenses for the company, in dollars and in worker time.

With Web tone, many products and services can now be demoed over the Internet, sometimes collaboratively. This medium provides for consistent and reliable demos on demand, supported from one location but available globally. If a collaborative demo raises a question, the collaborating agent can answer it at once. If a noncollaborative demo raises a question, the prospect can click a Call-Me button to have a customer service representative (CSR) call back at once.

Displaced costs will vary by the size of the sponsoring business; but, for Oracle, this new mode of automated marketing rings up savings of hundreds of millions of dollars. Not only that: it enables the sales cycle to move forward more smoothly, and it does so in a way that promotes standardization and thus enhances corporate control.

Direct vs. Relationship Marketing

The two major goals of marketing are to keep existing customers active and to secure new ones. Given this context, the advent of direct (or database) marketing was itself a revolution, furnishing a representative business with a tool whereby it could first pool all its data on customers and prospects, then segment them as appropriate to its concerns, and finally target them with specific campaigns. However, marketing of this type has two major limitations.

First, the focus on mass mailings that are generated using lists of undifferentiated prospects, though it enables one-time campaigns, offers no way of leveraging earlier interactions with specific customers. Second, as more and more corporations come to use such tools, customers come to feel harassed by indiscriminate mailings and telemarketing calls; response rates fall, often driving companies to purchase yet further undifferentiated lists from list brokers.

The era of mass marketing has passed. Marketers now aspire to *relationship marketing*, in which every interaction with a customer is an opportunity to learn more about that customer and to promote products or services in a way that is individualized. More than any other, the Internet is the channel that enables relationship marketing; it provides a medium to attract, to engage, to inform, and to learn from customers in an interactive way.

Attracting Customers

So—responses have evolved; but the challenge remains the same: to attract the customers that the company wants and to secure them for life. The key is interaction history.

A number of self-styled customer relationship management (CRM) vendors routinely vaunt themselves as providing a 360-degree view of the customer, while what they offer in fact is closer to 45 degrees. To vindicate the standard claim, a company must—at a minimum—capture all its interactions with a customer, across all channels (Web, call center, mobile professionals, professional clerks) and all applications (marketing, sales, service, self-service, unassisted selling, financials, procurement, managing, supply chain). It must effectively organize all the data captured, and it must enable the exploitation of the customer knowledge thus developed.

Interaction capture, and the history into which it matures, have become much more complex and potentially more interesting in the age of the Internet; they now embrace sequences of URLs navigated, browsing patterns within Web sites, shopping carts saved or checked out. The use of advertising within a corporate Web site or across affiliated sites gives marketers information about the routes followed by customers that brought them to the desired destination. The performance of a Web ad can be tracked in real time by counting customer clicks on the ad and collecting data on the orders that result from such clicks. Advertising can be placed on affiliate sites according to corporate strategies for market segmentation, and analysts can use the results generated by such ads to refine that segmentation.

After all this information has been captured, it can be analyzed for behavior patterns, and the results can be used to personalize subsequent interactions—to cross-sell, to up-sell, to recommend specific products. Where mass-marketing blitzes were a characteristic client/server business practice, true one-to-one relationships with your company's customers are a characteristic e-business practice.

Engaging Customers

Here the key is to understand the *current* customer, so that the corporate site can present promotions and information that he or she will find intriguing. This means that the site must be able either to recognize the customer as somebody returning or to secure some information specific to the customer. The latter is always possible to some degree, because the site has access to the customer's Internet protocol (IP) address, which carries geographic and domain-type (for instance, .edu) information.

To gather a broader range of information, the site may require that the customer log in, or it may deposit a *cookie* on the customer's PC. Either technique affords the site the near-certain recognition of a returning customer, even though the customer cannot be compelled to identify him- or herself correctly. The customer may be offered an incentive (such as a discount) to enter personal information or to participate in a survey. The site may also be able to identify and interpret the path followed by the customer to arrive at the site.

Customer information collected in such ways can be stored in a database, and then retrieved and used for reference on any later visit by the customer. This enables the site to present the customer with material that is individualized according to the customer's profile or preferences, and thus carries a high probability of engaging the customer's attention.

Using information from the customer's profile, installed base, and purchase history, marketing personnel or applications can deduce that the customer will take an interest in products like those purchased before, or like those purchased by other customers with similar preferences. Offerings also need to be related to the information that the customer is viewing at the moment, so that they will not be viewed as annoying distractions.

Data accumulated as to the customer's interests and purchasing behavior can serve as the basis for sophisticated rules governing automated promotional displays. Similar technology can be used for cross-selling and up-selling, or for offering products as substitutes for selections that would otherwise have to be back-ordered. Corporations can use these tactics to maximize their interactions with viewers (for "stickiness") and to enhance viewers' orientation toward purchasing.

Informing Customers

In the client/server world, information was pushed to an often undifferentiated public without regard for the interests of the audience, which was bombarded with direct mailings, postcards, catalogs, and dial-for-dollars phone calls that always (it seemed) came during dinner. The consumer generally had no idea what truly useful information was available, and the information actually being pushed was often entirely irrelevant to the consumer's concerns. Marketers spent enormous sums on these methods, though their impact was all too often to alienate the people targeted.

By contrast, the Internet enables a true publish-and-subscribe model. With little effort, every company can implement a Web page that consumers can use to convey to the company what information they actually want and how they want it delivered. Using check boxes or drop-down lists, consumers ought to be able to choose among a) delivery media, including e-mail, fax, conventional mail, and phone calls; b) materials including

- Catalogs
- Contract renewals
- Magazines and newsletters
- Preplanned maintenance notices
- Product announcements
- Product catalogs
- Product defect and recall notices
- Seminar and event announcements
- Other informational and promotional items

Learning from Customers

Traditional marketing methods, by their nature, have imposed limitations on interactions with customers, discouraging customer feedback. Improvements to products and services often depended on the results of expensive surveys and research. The Web, by contrast, provides an easy and cost-effective way to gather customer feedback on offers, products, and services, and to respond in real time to customer concerns. Companies will want to maintain permanent records of all customer input and to ensure that they are linked to customer profiles as appropriate.

Marketing at Oracle

Marketing at Oracle, as at most major companies, is a strategic center of activity. Oracle's marketing budget for fiscal 2001 is $500 million. The principal goals of the company's marketing automation effort are to automate as much as reasonable of the marketing and sales processes, to optimize return on marketing investment, and to facilitate management of the money involved.

Any major marketing effort at Oracle begins with the design of a campaign to be executed in one or more of eight languages (listed earlier). Proposals and target lists are created, a process that comprises review of installed-base information to ensure that related product configurations are accurately understood and that the correct language is being used. Proposals are then sent out with demos and draft quotes attached.

Oracle allocates to each country a marketing budget to be managed as appropriate; marketing management for the country has a measure of autonomy in relation to that budget, but its decisions are subject to approval by e-business software. Expenses go largely to dissemination of information through e-seminars, courses, Web broadcasts, and the like. Such initiatives, and the responses to them, are also monitored electronically. For instance, every company press release has an associated Web page that serves as a "landing pad," usually leading to a questionnaire and providing links to Oracle pages likely to be of interest to prospects, who can ordinarily react by conducting self-service demos, by searching knowledge bases, and—ideally—by purchasing an offering. Web-monitoring tools measure the effectiveness of campaigns, press releases, Web pages, and so forth.

Because of past difficulties in collecting and coordinating business information, marketing has often been conducted in almost complete isolation from the rest of the corporate enterprise. The advent of the Internet trumps most of the information problems, and in doing so makes it not only possible but nearly obligatory to integrate marketing tightly with the other major business activities—and to do so, for multinationals, on a global basis.

This integration is essential to automating the backbone of business, the process known as campaign-to-cash. This process links together budget allocation, selection of products and markets, identification of target segments, authoring and execution of the campaign, accommodation of customer response, purchase handling (e.g., through purchase orders or credit cards), fulfillment, and receipt of cash. For effective campaign-to-cash automation, marketing must be in touch with data and business processes originating with sales, service, pricing, manufacturing, finance, and order management. This integration may seem difficult; but it's easy compared to staying in business without it.

Pulling it all Together

We have established that customer information is critical and that technology enables companies to capture that information as customers navigate across Web sites or within the corporate site. Companies can collect data as to which ads the customer responds to, which pages secure the customer's attention, and which pages are the last to be viewed before the customer leaves the site. Customer ID and information as to customer address, installed base, credit cards, and purchase and payment preferences—all these data can be entered and maintained by the customer, conducing to company records that are more accurate and current.

In the traditional marketing world, customer information is expensive. Because the Web enables customers to maintain their own information, without agent intervention, the expense of securing that information is slight, that of maintaining it even slighter. Companies can save huge sums that they would have spent on telemarketing surveys, list purchases, and list purging and merging operations to secure clean and current customer data. The strategic challenge now is to centralize and reconcile enormous volumes of customer information so that it is neither in conflict with nor redundant to data captured by traditional methods of marketing, sales, billing, and customer service.

Moreover, the Internet enables marketing technology to become nearly or fully automatic, enabling marketers to focus on campaign strategy and design. Promotions, once designed, can be automatically monitored for thresholds and results. Without intervention by the marketer, distinct promotions can be presented to distinct customers, having been selected automatically on the basis of the customers' profiles, requests, previous purchases, and/or responses to specific Web pages.

In sum, competition intensified by the Internet has heightened the challenges posed by the traditional marketing objectives—to retain existing customers and to secure new ones while constrained by tight marketing budgets. Customer loyalties will erode rapidly unless the companies they deal with focus intently on sensible collection and use of customer information. At the turn of the millennium, the Internet raises the marketing stakes; but it also deals the winning hand by enabling intelligent relationship marketing.

Selling

Selling has been revolutionized by the Internet. No choice remains for firms wanting to survive. Never before has it been possible for a company to reach a global audience with a single voice, or to enable customers to purchase goods and services with such ease. A business partner can now access its leads and submit its royalty reports over the Net. Executives can manage their businesses across all channels and geographic boundaries. Field sales personnel, no matter where they are, can use simple Web browsers to access customer and deal information critical to closing business deals.

The Internet is the backbone that makes all this possible. Before the Net, the prevailing client/server architecture dictated the design of software used to assist in the selling process; such software had to be installed and maintained on user PCs, as well as on a server. This resulted in high maintenance costs, painful and prolonged upgrade processes, and departmental systems that could serve only local areas. Some vendors obscured these problems by referring to their architectures as *n-tier*, but this meant merely that their software needed to be installed not only on multiple user PCs but on multiple servers, thus proving even more difficult for support personnel to maintain.

Thus, in the client/server world, the selling process—though advanced somewhat by sales force automation (SFA) software—was fragmented and difficult to manage. The basic problem was that information could not be effectively shared across the enterprise or along the value chain to customers, suppliers, and partners. Moreover, as enterprises grew, the management and maintenance of data became very expensive. E-commerce, as we now understand it, was impossible. Customers, suppliers, and partners had no window into the enterprise. Sales-force automation meant merely contact- and opportunity-management software that enabled sales reps to access local information about their customers, and sales managers to perform departmental forecasts. Companies could not generate up-to-the-minute forecasts across multiple countries or compile timely global account information for multinational customers. Servers used by multinationals were typically country-specific, which made it nearly impossible to share information across borders. A sales rep in the United States working on a deal for a U.S. subsidiary of a German corporation would have little idea of sales activities at the parent company in Germany. Worse, CEOs of multinationals could not view global pipelines or make enterprise-spanning forecasts.

Now, with the Internet, end users can use Web browsers to execute SFA software. This enables any company to:

- Run its business globally using one or a few installations, with a very low cost of ownership

- Enable its customers and partners to do business with it unassisted, and from any point on the globe

- Access accurate and comprehensive business information in real time

The selling process has benefited particularly in three areas:

- Sales-rep productivity

- Lead management

- Executive oversight

Sales-Rep Productivity

Sales personnel can now use sales portals for real-time access to information needed to close deals. Less time is spent collecting customer information in preparation for a site visit, or putting together proposals that can now be generated automatically and distributed via the Web.

An even more dramatic change is that a company's customers can now access its Web store to request quotes or even to create their own proposals. Customers will find it much easier to make relatively objective comparisons using the Web. This self-service model can be designed to notify sales reps automatically when reviews and approvals are needed, and to automate or simplify administrative tasks in order to minimize sales-force paperwork.

Order taking will come to prevail over traditional sales functions, and large direct sales forces will no longer be needed. Direct-sales personnel are likely to be converted in many cases into account or relationship managers or customer-support personnel as sales and service functions increasingly coalesce. Some sales agents will be retrained for new roles along these lines; others will be replaced.

Lead Management

The Web brings with it the ability to capture valuable information about customers' interests and behavior. This can help sales personnel to determine which customer interactions qualify as leads appropriate for follow-up by a field sales rep, a telesales agent, or e-mail.

And this is only the beginning. A centralized lead system conduces to standardizing the qualification and assignment processes. For example, a customer responding favorably to a Web survey may be an ideal target for a forthcoming promotion. Partners to whom leads are assigned can now access and manage those leads over the Internet. Companies can determine which partners are selling most effectively and can ensure that leads are routed to partners competent to exploit them (see Chapter 4, *Partner Relationship Management*). And companies can measure the effectiveness of their direct marketing activities by calculating rates of lead generation, costs per lead, lead conversion rates, and associated returns on investment.

Executive Oversight

A coordinated central repository for managing sales data makes it possible to share opportunity information across a global sales force, enabling team selling across country borders. Sales executives and managers no longer need to merge spreadsheets from their various organizations to get an accurate view of the company pipeline or to create a forecast. Further, forecasting information can be submitted to upper-management automatically in such a manner that it is accessible in real time. Through a single sales portal, executives can now see all the information necessary to run the business: forecast trends, pipeline activity, and top deals for the quarter.

By using the Internet, company executives can exercise more control over the selling process. Communications are increasingly in written form and can be validated in advance as well as in retrospect. Representations by customers and prospects as to commitments undertaken by the selling company can be more reliably confirmed or confuted. Ambitious commitments by overzealous sales agents willing to jeopardize their employers' broader interests to secure sales will increasingly be relegated to the annals of business history.

Selling at Oracle

Oracle has an aggressive sales force, highly regarded for its ability to execute. Traditionally, however, this sales force has had to function within and to cope with the complications imposed by a convoluted corporate allocation of sales responsibilities. The arrival of the Internet as a major business enabler militates for rationalization in this area, making it simultaneously easier to simplify and more difficult to perpetuate the existing complexity.

The sales effort within Oracle has traditionally been organized by three criteria. In order of importance, these are geography, industry, and customer size. In broad terms, these criteria have been segmented as follows:

- Geographically, sales responsibilities have been divided among Japan, (other) Asia/Pacific, Canada, the United States, Latin America, and Europe/Middle East/Africa.

- By industry, sales responsibilities have been divided among services industries, process industries, and general business, as follows:
  - Services industries: financial services, telecoms, utilities, and government/education/health care
  - Process industries: airlines, consumer electronics, hardware, high-tech, and retailers
  - General business: startups, dot-coms, and firms with less than $500 million in annual revenue

- The size (traditionally as defined by annual revenue) of the customer has qualified about 100 Oracle customers as *named accounts*; a specific sales responsibility has traditionally been associated with each such account. The class of named accounts has for some purposes been treated as a fourth "industry" category.

However, these three major criteria are not related hierarchically; each has been allowed to trump the other two when its doing so has been perceived as advantageous for some reason, often ad hoc. To add a further layer of complexity, Oracle has traditionally pursued sales through four media: direct sales; the Direct Marketing Division, which addresses accounts within the Department of Defense (DoD), advanced programs, the public sector, higher education, telecommunications, financial services, utilities, and healthcare; telemarketing and telesales; and the Oracle Store.

The result of these mutually interpenetrating heterogeneities has been what anyone would have predicted: a structure of sales responsibilities that is fragmented, decentralized, and confusing, and that is characterized by multiple distinct processes, disciplines, contracts, price lists, sales technologies, training organizations, and training standards. And, like any other corporate structure, it has been gradually encrusted and rigidified by issues of politics, personalities, and organizational dynamics that tend to counteract any reform.

Enter the Internet. Because it must be reckoned with, the Internet compels a reexamination of the preexisting structures, which is the first step in breaching their fortifications. More fundamentally, the transparency promoted by the Internet makes it hard to prolong a system that comprises pricing structures and prices that differ from one country to another. Further, the Internet makes it possible for transactions that used of necessity to take place in different countries to take place all—effectively—in one place, on a single central computer system.

Oracle has taken advantage of this singularity to push through a deep reform of its sales policies and practices. Now all products for all customers for all industries for all geographic regions can be purchased directly through the Oracle Store—which, incidentally, is an implementation of Oracle's iStore application. Products may be combined and configured in ways Oracle recognizes as valid, but the sales process no longer allows the effective definition of new products or redefinition of existing ones. The company has put forward a single sales process and a single price book, along the lines of what is now known as the Saturn model. Contracts, though not reduced to a single universal format, have been very much simplified. And the online system incorporates a single, consistent discounting process.

The Global Store

Global stores promise very impressive ROIs, to be achieved partly through automating and partly through standardizing the sales process. Definitions will vary, but a comprehensive global store for a major corporation will deal in all that corporation's lines of business and in all its products; in all the currencies it recognizes and the tax implications of every purchase; and in all the languages in which the corporation conducts business. It will serve all prospective buyers, and it will do all this from one central location—with order fulfillment handled at the appropriate one of many dispersed locations.

The global store serves not only the company's traditional (external) customers but also its employees, notably its order takers, direct sales agents, call-center agents, support-renewal agents, and a variety of clerical administrators. The company needs to ensure that all its employees whose business responsibilities include price quoting and order entry have continuous access to the store and use it reliably. This is because one of the store's most valuable functions is to enforce correct and uniform pricing, discounting, product configurations, and other terms from the electronic product catalog. Never before has there been so powerful a tool for ensuring that all employees present a single corporate face to customers and prospects.

The global store must enable any user to choose among the currencies supported (perhaps for a quote on a product or configuration, not necessarily for an order) and among the languages supported. It needs to present a broad range, if not all, of the company's products, accommodating the possibility that some products are available only in certain configurations or in certain countries, and that prices may have similarly limited applicability. The store needs to be able to compute tax consequences of any purchase, which in many instances will mean that its software must integrate with software from a third party that specializes in tax computation.

What does this mean for Oracle? The Oracle Store is designed to handle:

- All of Oracle's lines of business
- All of its products, in both current and earlier versions
- All of its contract types (standard, custom, General Services Administration, and so on)
- All of its services (consulting, support, Business OnLine)
- Education offerings and the associated systems by which credits are issued (e.g., to partners) for training accomplished
- Contract renewals
- Support renewals
- Online services, including Oracle Applications Network and Oracle Technology Network

External customers of the Oracle Store are billed appropriately; orders placed by employees are normally free. Once an order has been entered, from anywhere around the globe, fulfillment is initiated from a location reasonably close to the ship-to location entered by the order-placer.

Customer Care

In this area, the Internet enables truly dramatic changes. In "the old days," a customer seeking help from a company might write a letter or, more commonly, place a telephone call to a brick-and-mortar call center. After the usual delays—for delivery, or while waiting for somebody to answer the phone—both the letters and the calls had frequently to be rerouted within the company, with attendant delays and risks of loss.

Now the customer can use e-mail to communicate with service personnel. The process is more rapid, partly because any rerouting within the company is easier. The communication is less likely to be lost, because it can so readily be copied and stored as needed.

Moreover, it lends itself to easy incorporation in a database of customer concerns and complaints.

The service organization for an electronic business can choose whether to provide customer care solely via e-mail or to coordinate the Web channel with one or more call centers (in a hybrid model called *brick-and-click*). Such coordination can be effected through a universal work queue, which provides each customer-care agent with an overview of his or her entire workload, enabling the agent to assess incoming calls and e-mails and to make informed decisions as to priorities and trade-offs.

Other opportunities offered by the Internet may even preempt the customer's need to address the company. Companies can post frequently asked question (FAQ) lists the contents of which respond to the most important questions their customers have posed. Companies can also sponsor sites that a customer can use to compare a given problem or concern with those of other customers. In addition, companies can implement software that uses techniques for case-based reasoning to guide customers to the action(s) judged—or measured as—most likely to resolve any problem experienced.

Customers can also use a company's Web site to download—or to request, if necessary—support information they need. They may also submit—spontaneously or on request—information as to their installed base of the company's products, and the company can use the data submitted to confirm or correct its customer records. Assuming that company software can route requests of certain types through needed approvals, customers can even take the initiative in such matters as raising their own credit limits or scheduling service calls by company technicians.

For the company, the value proposition is compelling. When customers prefer self-service, the Web makes it available at the time and pace they choose; the displacement of phone support can cut service expenses by 50 percent or more without reducing the company's intimacy with its customers.

Together, these developments will have enormous effects on service organizations.

Specific Customer Self-Services

Among the services that a customer can now perform without human assistance are:

- Adding new products or services to the customer's list of interests or purchases
- Asking questions
- Applying for, and in many cases securing, a credit card, a specified credit status, insurance, or a loan
- Changing address data
- Initiating a dispatch operation
- Learning from other customers
- Maintaining personal data
- Personalizing a profile of collateral, information, and/or merchandise to be sent to the customer
- Personalizing a service agreement
- Registering for an event
- Renewing an order (for a magazine, for checks, and so on)
- Renewing a warranty
- Reviewing an account status or balances
- Reviewing billing information
- Searching a knowledge base
- Updating customer-install-base information

Asking a Question

Ask Jeeves (at www.askjeeves.com) is a company that provides answers to questions as its corporate rationale. The knowledge bases on which such services depend grow increasingly resourceful as questions continue to be asked and answers and solutions accumulate. Ask Jeeves has compiled more solutions in a year than most companies compile in their lifetimes. Primus exemplifies the companies providing technology to build the underlying knowledge repositories.

Observations on E-mail

E-mail from a customer may be structured—that is, generated automatically in response to the customer's completing an online form—or unstructured. An e-mail of either type can be accorded automatic processing that includes parsing its text, inserting it into a work queue, attaching a selected response, and sending that response to the customer.

Parsing programs score incoming e-mails on the bases of length, specific words found, questions recognized, and so forth. Each company using such a program decides on a threshold score above which the e-mail will be accorded an automated response and below which it will be queued for human attention. The challenges for such programs are the development of solid bases of knowledge and of relevant and reliable parsing methods; companies can profit by automating their responses to customers, but any irrelevant or unsatisfying response risks alienating them instead. Whereas unstructured e-mails will often need human attention, structured e-mails can usually be processed and answered automatically; they thus form the basis for an effective call-avoidance strategy. Moreover, any accumulation of them can be subjected to straightforward techniques for statistical analysis.

When an incoming unstructured e-mail is delivered to a human agent, it is vital that the agent be provided with productivity tools. These typically overlap with and may often be identical to the resources (knowledge base and others) used by automated-response systems.

Particularly important is integrating the e-mail channel with telephony and other ways in which customers can initiate communication. When Oracle first added inbound e-mail as a customer-care channel, it had no mechanism for blending CSRs' e-mail work queues with their telephony queues. The result was that CSRs often left callers in long wait queues while they responded to e-mail messages. The CSRs were understandably reluctant to pick up their phones in order to discover whatever unpleasant surprises might be in store for them—difficult problems, customers angry about software, customers angry about being put on hold. They naturally inclined to scan the next e-mail items: in doing so they were at least buffered from any customer hostility.

Renewals

In certain areas of business, including the following, both companies and consumers face a variety of renewal issues:

- Software development
- Electronic-goods manufacture

- Hardware manufacture
- Automobile manufacture
- Equipment provision

Picture a customer that has purchased a product or service not from the original manufacturer but through a third party, which may have provided a warranty as well. The customer needs to know, on a continuing basis, the answers to many related questions: What—and with whom—are my warranties? What are my entitlements? When and how do I renew them? If they involve distinct companies in roles that may overlap, how are problems resolved? How do I find out about new products and services that it would make sense for me to buy instead of renewing an expiring agreement?

The Internet reshapes the landscape in this area. It allows customers to renew warranties and service contracts, and to "up-sell themselves" by moving to plans that provide greater benefits. It enables customers and businesses to enter into or maintain direct relationships with equipment manufacturers, even though their warranties were issued by third parties. For the price of an effective contract-management application, the enterprise sponsoring the Web renewal facility accrues a number of benefits:

- Reduction of revenue leakage
- More efficient call routing for coordinated call centers
- Fuller understanding of the relationship and the commitments binding the enterprise to the customer or to another business
- Automated entitlement checking and enforcement across major customer interaction channels

Auto-Renewals at Oracle

Every year sees the renewal of 85 percent of Oracle's service contracts globally—representing an annual revenue stream of about $1.5 billion. At present, this activity requires the attention of some 200 support service representatives (SSRs).

Oracle expects to reduce its staffing needs to forty SSRs and to drive its renewal rate to 98 percent. A prerequisite step is to rewrite its standard service contract to add an evergreen clause authorizing Oracle to invoice and renew automatically. Then, ninety days prior to the expiration of every such contract outstanding, the company can generate a package comprising a quote, relevant collateral, and a pro forma invoice, and dispatch it to the customer. Once the company receives, in return, an e-mail acknowledgment, the customer can be automatically invoiced; once a check or purchase order is received, the contract can be automatically extended.

With most renewals automated, Oracle will be able to concentrate the efforts of its SSRs on instances involving custom or problematic contracts and contracts relating to situations involving customers and/or services of special value to the company. And it can concentrate the efforts of its programmers on extending its renewal automation to cover these exceptional cases as well.

Customer Care at Oracle

Oracle's customer care is highly regarded. It is centered on a single set of practices that have been communicated effectively through the ranks, worldwide, and it takes advantage of highly effective techniques for interpreting and acting on statistics relating to call volumes, customer wait times, and cost per call.

However, the entire customer-care system at Oracle has been undermined by the policy that each country unit owns all customer information for its country. Thus call data, customer data, contract data, renewal data, and call-tracking systems have been dispersed across country boundaries. Though this poses problems for transnational evaluation and comparison of customer-care efforts, these are overshadowed by the fragmentation of all data pertaining to multinational Oracle customers.

The Internet, of course, makes possible for the first time a thoroughgoing solution to this problem. Not only can all the data for any Oracle customer—no matter how large—be brought together into a single repository, Oracle can now extend to the customer the ability, as appropriate, to maintain, integrate, validate, and interpret the data. Country units may retain oversight responsibilities, but in the fundamental sense the data now belong to the Oracle Corporation and to the customer to which they pertain.

Every week Oracle responds to roughly 50,000 calls for service and support. The average cost to the company of handling such a call is about $125; the most expensive calls, which tend to be those relating to the products that provide the greatest business value (that is, the E-Business Suite), cost about $300 on average. So the total annual expenditure by Oracle on service and support calls is roughly $325,000,000.

Accordingly, Oracle is now deploying a self-service support center on Oracle.com. Any customer can use the center to:

- Enter an address change

- Inquire on contacts

- Search a knowledge base

- Create a service request or check its status

- Review or renew a contract or check a service level

- View news and alerts.

This support center will make it more convenient for customers to do business with Oracle; at the same time it will slash Oracle's support expenses. Over the year to come, as the system is deployed globally,[10] it is projected to cut the cost of handling an average call from $125 to a few dollars.

The single-instance-database approach will support an evolution in the customer-care model. In the old scheme, each customer enterprise would sign up for the Gold, Silver, or Bronze level of support—which meant, among other things, that a customer of relatively little value to Oracle could secure a level of support equal to, or even greater than, the level for a customer of crucial importance. The two higher levels also entitled the customers choosing them to an unlimited number of calls for support, which deprived both Oracle and the customer of the virtues of pricing proportionate to service.

Incident-based support is replacing this model. The integration of worldwide data for multinational customers will enable support personnel to refer every customer to an index of that customer's importance to Oracle, precalculated on the basis of revenues recognized and anticipated. Customers will be able to cash support coupons in order to advance within a support queue or to secure the escalation of specific concerns. For the first time, support personnel will be able to act on an informed understanding of the customer as a global enterprise, and services will be priced justly; no longer will any customer be able to parlay a fixed fee into virtually unlimited support, nor will more self-reliant customers be called upon, in effect, to subsidize the needs of others.

Payment Processing

Full Internet implementation of payment processing will mean the utter transformation of this business process. Where traditional payment processing was paper-intensive and required human involvement at both ends of the transaction, provider and customer, a full transition to Web-based processing will mean no paper, except on demand, and no need for any human involvement!

Vending machines of the latest generation can sense when their racks are depleted and generate replenishment orders across the Internet; the years to come will see this ability spread. Even so, most purchases will probably still be initiated by human beings; all physical goods will still have to be shipped, and most services will probably continue to be discharged in ways that require human involvement. But none of these reservations has any bearing on payment processing. To understand how payments come to be completely automated, consider what happens when you place a credit-card order at a highly automated site.

Authorization

Of course, you must provide whatever personal information the merchant requires to process the order; this will include your credit-card data and may include a coupon number, promotion ID, or some other mechanism for securing a discount. (At some sites, it might also include product configuration data.) At length, you click the order button. This sends the order data, with the price displayed to you, to the merchant's site for capture by an order-entry system. However, it also triggers the authorization process, by which the merchant's software forwards details of the transaction to an authorization bank or to a third-party authorization service.

Depending on circumstances, authorization can be more or less complex. It usually includes validation of the credit-card account number and certification that credit is available for the order. These steps are accomplished automatically by an authorization request forwarded (whether by the authorization bank or by the third party) to the credit-card association and by it to the issuer bank. Authorization will often include a comparison of the billing and shipping addresses specified. All of this can be done automatically, although a failure to authorize may lead to human intervention.

Settlement

By law, settlement may not be initiated until the merchant has shipped the goods or discharged the service ordered. This process typically (though not for electronic downloads) requires human participation; when it does, a human being must record the merchant's completion of its obligation. This triggers a capture-funds request sent to the merchant bank (or "acquiring bank"), then to an interbank clearing organization, and then to the bank or other organization that issued the credit card being used. The credit-card issuer remits the money to the merchant bank, debits the customer's credit line, and bills the customer at the close of the billing cycle. The merchant bank imposes on the purchase amount a discount rate that varies from 1.5 percent to 6 percent depending on the size and nature of the merchant; it then credits the merchant's account with the remainder. All these processes, following the initiating data entry, are normally automated.

Payment may or may not require action by the customer. In recent years, customers have been able to subscribe to bill-presentment services that aggregate bills for them and give them the option of paying those bills either after review or automatically on the due date. The payment itself travels simply from the customer (or bill-presentment service) to the credit-card issuer; there it stops, the issuer having previously transferred the corresponding payment to the merchant bank.

Out of the amount that the merchant bank collects, it must pay an average of 0.5 percent of the transaction amount to third-party processors (notably authorization services and bank payment processors), an average of 0.08 percent to the credit-card associations, and an average of 1.25 percent to 1.9 percent to the card-issuing organization. Again, all this processing is normally automated.

Problems with Current Methods of Processing Transactions

Several aspects of payment processing currently pose special problems, some of which may prove intractable to automation.

Registration

As a rule, any customer trying to order from two or more sites must enter all required personal information once per site. Although e-wallets meant to address this annoyance are available or under development by Microsoft, CyberCash, Yahoo!, Verifone, and others, each current offering will work only with merchants who subscribe—at a price—to the service in question. E-wallets have also been hampered by customer resistance because of difficulties in understanding them and concerns about their degree of security.

However, the industry appears to be moving toward a solution to this problem. In June 1999, AOL, IBM, Microsoft, and Sun Microsystems agreed to support ECML, the Electronic Commerce Modeling Language, a new single standard for e-wallets. The standard has been approved by Visa, MasterCard, and American Express, and a number of e-merchants have pledged to back it.

ECML uses a set of uniform field names to identify normal customer data, and merchants simply have to make sure that the corresponding fields on their Web pages have the correct names. The name set is expandable, to accommodate the introduction of new data—for instance, units of digital cash.

Fraud

Fraud can be reduced but not eliminated. To be perpetrated, it must maneuver around all the obstacles erected against it, and this generally means that it can be detected and dealt with only by human beings. Nevertheless, a great deal can be done automatically to prevent it.

By federal law, a consumer who has lost a credit card, but who has not reported the loss to the credit-card issuer, is liable for the first $50 lost when the card is used fraudulently; the merchant is responsible for the remainder of the loss. In practice, merchants will rarely if ever pursue account holders for that $50, for two reasons: (a) the amount is too small to repay the pursuit; (b) in most cases of fraudulent card use over the Internet the card has probably not been lost.

Thus, the merchant either assumes full liability for fraud or pays a third party to assume some degree of liability ranging up to 100 percent. The payment normally ranges from 1 percent to 6 percent of the purchase amount, depending on the thoroughness of the measures that the third party guarantees.

Human and mechanical measures to combat fraud are known collectively as risk management. In relation to automated payment processing over the Internet, such measures fall into five main categories:

- Address analysis, which compares the bill-to and ship-to addresses to each other and to the billing address for the credit-card account to be billed

- For foreign addresses, association of distinct levels of risk with distinct countries or regions (declining to authorize a purchase solely on the basis of an address within the United States is illegal)

- Confirmation that credit for the purchase amount is available in the account

- Weighing whether the method of shipment requires the recipient's signature

- Examining the payment history for a known customer and/or the purchaser's credit record

Settlement

This area poses relatively minor problems. Payments other than by credit account may compel manual processing, and every payment will require manual processing if the merchant does manual reconciliation of payments to accounts receivable. The challenge is to automate all settlement activity and to do so at low cost with high reliability. This automation implies the integration of the merchant's store, financial system, and order-management system, which, in turn, implies an e-business software suite for automated cash collection.

Return Management

The most costly part(s) of every Internet transaction involving physical goods are shipping the goods to the customer—which merchants accept as an inevitable cost of business—and processing the return of those goods when the customer, for whatever reason, is not satisfied with them. Human involvement in return processing is in most cases probably essential, and it is not obvious that much of the processing can be cost-effectively handled by automation.

Conclusion

Payment processing is extremely complex. The point of this section is *not* that online processing has made it possible to automate any number of component processes that would otherwise have to be done manually. At one time, many of them *were* done manually, but many others came into being only because automation had already advanced to a point at which it could accommodate them. Not only the Internet, but information technology in general, is transforming preexisting processes; beyond that, it is making possible new ones that had no counterparts in the world of 1950.

Business Intelligence

The term *business intelligence* (BI) has three meanings , which partly overlap:

- *Competitive intelligence.* This meaning, analogous to *military intelligence*, is the oldest; it refers to the analysis of the business activities of one or more companies competitive with one's own.

- *Market intelligence.* Intelligence of this kind relates to the market or markets in which a company operates or invests, or may in the future.

- *Operating intelligence.* This meaning, now prevalent, refers to the analysis of the operations of one's own enterprise, with the goal of making those operations more cost-effective.

Common to these three meanings is the goal of transforming data into information, leading to more comprehensive and useful information bases. The objective of BI is to enable a more thorough understanding of business processes, resulting in more effective decision-making, both strategic and tactical. BI serves a broad range of users: the shipping clerk validating a packaging order that depends on customer profitability; the CSR selecting a product in an up-sell situation; the sales rep analyzing the effectiveness of his or her interactions with customers; the manager determining marketing budgets on the basis of campaign success rates; and, ultimately, the C-level executive basing the direction of high-level corporate initiatives on strategic data from applications that, taken together, span the company.

Traditionally, companies have addressed the need for business intelligence by producing reports, the purpose of which is to cumulate data and to present them in ways relatively easy to understand and to act on. Such reports are often automated to store parameters for data selection and presentation and to run at defined intervals; they are often complemented by graphs and by links between and among reports. Despite many new and powerful BI offerings, and regardless of all predictions of "the paperless office," reports still provide the basis for most business intelligence.

An obstacle to BI has been the fragmentation of data across applications and geographies, often resulting from the use of multiple unrelated applications. A multidivision multinational might implement one instance of a marketing automation suite, supported by one database, for each division in each country. To pin down the ROI on a widespread campaign would require battalions of DBAs and business-process experts, supported by harried programmers trying to write interfaces to dozens of applications that other programmers were busy updating. If the task force did indeed emerge with a plausible answer it was likely to be too late: it might hold some value for the next campaign, but the campaign in question was probably long since concluded.

Data warehouses (DWs)—which typically require huge amounts of storage, often reaching multiple terabytes—came into existence as a solution to this problem. Such warehouses pose challenges of their own. The enterprise must normalize data and data formats from multiple applications in order to analyze those data constructively; it must ensure that those applications regularly feed their output to the warehouse; it must operate and maintain the DW environment reliably; and it must implement mechanisms to display and analyze data and to propagate them across the enterprise. Ideally, the first data warehouses would have prefigured the databases now enabled by the Internet, comprising a single instance of every datum needed by the company. In fact, because of the complexities attending their implementation, many DWs remained to some extent application- or region-bound, falling short of their full potential.

Nonetheless, some DWs served as early showcases for the benefits to be derived from the aggregation and correlation of data provided by disparate applications: common views of business results and synergetic presentation of information, leading to recognition of unexpected correlations—like the well-publicized observation that beer and diapers were frequently purchased together, often on late-night shopping trips by young fathers. These benefits argue for the centralization not merely of data but of data-generating applications: If the analytical benefits are persuasive, what about the transactional benefits?

Ubiquitous use of HTML (HyperText Markup Language) and HTTP (Hypertext Transport Protocol), reducing extensively the degree of discrepancy among data formats, has advanced the use of data warehouses. Meanwhile, the Internet has made it easier to aggregate data across regional boundaries and to access the results, using a browser, from anywhere in the world. The results for DWs have been unprecedented levels of usability and reductions in total cost of ownership.

Data warehouses now provide the basis for more advanced information-analysis techniques, known collectively as data mining. These techniques support the development of data-exploration models and their application to DWs, taking advantage of the enormous amounts of data stored and of their normalized formats and dimensions to uncover patterns and relationships not previously recognized.

Business intelligence is further enabled in the age of the Internet: BI software can now exploit the ready flow of information to offer marketers not only new marketing techniques but also new ways to measure their effectiveness. Real-time measurement is becoming a key component of the marketing equation. Testing the effectiveness of a campaign has always been critical, but now it can be tested while the campaign is still under way, allowing companies to save or generate large sums via midstream corrections. Consider a banner ad that is generating fewer click-throughs than were expected: the marketer can review the response rate in real time and can adjust the campaign after a day or two by changing the design or placement of the ad. Likewise, a Web promotion that is generating too few sales can be redesigned with different targeting or to offer a different product or a steeper discount. (On the other hand, businesses are coming to recognize that they must not enslave themselves to real-time data: making and changing decisions frequently can be counter-productive, and only a few applications call unequivocally for prompt action; examples are fraud detection, Web-experience personalization, and network monitoring. BI has put more tools in the decision-making toolbox, but executives still need to know how each tool can best be used.)

Given the Internet environment, sophisticated BI software can facilitate prompt and reliable answers to difficult questions that are central to the strategy of every major business:

- How do we measure campaign expenditures and effectiveness?
- What is our global sales forecast?
- How reliable is that forecast?
- Who are our customers?
- What are our commitments to customers?
- Which of our products do our customers own?
- What value should we assign to customer X?
- Who are our most/least profitable customers?
- Which are our most/least profitable products?
- Which are our most/least cost-effective channels?
- Which are our most/least effective business partners?
- Who are our top (field, call-center) sales agents?
- What is our revenue by channel?
- What is the global pipeline and order position?
- Which campaigns have generated the highest numbers of qualified leads?
- How many leads is the sales force getting, and what are the trends?
- Which are our pivotal customers?
- What does it cost us to process an order?
- What does it cost us to serve a customer?
- Which demographics are crucial for us in targeting our products and promotions?
- What percentage of qualified leads turn into orders?
- How long does that take, on average?
- What is the average interval between a quote and an order?
- What is the average order amount?
- How effective are our compensation plans?
- How long does it take us, on average, to resolve a customer concern?
- What does it cost us to acquire a customer?
- What are our true levels of customer satisfaction?

- Who are our top business partners—by product, by region, and so on?

For companies with call centers:

- What is the average call length?
- What is the call-abandoned rate?
- How effective are cross-sells and up-sells?
- What strategy is most effective for real-time product recommendations and ad presentations?

More broadly, business intelligence supports the measurement of

- Call-center agent productivity
- Lead aging and conversion
- Product profitability and trends, by geography, channel, or period
- Revenue by channel (call centers, partners, direct sales, resellers, the Web)
- Win/loss trends by competitor, product, product line, or sales group
- True ratios of revenues to cost of sales—including commissions, expenses, salaries, training, and the like
- Revenue amounts and trends by geography, product, product line, channel, or period

Problems and Potential

A persistent problem for BI has been duplication of information, particularly of customer data. This problem has been aggravated by the consolidation into central DWs of records from multiple sources. For instance, in a company of three divisions, each division may have been maintaining an autonomous database; when the company tries to bring these together and to reconcile them, it may find that it has three—or even more—records for almost every customer it deals with. In their ongoing struggle to purge superfluous records, companies have been aided by increasingly sophisticated applications; in addition to direct removal of identical and other obvious duplicates, these applications use fuzzy logic, phonetics, and other techniques to identify and weed out redundant records.

Business intelligence offers dramatic possibilities for extension in various dimensions. One is for the incorporation and exploitation of information external to the enterprise using BI—extending BI's warrant to embrace competitive and market intelligence more effectively. Such applications lend themselves to hosting by neutral third parties whose business is the aggregation of public and proprietary information about the business community. A specific use for such information is for benchmarking a company's internal performance with reference to the performance of its competitors or of a cross-section of companies in the same industry segment or the same geographic region.

A second extension would make BI a more pervasive phenomenon, enabling the results it produces to be accessed from anywhere by using any suitable electronic device—PDAs, cell phones, and the like. BI applications can also be developed to generate alerts that will be sent automatically, as appropriate, to such devices—so that, for instance, a marketing manager, even on a golf course, could be alerted to automated recognition of the failure of a campaign.

Regardless, all applications of BI will gain strength as the discipline develops more sophisticated methods for identifying and distinguishing the data that users truly need to focus on. The massive growth of data available makes it crucially important to winnow the wheat from the chaff, sparing executives the chore of having to decide to ignore information that the ideal application would never have presented.

Executives savvy to BI will be aware that it can also be used against them. An interesting example is provided by Mind-It, an application developed by NetMind Technologies, which was recently acquired by Puma Technology. Mind-It, available at http://mindit.netmind.com/, enables a user to specify Web pages to be monitored; it then alerts the user when their sponsors change those pages. Although the product accesses only public information, it can be helpful in alerting users to changes in competitors' products, presentations, and strategies.

Corporate Infrastructure

Information

The development and transmission of information within and beyond the corporation continue to depend heavily on manual processes and large labor pools. As examples, Apple maintains a customer-support call center staffed by 100 people, while Oracle—for Internet-related issues *only*—maintains one with 50 people. In some respects, the burdens for vendors have grown heavier: with the growth of business volumes, the incidence of errors and exception conditions has increased. Moreover, the rise of technology has brought a decline in direct individual contact, which adds in many ways to difficulties in identifying customers and understanding their concerns.

The challenge in this area is for companies to evolve their call centers into customer contact centers, such that all customer-initiated communications, via whatever media, funnel into a single queue—where they can be sensibly prioritized and from which they can be forwarded, under the direction of predefined business rules, to the software, CSR, or technical rep predicted to be most cost-effective in dealing with them.

Another problematic area for information flow is the Internet. Corporations need easy and economical ways to post and maintain Web content, so that it can stay comprehensive, timely, and accurate. This means that, ideally, the owner of the information must be able not only to write, review, and approve the material but actually to post it to the Web. This is generally not the case today, when major Internet-enabled enterprises typically maintain or contract with large teams of Web designers and organizers. Large labor pools, handling processes that are largely manual or require serious technical training, inevitably mean high expenses and lower profit margins.

Technology for information management is not yet mature. This area will see vigorous activity in the coming years.

Contract Management

The Internet will bring about a revolution in contract management. Consumers and businesses alike contract for goods and services, but the actual contracts are typically visible only on paper. Suppose you have a maintenance contract for your refrigerator. Do you know where your copy is? When it expires? What conditions it covers? If you have a question about the ice-making unit, wouldn't it be easier to identify the relevant clauses online than by scrutinizing six or twelve pages of fine print?

Companies will begin to maintain extranet sites for their customers such that any customer can log in and see at a glance what contracts or warranties are in force and when they are due for renewal. A customer with a warranty-covered drive-train problem will be provided one-click access to nearby service locations and will be enabled to solicit competitive bids for the repair work.

Customers with e-mail addresses on record will be sent automatic notifications of renewals and of opportunities to upgrade existing contracts and to extend their contractual coverage. Customers without e-mail addresses will get phone calls or USPS mailings triggered by the same notification programs. Consumers using older products that are more expensive to maintain may receive special promotions for replacement products.

Contracts at Oracle

Contracting systems must be industry-specific: contracts for a software-and-services company are different from those for a leasing-and-rental company. Contract complications, each specific to one or a few of a host of industries, conspire to make comprehensive contract processing extremely complex.

Oracle's contract negotiations typically begin with a quotation for a license or service and move to a license sale or an agreement as to a service level, in either case specifying associated guarantees. Every contract covers a stipulated period, at the end of which it may be renewed. Given that Oracle has some 1.2 million customers, with an average of 10 license contracts each, we see that Oracle must deal with some 12 million contracts merely for licenses, with every contract associated with some number of quotes and proposals whether for new business or for renewal. This means megatons of data.

Oracle's eBusiness Suite 11*i* moves the company's contracting processes onto the Internet, in the process striking an emphatic blow for a paperless world. Proposals, license sales, renewals, all are now accessed over intranets and extranets. Contract terms—license type, duration and renewal date, location, and so on—have been standardized across all industries and offerings to a degree approaching the logical limits. More readily now than ever before, executives can retrieve useful answers to important and complex business questions: What contract options are the most popular? What liabilities does the company face due to legislation in a specific state?

Rights Management

Rights management and contract management are tightly intertwined. Both affect every industry on the planet. For an interesting example, consider the entertainment business. The managers of a film studio need to know what titles and rights the studio owns and what titles it has under development; for instance, who owns the rights to *Toy Story* peripherals in Brazil? Only with comprehensive information can managers formulate sensible strategies for exacting rents from their titles.

During 1998, it became general knowledge that Pixar was shooting *A Bug's Life* while DreamWorks Studio was working on *Antz*, and there was widespread speculation that two animated features on such similar subjects might damage each other at the box office. DreamWorks evidently advanced the release date for *Antz* by several weeks in order to beat *A Bug's Life* to the theaters. In fact, both films proved to be hits. But it is clear that early, comprehensive, and reliable information on competing properties can have a pivotal impact on executive decisions across a wide range of corporate activities, from research and development to marketing.

Call Center Operation

Before the Internet became indispensable to business, call centers were the area in which automation had penetrated most deeply. So, either it's ironic or it makes perfect sense that call centers have largely avoided the impact of the Internet. Whichever, this will change.

Hardware Issues

The central piece of equipment for a call center is an automatic call distributor (ACD), which usually consists of proprietary hardware with proprietary interfaces. Major ACD providers are Alcatel, Aspect, Ericsson, Fujitsu, Hitachi, Lucent, Nortel, Oki, Rockwell, Siemens, and Toshiba. Repeated industry attempts to rally around a single standard (JTAPI, TAPI, or TSAPI) have consistently failed, with the result that the greatest expenses attending the deployment of a new call center are first, hardware; second, labor.

A potential solution to this problem is offered by Internet telephony, with its promise of voice and data transmission over the same network wire. This technology will lead first to the centralization within the network of proprietary ACDs and then to their replacement by standard network routers.

Positioning themselves to compete for future interaction-center business, major companies are currently acquiring smaller ones: Alcatel has purchased Genesys; Cisco has purchased Selsius; Lucent has purchased Ascend; and Nortel has purchased Clarify.

A decisive breakout from the current gridlock will require both hardware and software. To address needs including setup of call-center agents, skills-based routing, screen pops, and contract-entitlement checking and enforcement, call centers will continue to require software beyond what the Internet will make available. Regardless, Internet telephony will figure importantly in a general solution.

Support-Call Routing

Typically, a support call is routed to an available call-center agent according to a scheme based on the customer's service-level agreement. This practice, prevalent in the client/server world, will continue to be important; but e-business enables routing of a new type, based on the assessed value of the customer.

This new type depends on integrated Customer Relationship Management/Enterprise Resource Planning (CRM/ERP) single-instance applications, which will exploit opportunity-management functionality to assess revenue realized from—and to estimate future value of—the customer calling, then use these data as key input to a call-routing algorithm. The effect will be to move from "metal-based" (gold, silver, bronze) support models to incident- or coupon-based models. In general, customers perceived as higher in value will be accorded higher priorities in the work queue, reducing their wait time for limited agent resources. But customers will also be able to buy coupons that they may cash in to move ahead in the queue of inbound calls. Queuing according to this model, impossible in the client/server world, becomes possible in e-business.

Cisco Systems, although it does not develop such applications, is moving to consolidate the technology required to support them. It has extensively developed its platforms and has executed a series of complementary acquisitions: of Selsius Systems, GeoTel Communications, and WebLine Communications.

Employee Compensation

For reasons suggested by previous sections, structures for employee compensation will change in important ways. An interesting example arises in relation to sales personnel. In some cases, companies will elect not to compensate salespeople for sales executed across the Internet, but this may prove to be a strategic error. A company will generally gain by rewarding its sales staff for encouraging customers to place orders over the Net, and if the staff are not compensated for doing so the company may find that these two sales channels are in effect competing with one another, often to the detriment of both.

The Death of Software

Companies that engage today in software development will find not that this process has changed but that it has died. (Of course, we can think of death as the One Big Change.) Packaged software is fated to give way to online services.

The following is a representative development model for client/server software:

1. Gather requirements
2. Produce a Marketing Requirements Document
3. Produce a functional specification
4. Ensure the availability of a large and complex hardware infrastructure
5. Produce a detailed design
6. Produce a detailed project plan, identifying scope, resources, and schedule
7. Write the software
8. Write the setup procedures and administrative functions
9. Port the software, as appropriate, across x hardware platforms and y operating systems
10. Package the software for distributed installation
11. Manufacture the CDs, print the documentation, stock the warehouses, ship the product

12. Stand by for—or assist in—hundreds, perhaps thousands, or (with luck) even millions of installations

13. Translate the software and the documentation

14. Return to step (1)

15. Endure long, complex, and various upgrade cycles

Passing through the first thirteen steps of this model has typically taken software companies as long as 2 years. But 2 years is a geologic epoch; it is *not* an Internet development cycle, which is a period so brief that it dictates a development framework accommodating real-time software enhancements. This means enhancements in minutes, or hours, or days, or weeks—perhaps, at the outside, in months. In short, e-business means the death of packaged software and the irresistible ascent of online services.

The ability to upgrade one's online services as rapidly, and as often, as is required by the needs of the company or the pressure of competition—this presupposes a framework underlying the application that is flexible and skillfully designed. It is not an unusual experience to visit a site for eBay, eToys, E*TRADE, Netscape, or Yahoo! and to find that the user interface has changed dramatically. Likewise, you may visit Amazon.com and see that the site offers a new product line or a major new service. And when have you needed the training manual for E*TRADE or Amazon to complete your errand? This is a services model, and it comes with a new set of rules and methods. Software companies that do not evolve to live by this model will die by it.

Examples of online services that are emerging to displace packaged applications include:

- Account and contact management
- Customer care
- General ledger
- Payroll
- Spreadsheets
- Storefronts
- Surveys
- Word processing

Examples of sites providing robust, scalable, and reliable online services include:

- eTravel.com
- FormulaOne.com
- NetLedger.com
- OracleSalesOnline.com.

The following chart conveys an idea of the scale of venture-capital investment in Internet companies. What it does not show is that more than 90 percent of that capital, during 1999, was directed to online services businesses. What more needs to be said? Software, as we conventionally think of it, has one foot in the grave. Within 5 years the rest of the corpse will follow.

Maintenance Strategy

Prior to the Age of the Internet, most software maintenance got done on weekends and holidays. Typically, the workers responsible would take the computer system down at 5 p.m. Friday, or at 12 midnight, or 5 p.m. Saturday. They would then work more or less frantically, installing upgrades, adding users or functionality, tuning performance, adding patches, fixing bugs—sometimes beavering away until early Monday morning, trying to get the enhanced system up and running by start-of-business.

The Internet does not spell the end of working weekends for maintenance personnel. But its impact in this context is like that in many others: while it does not erase the lines that bound the world's time zones, it smudges them energetically. After all, the typical Internet-enabled company now has one or a few sites, accessible from anywhere on earth, each supported by a single software instance. Most such companies try to keep their sites up and running 168 hours a week, but when they need to make changes to the supporting software they are often compelled to interrupt some of the services that the site normally offers. (As an example, Oracle has 1.2 million subscribers to oracle.com; replicating an updated database to a production server can take as long as 4 hours, during which that server cannot support operations on that database.)

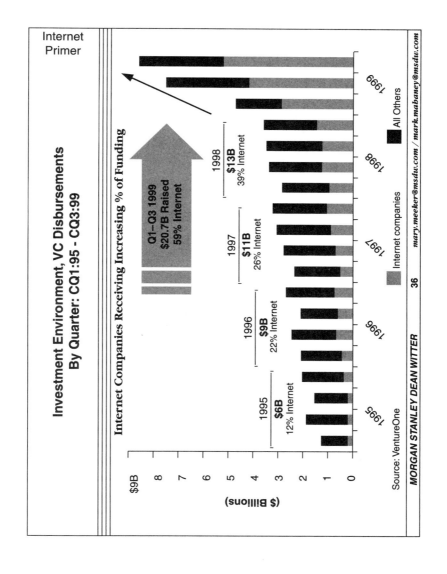

Now, however, there is no point at which services can be interrupted without risk of frustrating some would-be users. So companies will have to decide, probably on the basis of usage records, which periods are least sensitive. Holidays are now less promising: when they fall within the work week they provide windows that are too brief to be of much use—and are almost always specific to a single country. A fairly promising maintenance window begins at 5 p.m. Saturday, Honolulu time, and extends until 9 a.m. Monday in Auckland and Sydney; but this provides only 20 hours (18 when it's summer in Honolulu), compared to 40 hours if all that time fell (as "it used to") in a single location. Notably, even this period risks problems with Israel, where Sunday is a working day.

Furthermore, the maintenance stakes have risen sharply. I remember when one could apply a bad patch in the branch office of a bank and the tellers would shout, "Hey! It's not printing right!" One could then quickly back the patch out with no serious harm done. Such mistakes made in the workings of a global Web site could damage financial records for hundreds of thousands of customers before they could be corrected, and nobody would hear their shouts until it was too late.

Another complication: in the old days, each line of business had its own programs and was typically insensitive to those for the other lines of business. Finance, HR, order management, marketing, sales, service—each depended on software that had little or no impact on the others, so that changes could be made in one area without risking operations in another. Now, with single global software instances, this mutual independence is deeply compromised if not simply eliminated. Not only do all lines of business reside in the same instance, they compete for system resources: for disk space and for CPU cycles and memory. And they must serve, as appropriate, not only the company's customers, but its trading partners and its employees.

How then is maintenance to be done? We must begin by acknowledging that it comprises changes ranging across many categories, as tabulated and commented below. Application vendors might in general handle such changes as they would be handled at Oracle.

Type of Change	Remarks
Infrastructure modification	Infrastructure is discussed below this table.
Setup	Setup changes comprise changes to records for products, prices, and processes. These are usually straightforward.
Data migration	In many cases, a maintenance window—a suspension of service—is dictated by the need to migrate data from a legacy or bespoke system. This process normally requires that a data-migration script be written to map the data from the old to the production schema. The migration itself can be difficult and time-consuming, necessitating a substantial service outage.
Record addition	Data updates must remain enabled during data migration and must be flagged for replication as necessary.
Performance tuning	This is an ongoing process. In particular, long-running SQL scripts require tuning, and scripts need review to excise unnecessary database hits. Performance-testing scripts need to be created.
Functionality enhancement	Implementation of any significant new function (e.g., cost accounting, global sales forecast) must flow through all six environments shown below.
Upgrade	When a software vendor newly releases a product that an IT implementation depends on in its out-of-the-box form, a decision must be taken whether to upgrade the production environment. Such changes are typically the riskiest and most expensive.
Bug fix	Fixes can typically progress directly from quality assurance to staging, barring evident risks to performance.

Infrastructure

A typical software deployment involves a progression across six environments:

Environment	Remarks
Test	Changes of any of the types listed above can be performed in a test environment, although performance tuning is typically deferred.

Environment	Remarks
Quality assurance (QA)	Whereas test environments are typically distributed, QA environments are centralized. It is in the QA environment that setup changes, patches, data migrations, new user accounts, and so on all come together for the first time.
	Once a QA environment is stable, it is typically cloned for testing purposes. When testing has been completed, the clone systems are discarded.
Performance tuning	Here speed, reliability, and scalability are tested and "tweaked."
Staging	Once changes have passed through the preceding environments, they come to staging for system-integration testing. (A staging environment can be used for disaster recovery.)
Production	This is the "live" environment.
Disaster recovery	This environment, in a physically remote data center, provides "hot" backup in case of the failure of a production server or of access to such a server.

A representative physical configuration for the production environment at a large company might comprise the following devices:

- One Sun Solaris E6500, with 20 CPUs and 20 gigabytes of RAM, as the database server
- Five similarly configured E4500s as mid-tier servers, thus:
  - Apache server
  - Forms server
  - Reports server
  - Concurrent manager (scheduling and executing batch jobs, such as trial balances)
  - Redundancy server (performing disk mirroring)
- A set of routers for load balancing, and so on

Thoroughly conservative IT implementations would maintain a distinct disaster-recovery configuration exactly duplicating the production environment (but at a different physical location). Less conservative implementations, like Oracle's, might rely on the redundancy server for disaster recovery—a sensible if not ironclad approach, given that disk drives fail far more often than CPUs. In Oracle's implementation, every write to disk is performed simultaneously to two distinct disks; a production implementation that incorporated a disk redundancy server and was exactly duplicated by a disaster-recovery environment would perform every write simultaneously to four disks.

The normal IT shop for a major organization will also feature a staging environment that (again) exactly duplicates the production environment. For many corporations this means a capital outlay for hardware that at least triples the cost of the production implementation. This can mean very substantial expenses: at roughly $200,000 per server, the 18 servers required for staging, production, and disaster recovery would total $3.6 million. Testing, quality assurance, and performance tuning can typically be conducted on smaller machines or on the staging system, but in any case do not need any configuration as complex as that required for the production environment.

However, the maintenance window that concerns us does not relate directly to the machines used for testing, quality assurance, performance tuning, or disaster recovery. Its necessary duration is simply the time required to propagate updated code and data from the staging to the production system.

The Internet: Organizational Structures Changed

Sales and Service will Blend

Today, a typical multinational corporation has a chief sales officer with global responsibility or one such officer per global region (often a continent). Global responsibility for service is allocated similarly, though it is more likely to have a single global chief officer.

This model is likely to change, progressively, as corporations ask themselves questions during the transition to enablement for the Internet. The questions are: What happens . . .

When the e-business operates from a single global instance?

When common business practices are simplified and codified?

When we have a single global price list?

When our call-center agents receive service requests?

When service agents can view global sales opportunities?

When customers can use self-service to place orders, renew services, and register for events and seminars?

The answers to these questions will shoot full of holes the prevailing partition between sales and service. When quotes, orders, configurations, and customer care are handled directly by customers and business partners, the enterprise's sales and service agents will metamorphose into client-relationship managers, and electronic businesses will increasingly orient their sales and service organizations toward such blended responsibilities.

IT Organizations will Wane in Size, Wax in Importance

IT is like welfare—the goal is to get off it. But IT will never go away entirely. The realistic goals within the context of e-business are these:

- One centralized data center
- Online services and/or generic (out-of-the-box) applications
- A small but highly skilled team of professionals
- Lights-out operation

Consider a world in which hardware is centralized within the network—where all applications are online services configured as necessary through self-service by the line of business owning the business processes involved. Is this world realistic? Is it achievable? Yes!

For the typical large company, the IT organization must serve as a vehicle of change, conducting its parent enterprise toward cost-effective e-business automation. As such, the IT group will gain in importance even as, approaching the goals listed above, it contracts in size. The resulting team will be small but well formed, with technical expertise distributed among its members but with some overlap. Although some of its current responsibilities will persist, its transformation from the accustomed form to the e-business model will be dramatic and painful, and there *will* be casualties.

For small to medium-sized businesses, the Internet makes it possible to outsource full responsibility for IT, with the exception of desktop support. Soon that, too, will be a candidate for outsourcing.

Executives will Grow More Involved in Their Businesses

Business information available to company executives continues to proliferate. The challenge they have already faced for many years is to filter out data they cannot use effectively in order to concentrate incisively on tactical and strategic issues.

Business intelligence systems will intensify the focus that the executive can train on critical business information. The impact of these systems will be reinforced by the advancing consolidation within one or a few databases of records relating to all aspects of the company's business. Every manager will have immediate access to up-to-the-minute information for all areas within his or her authority: sales forecasts, order levels, inventory balances, customer records, and so on. Effective executives will know at once when a marketing campaign ceases to be cost-effective, when a supplier fails to deliver, when a customer ceases to be profitable.

The Web-enabled C-level executive (CEO, CFO, or other) can now define the specific performance indicators that he or she considers key and can manage the business (in part) by monitoring those indicators—because the Web makes it possible to gather and organize up-to-the-minute data from around the globe and to access those data easily through self-service. With executives as with enterprises, those that cannot leverage the Internet to promote their performances will find themselves falling behind, or compelled to retire from the field.

Companies will Increasingly Specialize

Intranets have greatly facilitated communications within the companies that have implemented them. An effect of the Internet is to extend this enhanced ease to communications between companies. Intercompany communication will continue to be circumscribed by security provisions; but, within constraints designed to protect each company's core assets, employees of one company are already empowered to communicate freely with those of another, and the next step in the same direction will be toward greater integration of the Web sites of distinct companies.

An example is provided by the major American automobile manufacturers. They are not dealers; and, while their Web sites provide prospective buyers with a great deal of information about the vehicles they manufacture, they do not allow a prospect to purchase a vehicle. Yet they certainly don't want to discourage purchases. So they face the challenge of enabling the prospect to transit seamlessly to a dealer site.

In the short run, the manufacturer sites can and do provide hot links to dealer sites, and they have done an effective job of implementing a uniform look and feel across those sites. However, this approach still suffers the shortcoming that the prospect is reminded that he or she is now dealing with a different business entity. This is not the desired effect, and software is under development to impose on this entire process a more compelling sense of unity.

The Internet: Customer Loyalty

Most obviously, the Internet will undermine customer loyalties based on geography. Its other effects are likely to include a leveling of prices for identical and comparable goods and services, as prospective consumers find it easier to make comparisons. On the other hand, would-be sellers will increasingly find ways to adjust their offer prices, ad hoc, to compete more successfully for especially alluring sales or customers.

If distinctions of geography and price are both blunted, it stands to reason that companies will turn increasingly to other means of competition. Internet advertising and alliances with related Web sites, in addition to Internet-related publicity, provide such means; though they are not new in concept, they are enabled by the advent of the new medium.

But it is likely that competitive measures already familiar to established businesses will weigh more heavily in promoting and securing customer loyalty. These will include frequent-buyer programs, attempts (especially through service and support) to promote customer satisfaction, and progressive broadening (if sometimes through alliances) to related ranges of products and services so that a visitor to Web site X will not be compelled to leave the site in order to gratify his or her next whim.

While brands will continue to influence consumer decisions, the key differentiators for companies determined to prevail will be exemplary service and a commitment to building and maintaining a strong and mutually rewarding relationship with the customer.

The Internet: Market Efficiency Enhanced

The year 1776 witnessed, among other things, the publication of a book by Adam Smith entitled *An Inquiry into the Nature and Causes of the Wealth of Nations.*[11] This event was, for practical purposes, the start of 224 years of labor by economists on defining markets and characterizing their workings. Much of that labor has addressed markets that are "ideal" according to one or another economist's ideas and, in doing so, has proceeded as if markets could exist in the absence of human beings as we know them. The value of such work is not merely open to doubt; it has been widely depreciated, by economists among others.

However, a consensus has developed that is of interest to us here. That consensus addresses the characteristics of markets that contribute to the efficiency of their operation, where *efficiency* is defined principally in terms of the socially desirable allocation of resources. Among those characteristics, some of which are identified in Smith's work, are those listed below.

- Numerous potential buyers and sellers
- Information freely available to all participants
- Low barriers to entry into competition
- Free movement of workers among regions and industries
- Low interference by government

At best, each of these is a matter of degree—one of many reasons for which discussion of perfect competition and perfectly efficient markets will remain forever a strictly academic pursuit. Yet readers will see that the Internet tends to promote every one of these characteristics:

- It broadens enormously the ability to participate in market operations.
- It floods participants with free information.
- It lowers barriers to entry to such a degree that thousands of businesses have been launched each on the strength of a simple Web site—in many cases, of a Web site created using free business-oriented software.

By the same token, it makes it much easier for workers to move into new lines of business. In various ways it also makes it easier for them to move physically, though it has not lowered official barriers to immigration: it helps to propagate a common language, and it supplies information useful for legal migration. (No doubt it also supplies information useful for illegal migration.)

The Internet does *not* militate against government interference. To the contrary, it presents a wholly new area into which legislators and bureaucrats may intrude their services to the public. However, the flows of information, communication, and commerce that the Net does so much to promote tend to contravene the constraints and intrusions that governments so like to impose. Remember this line from John Gilmore, a cofounder of the Electronic Frontier Foundation: "The Net interprets censorship as damage and routes around it." China, take heed!

I must add that, in less repressive societies in which broad electorates choose the legislatures, governmental intrusion into the marketplace is legitimate, both literally and figuratively. (Some examples of how the marketplace can work when unencumbered by bureaucracy are referred to in the section *Employment Laws*, later in this chapter.) For this reason, we want to bear in mind that any medium the subtleties and intricacies of which tend to foil the blunt instruments with which even freely chosen governments habitually attack is sure to obstruct, in some degree, the will of the majority—to say nothing of minorities.

The Internet: National Sovereignty Diluted

By easing the flow of goods and money across national boundaries, the Internet undermines in many ways the traditional sovereign powers of the state.

Importance of Business Location Diminishes

This item could easily be overstated. The geographic location of a business will continue to matter, though for some businesses more than for others. Manufacturers will continue to profit by locating their plants close to supplier and subcontractor locations, and close to their market populations. Because of delivery costs, this is especially true for those (for instance, automakers) whose output is unusually large as measured by gross weight. Other considerations that will continue to apply to all businesses include:

- Access to pools of qualified talent, which will increasingly mean proximity to major centers of education
- Nature and enforcement of relevant laws, particularly with regard to
  - Taxes
  - Employment
  - Tariffs
  - Contracts
- Broader issues of language and culture

The combined effect of these considerations is to defend the importance of national borders even as the growth of the Internet dilutes the impact of any given location within those borders and, to a lesser extent, beyond them. However, the very great importance of language, together with the worldwide growth of English, means that the borders of nations whose principal language is English will always be more porous for business purposes than other borders. In this respect, the Internet accelerates a trend that began with plunging long-distance telephone rates, which made possible such phenomena as call-center agents in India placing calls to customers and prospects in the United States.

That said, it remains clear that the Internet vastly increases companies' flexibility in siting. Why did Amazon locate in Seattle? According to *The Seattle Times* (January 5, 1997), "Bezos considered Boulder, Colo., and Portland, but chose Seattle for the company's headquarters. It is close to major book-distribution warehouses and offers a rich pool of technical talent and a lifestyle appealing enough to draw New Yorkers and San Franciscans." Fair enough; but it seems likely that many sites in the United States, and in Canada, would have served as well.

In fact, it's not obvious that Amazon's headquarters couldn't have been located just about as successfully in Dublin or Canberra. Tax and employment laws would have been different, of course, and the supply of workers literate in high tech would have been smaller. On the other hand, Amazon wouldn't have had to compete for such workers with Microsoft, Boeing, Nordstrom, Starbucks, and others. Customers would experience no meaningful difference—I can access www.amazon.com in about 2 seconds and amazon.de (the German site) in about 2.5 seconds. Communication with an appropriate distribution center would be unaffected.

Significantly, Amazon's distribution centers have been sited in accord with obvious business logic:

- In Seattle (but it's clear from what follows that the first distribution center did not have to be close to Amazon headquarters).

- In New Castle, Delaware, to reduce shipping times to the eastern states and beyond.

- In Nevada, probably for low rates per square foot of warehouse space. (A disadvantage to locating a distribution center in Nevada is that Amazon customers ordering from Nevada must now presumably pay state sales tax. The corresponding advantage is that Amazon won't have many customers there!)

- In England and Germany, to reduce shipping charges for customers in Europe and to establish Amazon's presence in those national markets.

(By now, Amazon has added distribution centers in several additional states with low or nonexistent sales taxes.)

By broadening a company's flexibility in the choice of its physical location(s), the Internet increases the extent to which private enterprise can respond to variations in the business climate, whether from state to state or from country to country. In particular, companies may be expected to seek out locations where local, regional, and national governments have set low, stable tax rates and have held to a reasonable minimum the bureaucratic burdens on businesses.

Money Flows Faster in Greater Volumes

Money crosses national borders for many reasons: purchases, settlements, investments, speculation. Broadly speaking, to exchange a country's currency for anything else is to bet against that currency—to bet that the thing for which it is being exchanged will prove to be of greater value to the exchanger.

There was a time when the scale of such exchanges was very small—when the overwhelming majority of all trade took place within, not across, national boundaries. That was the time when, for westerners, China was Cathay—a source of tea and oranges—and Japan was Xipangu, which from 1639 to 1854 was closed by imperial edict to western traders (except from the Netherlands). With the rise of international commerce and communications, that age ended forever.

National governments can still place their own wagers in the currency markets. But they have neither the cash resources nor the influence to prevail when a strong tide is running against them. This is the lesson of many financial crises over the last few years—in Mexico, in Russia, in southeast Asian countries—in which investors decided to exchange the currencies of those nations for other currencies—often the U.S. dollar. Likewise, the value of the dollar itself is being eroded constantly by the following two items, which at second glance prove to be identical:

- The enormous outflow of U.S. dollars
- The prolonged U.S. trade deficit

In short, the ability of governments to control (and usually to degrade—but *gradually!*) their national currencies has fallen sharply and will continue to decline. Populations of millions can be plunged overnight into misery and privation because every currency speculator is anxious to sell before the speculator in the next time zone. Such a crisis can cripple a nation's ability to make war and can topple its government.

Central Banks Wane in Importance

A widespread trend in recent years has been to increase the independence of central banks from other governmental institutions.

As that independence has grown, the strength of central banks has grown with it. At the same time, their strength is being undercut by international flows of funds.

The traditional roles of the central bank have been to manage monetary policy (typically with the principal goal of confining inflation to a range between 0 percent and 2 percent per year), to supervise the payment system, and to promulgate regulations. A few central banks (including the U.S. Federal Reserve Board) also supervise the banking system as a whole. Every one of these roles has been, or will be, deeply disturbed by international monetary flow.

A nation's central bank can control the national rate of inflation very effectively if that nation is isolated from the rest of the world. In real life, international trade in currencies and fluctuations in foreign direct investment can influence the inflation rate, each roughly in proportion to its relative importance in the economy. A nation that depends heavily on international trade and/or in which foreign direct investment is (at times) very great, can find that its inflation rate responds dramatically to international views as to the soundness of its economy. Southeast Asia has provided several examples over the last 2 years.

The role of the central bank in issuing regulations and supervising the banking system is already jeopardized by international flows of money, again as illustrated by Southeast Asia. The international monetary system probes constantly for weaknesses in national banking systems, any one of which may be punished severely if its rules are judged inadequately rigorous. Thus international standards, though implicit, have widely superseded the lax standards of oversight previously enjoyed—and presumably vigorously lobbied for—by bankers in many nations.

Supervision by a central bank of the country's payment system, though not a logical necessity, is very likely to continue while traditional money remains the principal, or final, medium of payment.[12] But the Internet is pushing the world's economies toward electronic-payment systems, which, as *The Economist* states, will provide the seller with a guarantee that the buyer is solvent, eliminating "credit risk, interest-rate risk, and operational risk attached to payments." The magazine adds that a systemic conversion to electronic money will deprive central banks of their ability to set interest rates.

Laws Weaken

Anything that can be communicated over the Internet can travel as readily across international boundaries as within them. National governments can, of course, pass laws intended to regulate such traffic, and they do. Let's consider a few instances.

PGP

PGP (Pretty Good Privacy) is a program for public-key encryption and decryption written by Phil Zimmermann. Zimmermann uploaded PGP to Usenet (once a distinct network, now a subnet of the Internet) in 1991. This attracted the attention of the United States Department of Commerce (DoC), which classified PGP as a strategic asset and took the position that Zimmermann had violated federal International Traffic in Arms Regulations. For several years, the DoC threatened Zimmermann with indictment and extended imprisonment, but in 1996 it finally dropped the case.

Ironically, U.S. courts had held (presumably in deference to the First Amendment) that it was legal to export the same code in printed form. While the DoC was pursuing Zimmermann, the PGP code was legally exported in book form to the Netherlands, where it was re-entered into computers and the program reconstructed. (Ironically, the result is a faster version of PGP—which cannot legally be imported into the United States!) The DoC then took the position that reexport of the program from the Netherlands would violate U.S. law and render the responsible parties liable to prosecution.

Setting aside reasonable questions as to the wisdom of the DoC's position, consider the difficulties such cases pose for law enforcement. Prosecutors need to be able to

- Prove who posted the forbidden item to the Internet
- Persuade the courts to overrule First-Amendment rights
- Arraign foreign nationals

More broadly, the federal government must face serious foreign-policy questions as to trial of foreign nationals that may be innocent under the laws of their own countries.[13]

As relates to encryption, the tide is running against the government. There is an urgent and legitimate need for industrial-strength encryption to protect trade secrets in the global marketplace, and big business is unlikely to accept a system that enables government to monitor its most sensitive information. In any case, to quote Bob Kohn, former vice president and general counsel of PGP, Inc., "The export law is like building a chain link fence in the middle of the ocean to keep the water out."

Communications Decency Act

The Communications Decency Act of 1996, of which Section 507 was ostensibly intended to outlaw indecent material on the Internet, was struck down in June 1997 by the U.S. Supreme Court. Had it survived, the act would have posed for law-enforcement officials, in addition to the challenges posed by the PGP, an additional one: to persuade the courts that one or more items posted were indecent. This challenge might have proven negligible, but the others would not.

Taxes and Duties

The Controversy

There is wide agreement that taxes specific to electronic commerce are currently a poor idea. They promise to be difficult to enforce; to erect an additional obstacle to the viability of e-commerce; and, if imposed before a sensible tax policy has been agreed upon, to be ill-coordinated and unfair, as well as burdensome in the usual bureaucratic way. The controversy relates mostly to the long term.

If Internet commerce is exempted from all taxes, it will enjoy an additional competitive advantage over traditional nonelectronic competitors, which will hasten the demise of the latter and deprive tax authorities at all levels of revenues that would otherwise have accrued to them from traditional sources. If Internet commerce is taxed equally with traditional business, the new revenues will be spent in part on social infrastructure (roads, for instance) that is degraded much more heavily by traditional business. (Compare a small fleet of grocery vans making deliveries over rationalized routes at efficient times with the old model, in which every family drives a car to the grocery store and then home again. Or compare downloading a program from the Internet to driving to a local computer store to buy it.) Even if this were fair, taxing Internet commerce by the current model for mail-order companies would divert additional business to out-of-state suppliers, reducing total tax revenues and aggravating the competitive burden on local businesses.

Many people oppose any tax on e-commerce (beyond, presumably, state taxes on intrastate transactions) on the grounds that e-commerce is driving, and will continue to drive, the national economic expansion; that it will increase tax revenues from computer hardware and telecommunications; and that it will create millions of additional jobs. This amounts to a claim that e-commerce, without being taxed directly, will nevertheless augment federal tax revenues. Yet it is clear that the less we tax electronic business the more we must tax something else if we are to maintain a given level of government spending. Some people plausibly interpret this to mean that imposing no new tax on Web commerce will add to the disadvantages of the poor, who have less access to the Internet.

Any solution to the tax problem will be arbitrary—and, for that reason, will be fiercely opposed by groups that consider themselves victimized by it. From where we stand, the good news is that any difficulties experienced within the United States are likely to prove tiny by comparison with international predicaments to follow.

The United States

On October 21, 1998, the U.S. Congress enacted the Internet Tax Freedom Act (ITFA), which legislates a 3-year (10/1/1998 to 10/21/2001) moratorium on new, multiple, and/or discriminatory taxes on electronic commerce. Internet-related taxes enacted before October 1, 1998, by thirteen states and by various municipalities were unaffected by the ITFA.

ITFA proponents argued that there are approximately 30,000 taxing jurisdictions within the United States, that those jurisdictions had the authority to create a snake's nest of regulations, that it was in the public interest to protect electronic commerce from such a threat, and that e-commerce pioneers in particular should not be confronted with more challenges than they already faced. The moratorium, they reasoned, would provide time for electronic business to grow robust and for the Congress to formulate a sensible approach to taxing business conducted over the Web. On the other hand, the ITFA was opposed by some states and municipalities because of suspicions that its intent was to reserve to the federal government any tax revenues to be derived eventually from electronic commerce—or to defer such revenues forever.

The ITFA left unaffected a status quo within which e-commerce was taxed similarly to other intranational commerce that might cross state boundaries: merchants doing electronic business would collect and remit state sales taxes on purchases made by consumers in states in which the merchants had a "physical presence" (a phrase that itself leaves some uncertainties to be resolved by the courts). So—other laws apart—Internet enterprises were left on equal terms with mail-order catalog companies, but both arguably had a tax advantage by comparison with companies that do most of their business within a single state.

Meanwhile, online retailers have an incentive to confine their physical presences to the five states (Alaska, Delaware, Montana, New Hampshire, and Oregon) that impose no sales tax; and those states, though they forego sales taxes as they are accustomed to do, have an incentive to lure such businesses, which will provide additional employment, inject cash into the states' economies, and raise corporate state tax revenues.

In hopes of determining federal policy conclusively, the ITFA created an Advisory Commission on Electronic Commerce. The commission, which concluded its work on April 12, 2000, made several relevant proposals, but could not muster the needed two-thirds majority either for the imposition of an Internet sales tax or for a permanent moratorium. Instead, it recommended a 5-year extension of the current moratorium. Congressional action will be required to implement this and any others of the commission's recommendations.

Europe

The European Union approaches the issue of Internet taxation from a position that seems at this time to ensure failure, and, by doing so, it inadvertently provides the United States with a usefully horrifying example. Europe's problems are discussed next.

For tax purposes, the EU distinguishes broadly between products and services. According to the European Commission (EC), a digital product (for instance, a downloaded program) is to be taxed as a service—even though the same program, if bought at a store, would be taxed as a product. Meanwhile the Organization for Economic

Cooperation and Development (OECD)'s Committee on Fiscal Affairs contends that classification of something as a good or as a service should not depend on the means of distribution. Though the OECD position conflicts with European tradition, I judge it likely to prevail on the basis of common sense.

For some time, European lawmakers were considering a bit tax to be levied on every digital bit transmitted over the Internet. The rate would have approximated 1 cent per megabit. Since 1997, however, EU officials have repeatedly deprecated the bit tax, and it seems unlikely that such a tax will ever be imposed. Critics have noted that children's games would often be taxed much more heavily than crucial business information, and that the tax on a downloaded 2-hour movie would approach $150.

All nations in the European Union have value-added taxes (VATs), but their VAT rates vary wildly from nation to nation, between a minimum of 4.8 percent and a maximum of 24.2 percent. Furthermore, the minimum purchase amount that triggers the imposition of a VAT varies widely—and only Denmark has a single VAT rate.

The EC at first took the position that, notwithstanding their diversity, VATs and customs duties were to be applied to Internet as to traditional commerce; but this meant no imposition of VAT on any transaction involving a purchaser outside the EU. On June 17, 1998, the EC reversed itself on this last point, noting that such exemptions would put corporate purchasers within the EU at a competitive disadvantage to those outside the EU. If VATs are not imposed on purchases made from outside the EU, business from within the EU will be driven outside the union. If VATs *are* imposed on purchases made from outside the EU, business from outside the EU will be driven away from the union. The only obvious solution to this quandary is for the European nations to give up VATs altogether, but this seems unlikely in the near term.

Regardless of the resolution of this point, the discrepant VAT rates within the European Union continue to pose problems for Internet legislation. If discrepancies are allowed to persist, they will drive many transactions across national borders and will confer unfair advantages on citizens who live close to borders and can choose among two or more tax rates. (Though this problem preexisted the Internet, it is aggravated by the Net's tendency to obviate travel.)

The EU's and OECD's continuing uncertainty as to tax policy for e-commerce means that fledgling e-businesses and e-business enablers within the EU cannot confidently assess their prospects for success. This distinguishes them from their competitors outside the EU not in kind but in degree, and the distinction has the effect of (relatively) discouraging entrepreneurship in relation to the Internet. Entrepreneurship in Europe has no need of additional government-imposed discouragement.

Because the Internet promotes disintermediation, the sheer volume of commercial transactions across the Internet threatens to become enormous. This will add to the burdens of administering any relevant taxes, and—to the extent that tax structures are more complex within the EU than they are in other places—the administrative burden will further disadvantage European companies. Purchases by citizens of low-VAT nations from companies in high-VAT nations will decline proportionally, putting pressure on the high-VAT nations to lower their VAT rates.

In sum, the soundest strategy for the EU appears to be a harmonization and a broad reduction of VAT rates in order to shore up its competitive position—not currently robust—in relation to the rest of the world. But for the nations of the EU to follow this path means a widespread retreat from sovereign discretion, not only for individual European nations but for the European community as a whole.

The World

In negotiations with the United States, the EU has agreed on the undesirability of imposing new taxes on electronic commerce. Japan has joined the United States in deprecating any bit tax (in particular) and in recommending the OECD as the appropriate body to preside over the development of a common international framework for Internet taxation. But the United States appears to have adopted, characteristically, the position most strongly in favor of minimal taxation—or none.

This position does not recommend itself as the basis for an international harmonization of Internet tax policy. First, the United States is one of only two (among twenty-nine) nations in the OECD with no VAT structure, the other being Australia. Second, any U.S. attempt to secure relative tax freedom for e-commerce will be perceived by the rest of the world as tending to promote American commercial hegemony on the Internet and in relation to its entire substructure—hardware, software, telecommunications, and so on. The world will view this tendency partly as dictated to the U.S. government by the formidable domestic Internet lobby and partly as a characteristic effort by Washington to impose American standards around the globe. And, in these perceptions, the rest of the world will be correct.

We have witnessed the recent rise of American exceptionalism (with regard, for instance, to land mines and war crimes), and we cannot reasonably expect many concessions by the U.S. government in this matter of the Internet. One can already find on the Web numerous diatribes from American groups against "foreign" taxes and tariffs and in favor of "promoting freedom abroad." Perhaps the most we can hope for is a perpetuation of the booming American economy of the 1990s, but at the growing expense of other nations and especially of the EU, with the corollary of further advances in the already swelling tide of anti-American bitterness abroad.

By contrast, the ideal outcome would require that the United States enter into international negotiations in a spirit of compromise so earnest that it would go more than half way toward meeting the concerns of the world community. If the Internet can effect, or can merely profit by, such an outcome, then the world will have taken a giant step in the direction of world government, and national sovereignties will have been struck a blow from which they may never recover.

By the summer of 1998, U.S. officials had succeeded in securing an agreement within the World Trade Organization (WTO) that no customs duties would be imposed on electronic transmissions before the WTO meeting in Seattle; one of their goals for the meeting was to extend that agreement by at least 18 months. Yet many would view such an extension as another 18-month installment toward an unofficial U.S. goal, an Internet now and forever without such restrictions. The collapse of the Seattle Round ensures further uncertainty as to international policy toward Internet commerce.

Employment Laws

Probably there are people that want governments to rescind all laws restricting the conduct of business. Some of these people would change their minds if they got their wish. After all, such laws—in the United States, at least—usually originated in popular revulsion against what businessmen sometimes do when left to their own devices.

We have been protected by law from many of the most exploitative and destructive practices of businesses for so long that most of us have very little notion of what businesspeople can do when unrestrained. Luckily, the Internet makes possible a refresher course in this subject—a course that might start with the story of the deaths of 146 victims of the Triangle Shirtwaist fire in 1911.[14] Course materials might be supplemented from the older media; I recommend *Night Comes to the Cumberlands*[15] and *Silent Spring*.[16]

But suppose, for argument's sake, that we agree that government *must* regulate the conduct of business. We must then concede that it cannot do so without imposing grave social costs. Laws, being general, will sometimes prevent practices we might wish to encourage as exceptions; they require expenditures of time and money to determine whether and when they are being broken, and further expenditures if they are to be enforced. And they are often so drafted as to have unintended and deplorable consequences. There is no such thing as a free law.

Employment Laws and the Internet

Typically, governments pass laws restricting business practices because they seek to promote social ends that businesspeople cannot be relied on to favor. In the United States, for instance, millions of people want to restrict immigration, many of them because they believe what they have been told by politicians eager to use social divisions and hatreds to advance their own careers. One law passed to restrict immigration limits the number of H-1B visas to 195,000 per year. This caps the number of skilled workers that may immigrate to the United States, and administrative delays in processing these visas delay, often for 6 months or more, employment and reemployment within the United States. Linus Torvalds, the founder of the Linux operating system, who has an H-1B visa, applied for a green card in 1997; he is reported to be effectively unable to visit his parents in Finland until his status is clarified by the Immigration and Naturalization Service (INS).

Silicon Valley is the principal destination of foreign nationals who secure H-1B visas, and a principal consequence of the annual limit is to put a brake on high-tech development in California. However, this impediment is nothing compared to the burdens imposed by governments in Europe on high-tech initiatives originating there.

We have already seen that issues of Internet taxation make Europe somewhat inhospitable to e-commerce, with the threat of lost business revenue exceeded only by the uncertainty as to how much revenue is likely to be lost. But the climate for e-business is made still more threatening by constraints imposed on business in general; and the most important of these, which are manifold, relate to terms of employment. In most European countries, workers cannot be dismissed except with many months' notice or compensation, whereas in Silicon Valley employment is typically at will and can be terminated at once by either the employer or the employee. European minimum-wage standards are relatively high, raising an obstacle to the hiring of the marginally qualified. Unemployment benefits are generous, so that incentives to return to work are reduced.[17] European vacation allowances are high, by law, and working hours per week are low. (France has recently legislated an ill-considered limit of 35 hours per week, which at the start of 2001 will become compulsory for all companies with more than 20 employees; it is already in force for larger companies, and the employment police have begun to raid corporate offices after 5 p.m.)

In large part, this pattern was established in Western Europe in reaction to the threat of Communism, which put forth the empty promise of a workers' paradise. Communism held many real benefits for those who experienced it, but the evidence suggests that, as an economic system, it was lucky to last as long as it did. The prevalent pattern in Western Europe, which we may call socialism, holds many real benefits for Europeans, who are understandably reluctant to see it undermined. However, with the fall of Communism, the continental European economies now cluster at the left end of the market spectrum. Like Communism, the European model will try to compete and will fail, dragging the European standard of living gradually downward except to the extent that the model is abandoned—something that will not happen overnight.

European business conditions are particularly hostile to Internet initiatives. Venture capital there has traditionally been hard to secure. Stock options are a very recent innovation, and getting rich via stock options is said to be regarded in France (for example) as contemptible. In October 1999, the unemployment level among the Euro-11 crept below 10 percent for the first time in 7 years; the latest figure is 9.5 percent. Euro-11 unemployment for would-be workers under 25 is 17.9 percent, but ranges up to 21.5 percent in France, 23.4 percent in Belgium, and 28.4 percent in Spain. Meanwhile, the same generation serves as a prime resource for Internet enterprise in the United States, where many high-tech employers are desperately seeking qualified labor.

Although everybody in Europe agrees that unemployment is a (perhaps the) crucial economic challenge for the EU, French political leaders have sworn that they will never allow "heartless Anglo-Saxon" ways to prevail in Europe. If this is true, Europeans may recognize too late that the EU has become the economic bellwether of the third world. To quote Byron Wien of Morgan Stanley Dean Witter, "Europe is becoming a Latin American republic: Weaken the currency, export more, provide more jobs, and relieve certain social political pressures."

Enacting that role, Europeans may turn out to be happier than their American counterparts. I do not presume to judge that the quality of life in the New World, however measured, will prove superior to that in the Old World. But Europeans are likely to find themselves falling farther and farther behind in wealth, and if they are to be reconciled to such a condition it must be because they have more time than Americans to spend with their families and on their (modest) vacations. They are trading money for time; we are trading time for money.

4

Partner Relationship Management

Managing relations with partner companies is a vitally important business practice. But the most important elements of partner relationship management (PRM) have always pertained to sales; moreover, most of the PRM software now in existence focuses on the sales process. For these reasons, this chapter will concentrate on PRM as it relates to sales.

But it is important to bear in mind the potential scope of partner relationships in business. Partners may undertake almost any business responsibility on behalf of the companies they partner with: the most obvious of these fall in the CRM areas of marketing, sales, and support. If the archetypal beginning business is a youngster's lemonade stand, then in such a business the proprietor is directly responsible for all business functions, notably marketing, sales, and fulfillment. But businesses don't have to grow much beyond infancy to encounter a point at which some of their work can be discharged more cost-effectively by somebody else: by newspapers running ads, by listings in the Yellow Pages, by radio or TV commercials, or by delivery services.

Companies spring up whose entire *raison d'être* is to perform some business function more effectively than it can be performed by firms that have been trying to do everything for themselves. These include, in marketing, advertising agencies; in support, companies such as IKON, which provides printer and copier support for many large corporations; in fulfillment, companies such as Federal Express and UPS. A company like Amazon obviously must attend in some way to its own internal business functions; but, having done so, Amazon clearly has much to gain by coordinating its business carefully with FedEx, and vice versa.

What is Partner Relationship Management?

PRM is a strategy for managing indirect channels in relation to the overall business enterprise. As an adjective for software, it designates applications intended to help a company manage its partner channels. Ideally, such software increases the effectiveness with which channel partners can sell goods and can service customers.

More than 45 percent of the world's commerce is conducted through indirect sales channels, and this figure is almost certain to increase. Yet less than 1 percent of packaged software sold helps companies to manage indirect selling. CRM will remain largely a charade until it provides substantial support for this "dark" half of sales.

What are Channels?

Channels are the methods that companies use to get their products and services into the hands of users. Every channel is either direct or indirect.

Direct channels comprise sales made by a company's own employees—most often by field sales or telesales agents—or through the company's own Web site. The purchase of a PC from the Dell Web site, of makeup from the Avon lady, of a commercial software system typically involves, for the manufacturer, a direct sale.

Indirect channels make up the rest of the sales world. You buy Tide from Kroger or Safeway, not from Procter & Gamble. The woman that calls you to sell you a credit card probably works for a call center in Omaha, not for Discover. And the furniture you purchase for your office probably made a few stops between North Carolina, where it was manufactured, and the furniture wholesaler from which you bought it. Indirect channels are home to fishes of many kinds: agents, brokers, distributors, manufacturer's representatives, private labelers, stores, value-added resellers, and wholesalers—among others.

Why Use Indirect Channels?

One might think that companies would prefer to deal directly with consumers and to steer clear of third parties that they cannot fully control. However, indirect channels offer numerous advantages. A company just setting out in business will often find that using an established and fully functional channel makes selling much easier and less expensive. But channel partners can be of value in many additional ways. They can provide regional political or legal knowledge or cultural savvy; finance inventory and/or ensure product availability; take advantage of established relationships; and undertake local promotion and advertising or accept responsibility for local credit and collection. They can also add value to a product or service through a variety of undertakings. Channel resellers are often small and flexible, making them easy to do business with.

Who Uses Indirect Channels?

Use of indirect channels varies enormously across industries. In insurance and computer-hardware manufacture, more than 80 percent of goods and services are sold indirectly. For large-enterprise software and for microprocessor-fabricating machinery, less than 15 percent of sales volume is indirect. As a rule, the more complex and expensive the product or service, the less likely is it to be sold indirectly. Yet even Boeing, with its extremely complex and expensive main products, uses indirect channels extensively for sales of aftermarket parts.

American companies, and perhaps most multinationals, tend to use indirect channels especially when attempting to penetrate foreign markets. It is in this process that a channel partner's political, legal, and cultural knowledge, plus its established business relationships, can be of outstanding value.

Why Is the Importance of Indirect Channels Growing?

The tighter integration of the sell side that is enabled by the Internet implies that channel resellers will collaborate much more extensively in, and will exercise more influence over, the processes of the demand chain. By simplifying and clarifying channel operations, these trends will augment the general impact of the Web in increasing indirect sales volumes.

What Problems do Indirect Channels Pose?

re Corporate Strategy

The corporate boardroom offers a view of the world that uses the products and services that the corporation markets. The reliability of that view is often in doubt; what is not in doubt is that indirect channels tend to reduce its visibility. Corporate officers often lose sight of their goods as these move through the channel: they may not know who is buying them, or where, or why; they may have no idea when or how the consumer wants to buy the goods, or how those goods are being used. Yet such information is crucial to any corporation that needs ideas for new products or services, or wishes to understand its potential for profit in markets it has yet to enter.

re Information

Information, of course, relates to corporate strategy. While the channel reseller has information needed by the original provider, the reverse is true, too, and each has reasons to withhold information as well as to share it. Conventionally, channel partners may withhold information about end users to prevent the provider from dealing directly with those users; channel partners occasionally return to the provider very shallow numbers—sometimes merely units sold per zip code. A recent industry study shows that the items providers most want from channel vendors are market intelligence, lead-distribution data, and information enabling forecasting and marketing-campaign management. The items the vendors most want from providers are price and availability data, postsales support, training, and configuration and quote assistance.

re Service Visibility

When an original manufacturer provides support for its products, this support gives it direct contact—not necessarily happy!—with some of its customers; and prospects and customers may also contact the manufacturer directly through bingo cards, Web hits, and channel referral calls. Because indirect-channel vendors typically are not privy to returns, complaints, or other problems that consumers have taken up directly with the manufacturer, they can be unprepared for disconcerting encounters with unhappy consumers.

re Compensation

This can be a delicate issue for a provider's in-house indirect-channel managers. Motivating a channel partner to sell the goods is a challenge often radically different from motivating the direct sales force. Nevertheless, channel managers are often compensated according to the partners' sales to consumers, not the partners' purchases from the provider. Methods of compensation commonly associated with management of indirect channels include spiffs, rebates, and design-win bonuses for reps who succeed in getting the provider's product designed into a product originating with another manufacturer.

re Human Resources

The original provider has a stake in the employees of its channel vendors. For instance, a partner employee may need training and certification to sell the provider's product, and the provider may wish to track the employee's qualifications. Alternatively, the provider might want to implement a special program under which a sales agent receives a specified bonus for every unit sold during a given month—and might want the program to reward not only the provider's employees but the channel vendor's as well. Considerations of this kind raise issues of accountability and may provoke conflicts with the vendors.

re Contracts

Business agreements between original providers and channel vendors are potentially very complex, involving territories, training, marketing support, pricing, inventory levels, payment terms, postsales support, service levels, and many more issues. Tracking and managing all the terms of a contractual agreement of this type can be extremely challenging.

re Marketing

Administration of and accounting for marketing-development funds, and propagation of integrated marketing campaigns through indirect channels, are challenges generally ill met. Even routine marketing support for channel vendors—such as supplying them with collateral, product samples, and demo units—raises slippery issues and is often fumbled.

re Distribution Management

Other things being equal, the manufacturer wants to sell channel resellers as much inventory as they can stomach; but the resellers want to buy only as much as they must to avoid losing customer business. Not only do they face carrying costs for storage, they face the risk—or the certainty—that the goods will lose value over time. Here, as in general, there are conflicts of interest.

Manufacturers can deal effectively with such conflicts—for instance, by offering price protection in some form to resellers. But this opens the door to further compromise and negotiation, and it becomes in effect one more arena for competition.

How Does a Channel Reseller Differ from an End Customer?

Channel resellers and end customers are alike in many respects. You provide products and/or services to each; you typically have agreed-upon pricing and discounting structures for each; you need to manage each and to keep records of your interactions with each.

But the differences are crucial. Of course, you want to encourage end customers, like resellers, to buy what you have to sell, but you don't care whether the end customers then resell it. For this reason, end customers do not have inventory commitments and territories, and they don't need to be trained as resellers. They don't get leads or give out quotes, and they don't do cooperative advertising with you; and they aren't paid to carry large quantities of rapidly depreciating goods. You often don't need to inform end customers of service problems, because they're the ones with whom those problems originate.

Moreover, the survival of a partner business often depends on its relationship with a vendor; end customers usually have less at stake. This distinction is closely tied to another: partners typically buy vendor products in large quantities or amounts, whereas consumers usually buy only one product from one reseller.

For manufacturers, danger lurks in the temptation to oversimplify and to treat resellers as end customers. The two groups are like apples and tomatoes, tasty red fruits of about the same size—both can be used in salads, but you don't put apple sauce on a pizza crust.

Why Is there So Little Software to Support Indirect Sales?

For the same reasons that CRM is so late to the party. The CFO has traditionally held responsibility for capital expenditures and thus for fundings for automation; most software spending has flowed, as one would predict, into applications meant to automate internal operations and to reduce corporate expense totals. Meanwhile the personnel responsible for driving revenues were not reporting to the CFO or even hanging around the back office; they were out on the road taking manual notes on contacts or trying to negotiate lower quotas, not stepping up to the plate for huge capital expenditures.

The second main reason is that, until the advent of the Web, dealing with third parties was relatively difficult. Evidence is provided by Boeing, which took 10 years to sign up 70 EDI partners, but managed to corral 300 Internet suppliers in only 9 months. In fact, the client/server model was antagonistic to partner networking. In many cases, a single channel partner represents multiple vendors, so that client/server integration of the supply chain would often have meant asking a partner to implement four or six distinct software packages to complete the links to all their suppliers.

This second reason was aggravated by the fact that many partners were not committed to any single vendor. This meant that a vendor investment in PRM software would often be rewarded only by a fraction of the partner's business, or that PRM applications would have to provide full support for the partner's relevant business needs at the expense of benefiting other vendors allied with the partner. With the Internet, on the other hand, a vendor can now implement a single application to support its entire range of partners; convergence on a single medium and the standards that have evolved for it has reduced total cost of ownership by an order of magnitude.

How Will the Internet Affect Indirect Channels?

The Internet is one of three forces driving distribution toward a greater reliance on channels. (The other two are outsourcing trends and intensified focus on end-customer management.) Thanks to the Net, automation of the buy side of the chain can now be extended effectively to the sell side, enabling the manufacturer to integrate the entire process that centers on its products and stretches from its suppliers' suppliers to its customers' customers. The Internet enables software that any provider of goods or services can use to support its entire selling chain in making the ultimate sale—software analogous to the system that provides Federal Express with a complete view of its distribution/selling chain, reading the contents of airports, warehouses, trucks, and whatnot.

As Internet technology makes information more fluid and frictionless, two things will happen. First, companies will come to focus more precisely on their core competencies and to outsource everything in the penumbra—often including sales, marketing, service, fulfillment, and other channel-related activities. This strategy carries value for all parties involved by directing every function to those who can handle it most effectively. Second, consumers will increasingly be able to buy from the party of their choice in the selling chain; if that party is the manufacturer, that's fine; if it's your cousin Vinny and two "yutes"—well, why not?

In sum, the increased availability of information will encourage outsourcing and streamline the selling function. It will also provide the consumer with more options for a comfortable buying experience. Sell-side monopolies will grow more difficult to maintain.

The Internet enables the enterprise to collaborate much more closely with its "trading partners": its customers, its employees, and its business partners. Ideally, all these will come to participate actively in the marketing, sales, and support cycles.

A company can use the Web to construct a partner network as an extranet—that is, as one or more sites external to the company's firewall that nevertheless require login using a password and thus are not part of the public Internet. Having prepared the site(s), the company then simply issues one or more ID/password combinations to each of its business partners, together with any appropriate guidelines on how the extranet is to be used. For an enterprise like Oracle, partners so authorized might include computer vendors, ACD vendors, network providers, system implementers, and software developers and resellers.

A partner network gives the sponsoring enterprise an additional channel useful for all of its major customer-oriented activities. Through this network it can distribute product and service information, and the network can funnel appropriate orders, inquiries, and service requests back to the sponsor. Beyond these task-oriented functions, the partner network offers value in that it constitutes a means to extend the sponsor's perceived presence on the Internet. However, if the network is to function effectively, the sponsor must address many pertinent questions and must craft the network's operation in accordance with the answers to those questions, including:

- How does a lead reach the sponsor?
- If the sponsor originates the lead, how is it assigned within the partner network?
- If a partner originates the lead, how is it assigned within the network?
- How does the sponsor measure the suitability of a given partner for a given lead?
- How do partners accept or reject leads?
- How are sales credits assigned?
- How are sales teams defined and assigned?
- If a customer places an order directly, what commissions are paid?
- Otherwise, who places an order: a partner employee or a sponsor employee?
- How does the sponsor measure partner performance?
- How do leads turn into opportunities?

- How do leads age and expire?
- Which partners are candidates for disintermediation?
- Can a partner log a defect on behalf of a customer?
- How can a partner contribute to the lifetime value of a customer?
- How can a partner contribute to customer satisfaction and customer loyalty?

The advent of the Web intensifies competition not only for customers but for partners as well. It is essential that the enterprise build and maintain a strong network of business partners, and the Web offers a variety of automated and interactive techniques for pursuing this goal; some examples follow.

Joint Marketing Programs

Prior to the Internet, the design and monitoring of joint marketing programs posed major challenges for coordination. Every major activity (planning, budgeting, execution, result measurement) called for information sharing in real time, but channels for such sharing were typically slow, cumbersome, and/or expensive. The Web makes it easy to communicate all essential data, in either direction, over a corporate extranet.

Training and Certification

Partner-management applications running on the Internet can serve not only to notify any business partner of corporate training events but also to deliver the actual training to the partner's office. Web collaboration tools make it possible to present and to demonstrate products to remote audiences.

Lead Management

A principal function of partner management is to ensure that every lead is directed to the appropriate partner, if possible through some automated rule for assignment. The partner targeted must be enabled to recognize the lead and to accept or reject it promptly.

Traditionally, an enterprise that has forwarded a lead to a business partner has lost track of that lead; while the enterprise may have been able to assess the partner's performance in the aggregate, any detailed assessment has typically been out of the question. Internet applications for partner management now make it easy to secure lead-specific feedback.

Sales Support

Such applications for tracking individual leads can be extended to sales support. When the company to which the lead has been forwarded needs such support, lead-tracking applications can notify the lead's originator automatically and can trigger forwarding of support tools and materials.

Team Selling

When the sponsor enterprise and a business partner are both involved in a potential deal and are working together on the lead, the Internet makes it easy for them to share critical information in a password-protected environment which, though outside the sponsor's firewall, is just as secure as if it were fully internal to the sponsor's direct sales organization.

Technical Support

Self-service applications implemented on the Internet can provide business partners, just as they would end users, with ready access to corporate support services. Such applications can answer the most frequent support questions without involving a human agent, thus driving down support costs. For more complex or unusual concerns, self-service applications can enable access to the corporate knowledge base, enabling a business partner to extract needed information. In cases in which such self-service proves inadequate, the applications can provide a "Call Me" button, which users can click to contact support personnel.

End-User Support; Demand Planning

As with leads, so with sales: a manufacturer's sale effected through a business partner has often meant that the manufacturer never secures basic information identifying the end user. A typical corporation that sold through third parties generally could not identify its installed base, had no way to communicate directly with its consumers, and thus could not reliably evaluate how its products performed or were perceived.

Again, the Web transforms this three-way relationship. As each sale moves forward from lead management to order capture, customer and status information can now be shared at every step. Manufacturers can use the timely sales and inventory data from their business partners to manage more effectively their manufacturing, shipping, and inventory cycles. The loop from manufacturer through retailer to end user is completed, building stronger relationships among the three parties.

Performance Measurement

Effective management of business-partner relationships requires that they be monitored and measured. By facilitating the collection of real-time data on lead management, revenues, training, and support, the Internet helps the enterprise to measure its partners' performances; to provide them training as needed; to exploit feedback from end users to improve its products and services; and to maximize its revenues by focusing on the profitable partners.

For corporations that depend on business partners, managing their partner relationships has always been a major challenge. The key to success in building and maintaining a robust network of partners is the World Wide Web.

How Can Providers Induce Channel Resellers to Cooperate?

Currently, the preponderance of power in the channel is held by channel resellers, by virtue of their proximity to the consumer and the access that this grants them to customer information. However, the majority of the information needed to close a sale—pricing, discounts, quotes, installed-base data, configurations, product availability, and customer history and credit status—resides not in CRM or PRM applications but in the database of the manufacturer. Channel vendors need this information, and we may expect manufacturers to leverage it with a view to restoring a balance of power with respect to channels.

How Big is the Partner Relationship Management Market?

Although studies by industry consultants project a $500-million market for PRM, PRM insiders estimate that the market may be larger by an order of magnitude. If PRM represents 50 percent of the entire process of manufacture and sales (supply chain plus demand chain) then the market presumably equals at least the combined revenues of all supply-chain vendors. This figure is already approaching $2 billion, though in a relatively young market. A plausible estimate for the entire PRM market segment is $4 billion.

Why is Channel Management the Next Great Software Space?

In 1999, software addressing this PRM market space totaled no more than $50 million of that $4-billion total. The potential for growth is huge, and that growth will accrue to companies that can bring the full battery of enterprise information to bear on the indirect channel, as needed, in order to drive increases in sales. Though PRM systems must coordinate the efforts of the original provider with those of its downstream partners, those systems must ultimately look beyond the channel to the consumers to which the products and services finally flow. That focus on end-user visibility will undergird the new software products and markets that will drive corporate strategy.

The market segment for PRM software is currently contested by a number of competitors, each falling into one or another of three categories:

- Pure PRM players, including Allegis, NetActive, and Webridge

- CRM vendors offering PRM extensions; these include Onyx Software, Pivotal, SalesLogix, Siebel, and Vantive (now owned by PeopleSoft)

- A new breed of developers integrating CRM with PRM ; these include Asera, Eprise, MarketSoft, Radnet, and YOUcentric (formerly Sales Vision)

A fourth category, which would consist of ERP vendors turning to PRM applications, may come into being.

The Endgame

The endgame for any PRM aspirant is to sign up an Application Service Provider to host a complete, integrated, supply-and-demand-chain application. Implement a system that can manage the entire process from component manufacture to consumer purchase and extend browser access to that system to all suppliers and channel partners, and you can, in theory, start up a series of $50-million businesses. Choose a product category, sign up all the third parties, and give them a URL and a host, and then start thinking about what company you want to build *next* week.

5
Internet Exchanges

Terms

I hate to begin with terminology, but I must. This area of e-commerce is so fashionable and is developing so quickly that the terms can be ill-defined and confusing even for those who hear them daily. Bear with me: this will not be brief.

Electronic marketplace is probably the most inclusive of the relevant terms. To my mind, every site that enables sales over the Web is an electronic marketplace or a constituent of one. (The Internet as a whole is an electronic marketplace.) So this term covers businesses like Amazon and Nirvana Chocolates, which nobody would mistake for exchanges, and it covers exchanges as well.

So what is an **exchange**? Usage varies. Net Market Makers (NMM), whose site[18] is a useful resource for this subject, defines them as "two-sided marketplaces where buyers and suppliers negotiate prices, usually with a bid and ask system, and where prices move both up and down," a definition with which I agree. But NMM goes on to deal with lead-generation sites, catalog aggregators, and even auction sites as things other than exchanges; I prefer to use the term to include all such sites . . . and more. In fact, the only distinction between what NMM calls "exchanges" and what it calls "auctions" is that the former involve only one party on each side whereas the latter involve multiple parties on one side. Aren't exchanges (of goods and services) still what is taking place on all such sites?

Thus, I classify **auction sites** as one kind of exchange. In fact, a large proportion of exchange sites support auction activity as well as spot buying, and provide catalog aggregation and other services as well. (Surely it makes sense to offer one's customers options, instead of forcing them to go elsewhere to conduct business in the way they wish.) In any case, auction sites can support **seller auctions**, in which prospective *buyers* bid *up* the price of a good or service, or **buyer** or **reverse auctions**, in which prospective *sellers* bid *down* the price—or, of course, both.

Catalog aggregators bring together, rationalize, and reconcile catalogs from multiple vendors, facilitating comparisons by prospective purchasers. Prices for cataloged goods tend to be static, but are not necessarily so.

Private exchanges were the earliest electronic exchanges. Each was hosted by a single company inside the company's firewall and used for procurement from among a group of preauthorized suppliers. Many such exchanges were implemented using EDI, a costly technology that is rapidly giving way to the Internet. Now, as public exchanges become more and more common, some companies that sponsored EDI-only private exchanges, or none at all, are growing increasingly interested in implementing private Internet exchanges—often not instead of public ones but in addition, for the sake of enhanced privacy and discretion.

Vertical exchanges: each of these is specific to a single industry, broadly or narrowly defined.

Horizontal exchanges deal with goods and services that are not specific to one industry; office supplies is an obvious candidate for a horizontal exchange.

Branded exchanges: each of these is sponsored by one or a few companies and deals with goods and services of concern to the sponsor(s); they may be vertical or horizontal, or both. Instead of the many-to-many model prevalent with exchanges, branded exchanges conform to a sponsor(s)-to-many model.

Demand exchanges, **procurement exchanges**, and **customer exchanges** are distinguished by how they relate in time to the company-enabling sale of a good or service. Exchanges in which such sales take place I call **procurement exchanges**; these include the great majority of the exchanges now planned or already operating. **Demand exchanges** deal in what are conventionally categorized as presale assets and activities; they correspond, more or less, to what

NMM calls "lead-generation" sites. **Customer exchanges** are the analogous entities for postsale assets and activities.

E-hubs represent an evolutionary advance beyond conventional exchanges. Such an advance may take one or more of three forms:

- The provision of services beyond those required to execute simple transactions on the exchange

- The extension of transaction services beyond procurement into areas of CRM

- The progressive integration of transaction services with the existing ERP and CRM systems of exchange participants

Clearly, each of these forms is a matter of degree, and there is no obvious line of demarcation between exchanges and e-hubs. In general terms, an exchange morphs into an e-hub as it enhances its value to its participants, even to the point of rendering itself an indispensable element of their standard business practices.

An **e-spoke** is a logical path connecting two e-hubs. One of the many services that an e-hub—particularly a vertical one—can provide its users is to recognize any submission that is unsuited to its area of business and to reroute it, along an e-spoke, to a connected exchange that is designed to handle it. Such routing will be governed by preagreed business rules and will probably be directed by an electronic tag (perhaps using XML) attached to the submission. A major issue that such a tag must address is security, because security measures that the submitter expects from the first exchange must be matched in full by any exchange to which the submission is forwarded. No such mechanism is currently in operation, so far as I can tell, but Commerce One claims that its Global Trading Web has this capability and that it has users planning to exploit it.

Spot buying is ad-hoc purchasing from a supplier with whom the purchasing company has no formal relationship—and perhaps has never done business.

Direct goods are the raw materials and components used in the manufacturing process.

Indirect goods are all the other goods companies need to conduct their businesses, like paper and pencils and PCs.

Procurement Exchanges

A procurement exchange is a marketplace in which one or more companies offer goods or services for sale and one or more companies participate as purchasers of such goods and services. A company may figure on both sides in a procurement exchange. All, or nearly all, existing exchanges belong to this category. Procurement exchanges play an increasingly important role in supply chains, and the volume of this business is such that this category of exchanges will probably always be the most important.

Before the age of the Internet, corporate procurement took many forms. One of the simplest forms was that somebody consulted one or more catalogs of goods, made a decision as to item and quantity, placed a call or filled out and mailed an order form, and waited for delivery of the goods. That process is largely a thing of the past. Procurement will move increasingly to electronic exchanges, as implemented by Ariba, Commerce One, and Oracle. There the buyer will find multiple suppliers who will bid competitively for the order; the procurement process will be much more thoroughly automated and much more rapid. Manufacturers will post component specifications on the Web for all prospective suppliers; an electronic auction process will then identify the bidder offering the lowest cost and/or the highest quality.

Participants in such exchanges will include not only suppliers and buyers but partners, consumers, and company employees. Exchanges provide all participants with a forum within which they may combine forces to gain leverage in the marketplace. Combining forces means aggregating purchase orders, requisitions, service bids, and more. To leverage their corporate weight more effectively, many large corporations will want to use their intranets to consolidate internal purchasing initiatives that may originate with many departments and/or countries. Multiple companies will group their purchase requests to multiply their buying power.

Leverage to be gained will take the form of reduced costs, increased margins, and stronger demand. Early reports indicate that companies that enable procurement via the Internet typically realize immediate reductions in purchase prices. Though such reductions average perhaps 10 percent,[19] Commerce One reports that trading on its exchanges has resulted in savings ranging up to 50 percent.

Though bringing suppliers and purchasers together is the first service provided by procurement exchanges, it is rarely the last. Exchange sponsors are already competing vigorously to provide added value to their participants, understanding that they must grow rapidly and foster participant loyalty if they are to survive in a turbulent and highly competitive marketplace.

Rapid Proliferation

Procurement exchanges are multiplying with insistent rapidity. Companies spend a total of some $5 trillion per year on industrial parts and supplies (*only*). According to a study by Merrill Lynch,[20] the volume of electronic commerce transacted through third-party marketplaces will amount to about $450 billion by 2003. The reasons for this proliferation of exchanges are numerous. The most obvious is that, for both buyers and sellers of goods and/or services, an exchange simultaneously broadens the potential market and simplifies access to it. Exchanges also can normalize the sales information they provide, thus facilitating comparisons of similar products and services, and can provide a broad range of news and information relevant to their markets.

Most companies will not rely on exchanges for the procurement of everything they need in order to do business. Large companies, in particular, can often negotiate mutually beneficial agreements with some of their suppliers, and when they do so it will normally mean that some portion of their procurement no longer qualifies for submission to an exchange. But companies will not generally find it cost-effective to scrutinize every expense, even those for paper cups and adhesive tape. The party most motivated to watch these deals like a hawk is the current supplier, or the would-be supplier.

First-mover advantage is especially high among exchanges. Other things being equal, it makes more sense for a company 1) to join an existing exchange than to start a new one; 2) to join a large exchange than to join a small one. No company wants to complicate its business by belonging to multiple competitive exchanges, so each has an incentive to seek out, for each qualifying business need, the exchange representing the broadest existing market, and then to stick with it. Even so, exchange sponsors can provide a wide variety of services in order to ingratiate themselves with their participants, and any sponsor that does not work continuously to do so is potentially vulnerable to an upstart more responsive to participants' concerns and needs. The most successful sponsors will provide so much business value to their participants that the latter will come to take them for granted as part of their standard business procedures. By this process, exchanges will evolve into e-hubs.

General Exchanges

FreeMarkets

FreeMarkets, which dates from 1995, claims to be the original business-to-business (B2B) e-marketplace. Glen Meakem, the founder, actually peddled the idea in 1994 to GE—which declined. Partly as a function of its great age (about 135 Internet years), FreeMarkets is now publicly traded, unlike most of its cohort. Also because of its age, its dollar-volume figures are relatively very high, though this effect is enhanced by its not confining itself to a specific market category. It claims to have enabled $7.6 billion in total market volume and $1.5 billion in customer savings. Volumes in 2000—including $2.2 billion in the second quarter—have been running about six times those of 1999.

FreeMarkets' scope is too great to detail here, but it lists thirty-two categories of equipment and twelve categories of inventory; these range from agricultural equipment through packaging, metals, telecommunications, transport, chemicals, textiles, and semiconductors to office furniture and appliances. Inevitably, it competes with virtually every other exchange listed in this section.

As with most exchanges, FreeMarkets' basic transaction mechanism is the online auction, but FM invests much more work in its auctions than is usual. Its typical process involves working with the prospective purchaser to develop a detailed request for quotation (RFQ) that explicitly lists all terms and costs, including transport fees, taxes, and service and maintenance requirements. Would-be suppliers must then agree to all terms of the RFQ, and they are further screened by FM and by the purchaser-to-be. FM's scrupulous approach particularly suits transactions involving complex equipment. The entire process usually takes 2 to 8 weeks; only when it is completed does FM conduct a real-time auction.

These auctions are buyer-driven and are paid for by fees pre-contracted with the buyer—typically millions of dollars per year and sometimes including a percentage of savings realized. Suppliers, because they must agree to the buyer's specs, may participate for free. FreeMarkets has seventy-four large purchasers as customers, including Alcoa, Caterpillar, Procter & Gamble, United Technologies, Westinghouse, Frigidaire, and Whirlpool.

FreeMarkets is threatened by the possibility that major customers will found their own exchanges; GM, a former customer, did precisely that, dropping FM 2 months after announcing what was to become Covisint. But the company is protected by the expertise and dedication it brings to the auction process.

Oracle Exchange

Oracle Exchange, launched in late 1999, is a horizontal exchange open to any company that cares to use it. The exchange supports seller auctions, reverse auctions, and spot purchasing, and it provides catalog aggregation, a search facility for prospective purchasers, and a range of marketplace intelligence. Procedures for complex RFQs are also supported. The exchange enables purchasers to make payment using purchasing cards or on account.

As an open exchange, Oracle Exchange has no membership or registration charges. Its revenues are raised by transaction fees, which for auctions range from 1 percent down to 0.1 percent. Fees are posted in more detail on the site www.oracleexchange.com. The business scope of the exchange, effectively unlimited, is suggested by the catalog categories originally listed on the home page: Building and Construction Machinery and Accessories; Computer Peripherals and Accessories; Electronic Components and Supplies; Equipment Maintenance and Repair Kits; Laboratory Equipment; Lighting and Electrical Accessories and Supplies; Manufacturing Components and Supplies; Management, Business Professionals and Administrative Services; Office Equipment, Accessories and Supplies; and Tools and General Machinery.

The utility of Oracle Exchange is enhanced by the participation of the members of the Oracle Supplier Network, a preexisting organization comprising some 260 companies including Adecco Staffing Services, barnesandnoble.com, Boise Cascade Office Products, BT Office Products, Collabria, Inc., Compaq Computer, GE Supply, and Office Depot.

Oracle Exchange's logging facilities make it possible for both buyers and suppliers to check order history and status and related information. The exchange is designed to be open and standards-based so that participating companies can more easily integrate their exchange activities with their ERP systems. Standard technologies used include HTML, HTTP, SSL, and XML; business documents formatted in XML comply with Open Applications Group standards. Oracle uses its own Business OnLine program to support the exchange.

Oracle also uses the code and technology underlying Oracle Exchange as the basis of its offering to companies and consortia that want to sponsor verticalized exchanges, extending and specializing the model to suit the needs of the targeted industries.

Industry-Specific Exchanges

Procurement exchanges will emerge in every industry: aerospace, airlines, automobiles, consulting services, consumer electronics and other consumer products, defense, education, financial services, government, health care, high-tech and traditional manufacturing, paper and pulp, pharmaceuticals, telecoms, utilities, and so on and on. After direct and indirect distribution channels, they may be regarded as constituting a distinct third category of channel.

The last few months have seen a flurry of announcements of the implementation of online exchanges—for the automobile, chemical, convenience store, food and beverage, forest products, house construction, retail merchandise, and travel businesses.[21] Such exchanges are typically, though not necessarily, created by a buyer or by a group of buyers that are allied at least in this action. Once in operation, each exchange functions as an electronic bulletin board to which each buyer may post its needs; each posting identifies an item and may stipulate a quantity, a price, a timetable, and a delivery address. Items of many kinds may also carry physical specifications. Similarly, would-be sellers may post items to be sold; of course, they may respond to buyer postings, and vice versa.

The more leverage a buyer can exert, the lower the price and the higher the quality that buyer can expect to command; conversely for sellers who control a majority of the goods or services in demand.

Let's consider a few examples. (There are hundreds of such exchanges. Inevitably, the majority of exchanges are not mentioned below. Those that are, while among the more important, are cited partly to convey the near-universal proliferation of these online marketplaces.)

Aerospace and Defense

Exostar

This exchange addresses the global aerospace and defense industry. Founded in March 2000 by Boeing, Lockheed Martin, BAE SYSTEMS, and Raytheon, it was implemented by Commerce One using Commerce One's MarketSite Portal Solution. Technology developed by Commerce One and GE enables companies using EDI to migrate to the Internet without having to jettison their existing networks.

In total, the four founding companies have annual procurement outlays of $71 billion dollars; they deal with 37,000 suppliers, hundreds of airlines, and dozens of national governments; and they have invited all these associates to participate in the exchange.

Automotive

Covisint

One of the most important exchanges was launched on November 2, 1999, with announcements by Ford that it would implement AutoXchange with Cisco and Oracle and by GM that it would set up GM MarketSite (later TradeXchange) with Commerce One. Ford made clear that AutoXchange would welcome participation by other car manufacturers, and on February 25, 2000, Ford and GM announced that they would merge the two exchanges, the result to be called auto-xchange and to be joined by DaimlerChrysler. Two days later it was announced that Nissan and Renault would also join them, and that a number of Japanese manufacturers were considering joining. On May 16, 2000, the participants renamed the exchange Covisint (for connectivity, collaboration, visibility, and international scope).

The five manufacturers together spend $300 billion annually on parts and supplies procured from some 30,000 suppliers. Spokespersons suggest that roughly 35 percent of this business will move onto the exchange. The U.S. Federal Trade Commission (FTC) undertook an investigation concerning whether the exchange would function in restraint of trade, but approved it in somewhat guarded terms on September 11, 2000.

Although the auto manufacturers compete with each other for customers, parts, labor, and market share, they recognized that a single comprehensive exchange would provide the highest measure of liquidity and efficiency. The exchange has deployed firewalls and other security measures to ensure that sensitive information belonging to each participant is withheld from its competitors.

The new exchange, already in operation, is likely over the next few years to drive down manufacturing expenses, or at least to retard their growth, and the participants expect further savings from displacing transaction paperwork. The average purchase order currently costs $150 to process; this cost is expected to plummet to between $5 and $15. The effect for consumers may be car prices that actually decline.

Aviation

Aeroxchange

Aeroxchange, a marketplace for the aviation industry, was announced in July 2000 by thirteen airlines: Air Canada, Air New Zealand, All Nippon Airways, America West Airlines, Austrian Airlines, Cathay Pacific, Federal Express, Japan Airlines, KLM, Lufthansa, Northwest Airlines, SAS, and Singapore Airlines. Although the exchange, which went into service in September 2000, will exclude trade in aircraft and fuel, it is expected eventually to handle more than $45 billion of the airlines' annual purchases of goods and services.

Aeroxchange uses the Oracle exchange platform, which supports normal and reverse auctioning, catalog services, contract and spot buying capabilities, and collaborative supply-chain planning. Assets to be exchanged include airframe, avionics, and engine components; maintenance services; and a broad range of routine goods and services specific to the industry. The Aeroxchange market appears to overlap, in part, that served by Exostar, which was described earlier.

Chemicals and Life-Science

Chemdex

Chemdex, founded in 1997, was the first customer-driven online marketplace for life sciences. A catalog aggregator listing 1.7 million products from 2,300 suppliers, Chemdex provides scientific researchers, suppliers, and enterprises an open and neutral marketplace for life-science products, enabling wide market access and a frictionless trading environment.

Chemdex offers complete e-commerce solutions, including electronic procurement, systems integration, and comprehensive customer support programs, enabling greater levels of productivity for life-science researchers. Chemdex delivers integrated supply-chain solutions to 140 enterprise customer accounts and to 30,000 registered scientists from academic institutions and from major pharmaceutical and biotechnology companies.

In early 2000, Chemdex and three related companies metamorphosed into Ventro Corporation, of which Chemdex is now an operating company. Ventro also operates Promedix, an exchange for medical equipment, and holds a minority stake in each of four additional exchanges, but it derives 90 percent of its gross revenues from Chemdex. The company appears to be a cross between a marketplace operator and an incubator, and its market cap has suffered recently because Chemdex revenues have been below expectations.

Construction

Cephren MarketNet

Cephren, Inc., and Commerce One collaborated to develop this marketplace for the building and construction industry, which was announced in January 2000. The exchange enables buyers and sellers of construction products, services, and equipment to communicate and transact at will. Buyers can create bid packages and issue them to sellers, who can then submit their responses online.

Cephren itself was then a new company, formed by a merger between Blueline Online, Inc., a provider of Internet-based project collaboration services to the building and construction industry, and eBricks.com, Inc., a procurement network for buyers and sellers of construction products and equipment. Cephren presents itself as the industry pioneer in this market; it serves more than 800 firms and has 10,000 project collaboration subscribers on five continents. Potential competitors are discussed below.

HomebuildersXchange

The five largest American homebuilding companies, together with Encore Venture Partners and Oracle Corporation, have set up this exchange to offer increased supply-chain efficiencies to every party to the house-construction process—including builders, trade contractors, distributors, lumberyards, wholesalers, service providers, and manufacturers. The industry generates annual revenues in excess of $200 billion.

The exchange, which went online in the summer of 2000, provides normal and reverse auctioning, catalog purchasing, contract and spot buying features, and collaborative supply-chain planning to facilitate capacity and demand planning for participants. It is developing additional features including handheld wireless access, hosted job-cost management, hosted sales-force automation, and other services specific to the construction industry.

WhiteHammer.com

This exchange, intended as a competitor to HomebuildersXchange, was announced in June 2000 by a group that included SAP, Weyerhaeuser Real Estate, and six other homebuilding companies. Intended in general to provide services much the same as those of HomebuildersXchange, WhiteHammer differentiates itself via an information system, based on SAP software, that is designed to increase supply-chain efficiency across the construction enterprise. Use of this system will be offered on a subscription basis.

One of the exchange's founders cites industry experts to the effect that one of every three dollars spent in residential construction is lost to scheduling errors and related construction delays. He projects that the efficiencies enabled by WhiteHammer will go far toward minimizing wasted costs and improving the general financial performance of exchange participants. The exchange is expected to go live in late 2000.

Energy

Altra Energy

Altra, founded in January 1996, provides a marketplace in which more than 500 companies in various areas of the energy industry conduct transactions in natural gas, crude oil, power, and related information. Altra has grown rapidly, acquiring QuickTrade, a competitive exchange for natural gas; two energy companies, Energy Imperium and TransEnergy; a French IT firm, Sema; and Unified Information.

Altra, located in Houston, now employs about 260 people. Its significance is attested by its monthly volume records, set in August 2000, of 18.9 million megawatt-hours and 27.9 million barrels of natural gas liquids traded.

Enporion

Enporion, an exchange for energy utilities, was announced in August 2000, by a group of five companies: Allegheny Energy, Minnesota Power, PPL Corporation, and XCEL Energy. Participants are expected to include electric, gas, and hydroelectric energy producers and members of their supply chains. The exchange aims to enable reduced cycle times, lower inventories, reduced processing costs, standardized supply-chain practices, and improved information flows. To achieve these ends, it will provide e-commerce catalogs, auctions, Web-based RFPs, configuration tools, and a collaborative system for project management.

Operational on October 24, 2000, Enporion is the first exchange undertaken collaboratively by Commerce One and SAP, whose relationship is discussed later. It will presumably compete to some extent with Altra Energy.

Facilities

MyFacilities.com

This site, set up by Honeywell, is the third electronic hub in which the company is a sponsor or major player. For the moment, the site presents itself as an Internet community for facility-management professionals. It is gearing up to provide a full-fledged market that would bring together facility managers, solutions providers, service contractors, distributors, and material suppliers. It will feature full and secure product-search, order, and payment capabilities.

The site already offers information resources intended to keep its audience abreast of trends and technologies in facilities management. These include computer-based training programs, benchmarking tools, listings of codes and standards, industry news, case studies, and listings of upcoming trade events. In order to optimize its services to the community it serves, Honeywell is actively seeking other companies to share sponsorship and to provide additional offerings.

Food etc.

CateringX

This exchange was sponsored by the Lucio Tan Group, a Philippine conglomerate, and constructed by Oracle. Focusing its early growth on the Asia-Pacific region, CateringX intends to develop into a fully global exchange, streamlining the supply chains of industrial caterers, concessionaires, in-flight catering companies, hotels, and restaurants. It provides normal and reverse auctioning, catalog purchasing, contract and spot buying features, and collaborative supply-chain planning to facilitate capacity and demand planning for participants.

Covering the full range of catering needs, from raw foods through crockery to kitchen design, CateringX went live in June 2000, and is currently serving more than 700 suppliers and purchasers. Its services go beyond procurement to embrace fulfillment issues including document processing, storage, pretesting and preinspection, and brokering.

Transora

Transora is an exchange for consumer products—especially foods. Funded in June 2000 by forty-nine companies, it went live in mid-August; it is now sponsored by fifty-four major consumer-products companies with more than $500 billion in annual sales; these include Coca-Cola, Kraft, Procter & Gamble, and Anheuser-Busch. The exchange relies principally on the auction and catalog models, but its services span the entire supply chain, providing for procurement, online order management, supply-chain collaboration, and financial services.

The task of constructing the exchange site was directed to the Ariba-IBM-i2 alliance, but PricewaterhouseCoopers took over the integration and consulting responsibilities that IBM would normally have undertaken. The exchange has been marketed aggressively in Asia, Latin America, and Europe; this has lent impetus to a rival exchange, CPGmarket.com, a Euro-centric effort propelled by SAP, Nestlé, Danone, and Henkel. There has been speculation that the two exchanges will follow the Covisint path blazed by GM and Ford, choosing to merge rather than to compete.

Human Resources

CareerPath.FreeAgent.com

This co-branded exchange is a collaborative effort by CareerPath.com, the Internet's largest career-management site, and Opus360 Corporation, a provider of Internet solutions for bringing people and projects together. FreeAgent.com is Opus360's Internet service for free agents. The purpose of the exchange is to match the skills of consultants, contractors, and other independent professionals with the staffing needs of corporations. The two companies, with more than two million registered users, orient the exchange toward prospective employers as well as free agents. Users can post jobs or résumés and can search a database of job listings or résumés compiled from hundreds of sources. The site also provides free career advice.

OTN Xchange

In July 2000, Oracle announced that it was launching a staffing exchange under the aegis of its Oracle Technology Network. Like CareerPath.FreeAgent.com, OTN Xchange addresses the needs of projects that need additional staff as well as those of workers seeking employment; but the Oracle exchange is the first to target a specific workforce segment—workers with Internet-development skills. In August 2000, membership in the OTN reached one million, and the exchange aims principally to provide services to them and to those who might employ them.

Establishment of the exchange is partly a reaction to a severe worldwide shortage of IT professionals; an estimate for the United States projects a shortfall of 970,000 IT professionals by 2004. Goals of the exchange include enabling developers to enhance their skills and productivity and helping to direct available talent to projects for which it is most urgently needed; the exchange is also explicitly a promotional measure for Oracle. Services are free of charge. Users of the exchange can buy, sell, and auction technical services, and can manage individual, corporate, and open-source development projects.

OTN Xchange was developed in partnership with Collab.Net, a leading provider of collaborative software development services, which also provides hosting for the exchange.

Some Notes on Human-Resource Exchanges

For a number of industries, a major asset to be exchanged will be services not merely provided but actually embodied by people. A pilots' association might set up such an exchange; any agency providing temporary workers would be well suited to one. For an example of how such an exchange would work, we can consider the consulting industry (comprising Arthur Andersen, Andersen Consulting, Deloitte & Touche, Ernst & Young, KPMG, PricewaterhouseCoopers, and others).

From the point of view of the consulting firm, each consultant employed has a set of skills, a home location, a set of expenses (salary, benefits, travel and lodging, and so on), and a projected margin contribution (revenue generated less expenses incurred). A consultant when not booked may undergo training, the point of which would be to maintain or increase the revenue that consultant can generate in future; but, during the period not booked, the consultant generates no revenue. (Expenses, yes!)

When a company needs a consultant, the need is typically time- and location-sensitive: the company needs a specific skill or set of skills at location L by date D for time T. If the company posts its requirements to an exchange, all consulting firms using the exchange are able to bid competitively for the business: bids will be driven up as D approaches—especially if L is distant from any eligible consultant—but may be driven down as T increases and/or as the consulting firm experiences or anticipates an increase in nonbillable consultant time. Conversely, a consulting firm can post projected dates of availability for consultants with specific skill sets, and companies needing the skills specified can bid competitively for the consultants.

As a bidirectional auction, this mode of operation perfectly suits the exchange model. Some deals struck through such an exchange would burden the customer with higher rates, or the consultant with lower revenues, than they might otherwise be able to secure; but in this respect the exchange would be a zero-sum game. In other respects, it would be win-win, with all parties having access to information that was comprehensive and up-to-the-minute, and with negotiating time and expenses minimized; meanwhile any party dissatisfied with the rates or compensation on offer could always drop out of the bidding.

As happens today on eBay, customer companies could review and rate consultant firms and even individual consultants, and vice versa.

Metals

MetalSpectrum

This metals marketplace was announced in May, 2000, by a group of six specialty-metals producers—Alcoa, Allegheny Technologies, Kaiser Aluminum, North American Stainless, Olin, and Reynolds Aluminum—and two metals distributors, Thyssen North America and Vincent Metal Goods. However, MetalSpectrum presents itself as independent of these companies, offering an open and neutral marketplace for metals including aluminum, brass, copper, carbon steel, and stainless steel.

Implemented by Ariba and i2, MetalSpectrum opened for registration in September 2000. The site will provide online auctions, catalogs, and RFQs, and it is intended later to supplement these services with logistics and finance support; purchasing for maintenance, repair, and operations; and other features. In September 2000, MetalSpectrum announced that it had entered into alliance with MetalSite, a second metals exchange dating from 1998 and dealing mainly in guaranteed inventory of prime and nonprime steel. The alliance will presumably compete with a third exchange, as yet unnamed, that is being constructed by SAP and Commerce One for a group of sixteen metals and mining firms, including Alcoa, Anglo-American, Broken Hill, De Beers, and Rio Tinto.

Multiple

VerticalNet

VerticalNet styles itself "the Internet's premier owner and operator of business-to-business trading communities," and at least in quantitative terms, this is indisputable: the company owns and operates fifty-seven vertical exchanges, and there are more in the works. The company has built most of these; about ten it has acquired. VerticalNet classifies its exchanges under fourteen headings: Communications, Energy, Environment/Utilities, Financial Service, Food/Packaging, Foodservice/Hospitality, Healthcare, High Tech, Industrial, Manufacturing/Discrete, Manufacturing/Process, Public Sector, Science, and Services. These provide virtual neighborhoods for storefronts representing roughly 3,300 companies at an annual fee of $6,000 apiece. These storefronts are renewed at a rate of about 90 percent, indicating that participants are generally saving a lot of money.

VerticalNet is like FreeMarkets in that it was founded in 1995 and is now publicly traded. Its earliest sites had only rudimentary functionality, but the company has been adding functionality including auctions, catalogs, bookstores, and career services across its entire range of properties. In March 2000, VerticalNet acquired Tradeum Inc., a developer of software for implementing digital exchanges; the acquisition will help VerticalNet to enhance its existing exchanges and to set up new ones. The company has also been expanding aggressively in overseas markets, notably in Japan.

The most important of VerticalNet's exchanges is NECX, which deals in electronics hardware and which contributed 54 percent of the company's revenues in the second quarter of 2000. However, NECX continues to be principally an off-line brokerage and clearinghouse; only about 20 percent of the revenues it generates derive from online trades. Together with the fact that most of the company's other revenue comes from advertising, this has provoked some skepticism as to VerticalNet's claim to be an online enterprise. That claim is validated at least in part by the company's continuing to lose tens of millions of dollars annually, although its (suspect) revenues have been rising rapidly, at almost 100 percent year over year. Regardless, investors appear to be confused about the company's prospects, and its market cap of $2.6 billion in late September 2000 is barely 20 percent of its high early in the year.

Paper etc.

fp-xchange

fp-xchange attempts to do for the global forest-products industry what GlobalNetXchange does for the retail industry. Oracle is developing this exchange in collaboration with fibermarket.com, a leader in B2B e-commerce for the industry. The forestry-and-paper-industry supply chain deals in paper, pulp, recovered fiber, solid wood, and related building products, and amounts to some $600 billion annually.

PaperExchange.com

PaperExchange, founded in 1998, is a marketplace for the pulp and paper industry, serving more than 4,800 corporate and 7,000 individual members in 105 countries. The exchange does not charge for access to or use of its site, and it does not levy membership fees; it derives its income from fees imposed on transaction volumes. In return, it provides its users with industry-specific content, industry-events information, news headlines, job listings, and a resource directory.

Members buy and sell pulp and paper through private, secured transactions; the exchange does not release information as to its member list or their transactions.

Retail Goods

GlobalNetXchange

GlobalNetXchange (GNX) aims to bring online the supply chain for the retail industry worldwide. Announced in February 2000 by Oracle and retail giants Sears and Carrefour, it creates a common platform for the soft-goods supermarket/hypermarket space. The exchange was joined in March by German retailer METRO AG and British retail conglomerate J Sainsbury plc. The four retailers account for roughly $140 billion in annual purchases from more than 50,000 suppliers, partners, and distributors. Carrefour conducted a first auction on the exchange on March 13, 2000, and Sears conducted an auction on March 17.

RetailersMarketXchange

On March 8, 2000, Chevron, McLane Co. (a division of Wal-Mart), and Oracle announced the creation of RetailersMarketXchange, a medium for connecting small convenience stores with suppliers. Chevron's interest relates to the convenience stores associated with its service stations.

The new retail-goods exchange, in contrast to enterprises like Webvan, does not set up a new consumer service; it merely seeks higher efficiencies and lower expenses in business processes that already take place and that must continue to occur. This makes it simultaneously more conservative and more likely to endure.

Rubber

RubberNetwork.com

This exchange, announced in April 2000, is sponsored by Bridgestone, Continental AG, Cooper Tire & Rubber, Goodyear, Groupe Michelin, Pirelli, and Sumitomo Rubber. The seven companies represent about 75 percent of global tire-manufacturing capacity. Total industry purchases of raw materials, equipment, goods, machinery, and services amount to more than $50 billion per year.

The companies chose the Ariba-IBM-i2 alliance to build the exchange, which is expected to go into operation in the first quarter of 2001. Services projected include sharing of inventory and forecast data; standardized catalogs; order placement and fulfillment; factory and demand planning; logistics optimization; and dynamic trading mechanisms, including conventional and reverse auctions. A launch date for the exchange has yet to be announced.

Technology

eHITEX

eHITEX (or "The High-Tech Exchange"), was announced on May 1, 2000, and went into service on August 1, 2000. Focusing on the supply-chain needs of the computer and electronics industries, the exchange addresses a market amounting to hundreds of billions of dollars per year in high-tech parts and components. Its founders represent every stage of the high-technology supply chain: global OEMs, CEMs, suppliers, and distributors. The founders were AMD, Agilent, Canon, Compaq, Gateway, Hitachi, HP, NEC, Quantum, Samsung, SCI Systems, Solectron, Synnex, Tatung, and Western Digital.

eHITEX is built using technology from SAP and Commerce One. The services it provides include auctions, catalog management, value-added features including a news ticker, and marketplace adminis-tration. It plans to add support for supply-chain collaboration. The exchange generates revenue through transaction fees and through services, including consulting. It competes with e2open, a similar exchange developed by the Ariba-IBM-i2 alliance (discussed later).

Telephony

Arbinet

This exchange, founded in November 1997, deals in telephone-line capacity: in voice, fax, and IP minutes (each on a specific line) across PSTN, VoIP, data, and wireless networks. Arbinet (short for "Arbitrage Network") addresses the traditional misallocation of telephone bandwidth whereby some networks urgently need capacity they don't own, while others have ample supplies sitting idle. With thousands of networks around the world, and with conventional long-term contracts locking companies into supplies that may prove too great or too small, misallocation is an enormous problem for the industry.

Arbinet provides its members with on-demand transaction execution and with simplified invoice/payment processing. As a neutral party, it monitors the connections it brokers in order to resolve any disputes that may arise between buyers and sellers. The company makes money by charging half a cent to the buyer and half a cent to the seller for each minute sold, resulting in annual revenues in the tens of millions of dollars. Arbinet competes with RateXchange and with Band-X.

Transport
National Transportation Exchange

This exchange, founded in 1995, connects shippers with fleet managers who have truck capacity to fill. National Transportation Exchange (NTE) sets daily spot prices based on information from hundreds of trucking companies about which vehicles, with how much empty space, are going to which destinations. Then NTE brokers deals between carriers and shippers, issuing contracts and handling payments.

NTE constitutes the nation's leading online marketplace to drive productivity and profitability for buyers and sellers of ground transportation services. The company has multiple trading mechanisms to help member companies collaborate and manage their logistics.

Other Exchanges

Almost all the Internet exchanges that have been implemented are procurement exchanges, and the consequence is that there is much less to be said about the others. However, considering exchanges within the context of customer relationship management, it is clear at once that procurement exchanges deal with the broad area of sales but have few implications either for marketing or for support—the other two legs of the CRM tripod.

This means not only that there exists a business opportunity to colonize these neglected reaches of CRM with exchanges, but also that the sponsors of procurement exchanges need to be alert to that opportunity. If not, they face the risk that other firms will outflank them both upstream and downstream in the sales process, and will then evangelize for unified exchange suites in order to displace the relatively antiquated exchange in the middle. And, indeed, an integrated approach is called for here as strongly as anywhere in business, because the whole point of upstream marketing and of downstream support is—directly or indirectly—to drive sales and thus revenues. Demand and customer exchanges will play an increasing role in the future of e-business.

Demand Exchanges

I call the subjects of this section *demand exchanges* because their principal purpose is to create, stimulate, and increase *demand* for products and services. For this reason they are typically driven by the concerns of prospective sellers or suppliers, not—as with procurement exchanges—by those of prospective purchasers. They are nevertheless *exchanges* because they provide a forum within which marketing professionals and groups can interact to exchange information with the purpose of stimulating demand.

Because the assets exchanged on procurement exchanges are normally services or physical goods, a company participating in such an exchange takes no implicit position toward its counterpart in any transaction; Dell (for instance) will sell a PC to anybody who's willing to pay for it, except perhaps as constrained by national-security regulations. By contrast, the assets exchanged on procurement exchanges are informational. As such, they are assets that an originating company will distribute with care, if at all, for fear that they can be exploited by competitors to the originating company's detriment. For this reason, demand exchanges function primarily as a venue for collaboration, whether implied or explicit.

The information to be exchanged on these sites includes marketing information in general, but it focuses on customer information and specifically on sales opportunities. Within terms agreed to by its customers, a company's customer lists and profiles are obvious candidates for exchange. Other qualifying assets include courses and RFPs. Product specifications and installed-base information may be exchanged for use in cross-selling and up-selling.

Successful demand exchanges offer these benefits:

- They increase market penetration (by the use of campaigns, events, promotions, and lead generation).

- They enhance brand value and recognition (by the use of advertising management).

- They expand networks of distributors and affiliates and drive increased traffic volumes across those networks (by the use of PRM and affiliate management).

- They gather customer intelligence (by permission-based profiling and interest tracking).

- They increase marketing focus on the customer, enhance customer awareness and loyalty, and thus grow revenues (by the use of relationship management).

Demand that is driven by such exchanges may be directed to physical stores, Web stores, field sales, telesales, partner/OEM/distributor channels, or procurement exchanges. Customer and prospect companies can use demand exchanges to respond to campaigns or to direct sellers' attention to RFPs, RFQs, auctions, and bids.

Existing Internet-enabled companies offer a variety of online services that can add value to demand exchanges, including

- List management
- Permission-based or opt-in e-mail marketing
- Advertisement management
- Marketing content creation
- Loyalty building
- Mobile device support
- Demographic information

Demand exchanges can generate revenue in various ways, including by

- Selling advertising space
- Levying commissions on sales
- Taking fees for delivery of qualified leads
- Generating RFPs and/or RFQs for buyers

Customer Exchanges

The assets to be traded on customer exchanges, as on demand exchanges, are informational; but customer exchanges are logically closer to procurement exchanges, because the support and maintenance issues on which they focus usually relate to specific physical goods and often lead to demands on inventory, as when you visit a service station to replace a spare tire.

A principal resource for support and maintenance is technical information, and customer exchanges will typically comprise extensive knowledge bases. Companies originating technical information will treat these knowledge bases as depositories, and companies seeking such information will be granted access on a subscription basis or in return for a per-use fee. Alternatively, such a company may have a business relationship with the item originator because of which any such charge will be waived.

Customer-specific items to be shared on such exchanges will include contracts, returns, spares, and service levels and requests. For instance, a company receiving a service call from a customer might have no service staff available at the time near the customer's location. It could exchange the service call, on a tit-for-tat basis, with a business partner that had service personnel ready to go. Service contracts could be auctioned, and a winning bid might be either a positive or a negative amount, depending on the extent to which the bidder regarded the contract as a business opportunity and on the degree of liability attaching to the contract holder.

Given their focus on support and maintenance concerns, customer exchanges will generally provide support for scheduling and dispatch activities.

Exchange Builders

Competition among the companies that construct exchanges has been a hot topic throughout the year 2000. Currently, the major players in this arena are Ariba, Commerce One, and Oracle. I confine my remarks here to important recent developments and some of their implications.

Ariba and Commerce One

During most of the recent drama in this market space, the spotlight has been trained on the rivalry between Ariba and Commerce One. This is arguably not because Oracle figures less importantly in Internet-exchange construction, but because it has spread its efforts so broadly that it is not generally perceived as "an exchange company."

In any case, Ariba has largely upstaged Commerce One. Ironically, the main reason may be simply that Ariba reported its results for the second calendar quarter of 2000 about a week before Commerce One did. Those results were so impressive that they boosted Ariba's stock price by 42 percent in 2 days, but Commerce One's stock came up 41 percent in sympathy. When, 6 days later, Commerce One failed to deliver such a happy surprise, its stock plunged 17 percent in 1 day, but Ariba's declined less than 1 percent. Here are some of the relevant figures:

| Company | Revenues | | Market Cap (26 Sept. 2000) |
	1999 2nd Quarter	2000 2nd Quarter	
Ariba	$11.9 million	$80.7 million	$38.3 billion
Commerce One	$4.2 million	$62.7 million	$12.2 billion

Ariba's revenues clearly were greater than Commerce One's. But Ariba's absolute growth over the year was only slightly greater than Commerce One's, and its relative growth, though striking, was much smaller: 577 percent as against 1,392 percent. Both companies continue to incur net losses.

The revenue difference derives in part from the companies' distinct business models. Ariba depends heavily on software license sales, which, of course, produce up-front revenue. Commerce One aims to generate a larger proportion of its long-term revenue from exchange transaction fees, but the inflow of these will increase only gradually over many years.

Despite these various differences, the company's situations are similar in important respects. Each needs alliances, for two outstanding reasons: First, to exploit the resources of its business partners, especially their sales personnel and installed bases. Second, to move forward quickly on the task of integrating exchange transactions with the existing ERP systems of exchange participants. Each has acknowledged this need, has recognized that the ideal partner(s) would be large technology firms already deeply involved in e-business, and has entered into an alliance that appears to offer major reinforcement.

Ariba

Ariba's alliance, announced on March 8, 2000, was with IBM and i2 Technologies, the latter since 1988 an important name in supply-chain automation. The first collaborative undertaking of the triad, announced on April 12, was an agreement to develop an online marketplace for Volkswagen.

Before the announcement of the alliance, Ariba and i2 had been to some degree competitors, and analysts speculated that IBM was to function in part as a peacekeeper. Supporting this view was a condition of the alliance that IBM was to take an equity position in each of its new partners. IBM also brought its e-business know-how, its integration skills, its massive customer set, and its consulting force, while the other two companies contributed their specialized products and expertise. IBM has also contributed 210 members of the 250-member sales force for the alliance.

However, as noted above, the agreement to develop Transora, the food-products exchange, found PricewaterhouseCoopers replacing IBM as the consulting/integrating partner. An IBM spokesperson pointed to the flexibility of the triad, so demonstrated, as a source of strength; but there remains uncertainty as to whether the three companies will be able to work together over the long run.

Nevertheless, Ariba remains the strongest contender among companies focused on exchange technology. It has more than 150 marketplace customers and has secured contracts for 6 or 7 major exchanges, including e2open, MetalSpectrum, RubberNetwork.com, Transora, and the nascent Volkswagen exchange. Its high market capitalization gives it great leverage in acquiring companies with complementary technology, and it has done so with Trading Dynamics, TRADEX, and SupplierMarket.com.

Commerce One

On June 14, 2000, about 3 months after the Ariba-i2-IBM announcement, Commerce One launched a counterattack, announcing its own alliance with SAP, the world's largest vendor of business applications. This coalition was crucial for both companies: Commerce One was facing off against an Ariba that was much strengthened by its new partnership. Suddenly, Commerce One had the prospect of SAP's enormous installed base and was armed to exploit it with a $250 million SAP investment. As for SAP, it had been largely written off as an Internet force, but now it had an automatic online presence and a powerful tool for leveraging its customer list and technical expertise. (On September 27, 2000, SAP stock was up 31 percent since the announcement.)

This was an alliance with a difference. Instead of setting out to integrate their existing products, as the other team proposed to do,

Commerce One and SAP resolved to develop a new suite of products, called EnterpriseBuyer, using the most promising ideas and features of their previous efforts. Although this approach inevitably meant some delay before the new software could reach the market, it augured fewer problems with implementation once it arrived. The companies stated that the new products would enable a full range of collaborative commercial relationships between buyers and sellers, ranging from product design through fulfillment. They will also focus on direct goods, differing in this respect from Commerce One's BuySite, which is being rolled into EnterpriseBuyer.

The Commerce One-SAP alliance, like its main rival, has generated much industry gossip. SAP had been famous, or infamous, for self-sufficiency, seeming to disdain partnerships of any kind, and some analysts felt that Commerce One would find the bigger company overbearing. As the alliance has held together and generated positive results, speculation has shifted to a possible merger of the two companies; but the consensus is that this is unlikely. Culture shock would take on a whole new dimension.

Commerce One has strengthened itself further by a project to merge the new Commerce One/SAP product with Microsoft's .Net platform. The firms agreed to integrate their technologies and to collaborate on XML standards. All three companies view the agreement as helping to drive future revenues.

At this stage, Commerce One is involved in about 100 exchanges, 77 of which it implemented alone, the others with SAP. They include a number of major efforts, the largest being Covisint, which, because of the sequence of events, Commerce One is developing jointly with Oracle, otherwise a rival. Other noteworthy Commerce One exchanges include Cephren MarketNet, eHitex, Enporion, and Exostar. Commerce One has also been aggressively developing regional exchanges outside the United States, in Europe, Asia, and both Americas. Roughly half of the full 100 are operational.

Commerce One differentiates itself in part on the basis of its Global Trading Web, which is intended to connect all of its e-marketplaces worldwide; four are connected already. Buyers and sellers currently involved in the Global Trading Web control about $2.3 trillion in total spending. The company is probably correct in the view that a major next step for e-business is the global integration of the online trading structure.

Oracle

Oracle's strategy has been to differentiate itself by developing, on its own, all the software that global enterprise requires. The company does not forswear alliances, but its energies are focused on completing and evolving a comprehensive suite of software products for e-business, then leveraging the organic unity of this offering to woo customers away from the often complex and protracted integration efforts that they would otherwise confront.

This drive for self-sufficiency has lowered the company's profile in the exchange marketplace. The drama and gossip generated by the shifting tactics and alliances of Ariba and Commerce One are not matched by any Oracle exchange doings that have come to public attention, though there has been some conjecture about the inner workings of Covisint, where Oracle and Commerce One are working together on terms that must be uneasy.

Nevertheless, the Oracle exchange story appears to have been persuasive. Because Ford was won over, Oracle is helping to construct the exchange that may prove the world's biggest, with a possible volume approaching $800 billion per year. Notable exchanges using pure-Oracle technology include, as we have seen above, Aeroxchange, CateringX, fp-exchange, GlobalNetXchange, HomebuildersXchange, and RetailersMarketXchange—not to mention Oracleexchange itself, and Oracle's HR-oriented OTN Xchange.

Others

BroadVision

On September 20, 2000, BroadVision announced a new product, called MarketMaker, with which it is entering the Internet-exchange competition. The product, which enables its users to construct and operate Internet exchanges, is distinguished by facilities for content management and for CRM; it can track the actions of purchasers and adjust its behavior accordingly, as by offering a purchaser the products he/she usually buys and other related products.

MarketMaker exchanges will be hosted by Corio. At first, BroadVision will orient MarketMaker toward indirect goods, but it does plan to broaden MarketMaker's scope to cover manufacturing materials and components. It is too early to assess what impact the product will have in the exchange marketplace, but BroadVision is bolstered at least by the fact that it is a profitable company, a distinction neither Ariba nor Commerce One can yet claim.

Ventro

Ventro (introduced earlier under the heading *Chemdex*) is the exception—at the moment—among these stories of exchange successes. Recent revenues for both Chemdex and Promedix have been disappointing, and Ventro's investments in other online marketplaces are not looking promising. The company's exchange technology is its own, developed for Chemdex in 1997; Ariba's and Commerce One's offerings are now more attractive.

Ventro's shares closed September 27, 2000, at $9.09, down more than 96 percent from its high of $243.50 in late February. Vulnerable now to a possible takeover, Ventro is reported to have retained Broadview, a high-tech mergers-and-acquisitions firm, to help it find a buyer or a merger candidate. Unless it finds a powerful partner, the company appears unlikely to play much of a role in the evolution of the exchange industry.

VerticalNet

VerticalNet's position, as discussed above, remains ambiguous. The company is working to present itself clearly as an online enterprise, but analysts and investors remain dubious. Much of the uncertainty derives from the very light trading volumes flowing through the great majority of the company's exchanges.

Like Ventro's, VerticalNet's stock price in late 2000 continued to be severely depressed, about 78 percent off its high of $148.38. It, too, might be a candidate for acquisition, but the nature of its business appears not to suit the strategy of any company that might buy it. Regardless, VerticalNet continues to acquire existing exchanges and to secure contracts to build exchanges for new sponsors. It seems likely to continue in a quiet way, but not to pose any serious competition for the major exchange builders.

Ironside

Ironside Technologies is a provider of sell-side e-commerce applications. On September 25, 2000, it announced the Ironside

Network, a pseudo-exchange the purpose of which is to mediate between sellers and exchanges on a one-to-many basis.

Ironside recognized that the existence of hundreds of online exchanges using varying technologies, and the need for some companies to deal with multiple exchanges, called for an interface that would enable a participating supplier to address a single site in order to establish a presence in multiple markets. The company thus is providing not an exchange, as such, but a subset of the much-needed technology that will facilitate the integration of exchange operations into companies' existing systems for ERP and CRM.

The Outlook

Online exchanges will continue to form, industry by industry, although—for procurement exchanges—the pace appears so rapid that the dust may already have settled before this book is in the hands of readers. As with retailers, it appears that the number of profitable exchanges per industry may be limited to two or three of each type. Also as with retailers, the numbers may be further reduced by mergers, within the limits loosely defined by antitrust guidelines. This is especially the case for industries in which competition extends vigorously across national boundaries, allaying antitrust concerns and enhancing the efficiencies to be gained by consolidation.

Business is booming for the three main exchange builders, and there's every prospect that it will boom for their clients. Each of the three will probably still be in the exchange business 5 years from now, and the number of exchanges built will soar into the thousands, though a period of consolidation may later cause it to fall back. Clearly, what business needs are exchanges constructed with technology that is open and interoperable, so that the world of online commerce can be integrated to the same degree that the Internet itself is today.

6

Where We Stand Now

Clovis Man Meets the Giant Sloth

Clovis Man is named for Clovis, New Mexico. Near Clovis is Blackwater Draw, where, in 1932, extensive stone-age relics that date to about 12,000 years ago were discovered, constituting some of the earliest evidence for human presence in the Western Hemisphere.[22]

When human beings first came across the Bering land bridge from Siberia, they found a continent inhabited by large animals of many species: woolly mammoth, camel, horse, bison, sabertooth tiger, dire wolf, and others. Almost all of these species became extinct not long afterward, and there has been ongoing controversy as to the extent to which human predation did the dirty work. What is clear is that the extent was not zero: large-animal remains have been found together with Clovis-age spear- and arrowheads at no fewer than twenty-three sites in North America.

Those large animals included several species of giant ground sloth. The New World sloths known today are fairly small arboreal mammals; but the largest ground sloths stood 20 feet tall and weighed several tons. Originating in South America, these animals migrated north once the land link between the two continents was formed about 3 million years ago. Remains of sloths of several species have been found at the La Brea Tar Pits in Los Angeles. The last living species, the Puerto Rican ground sloth, was extinguished about 1500—by human predation—but there are occasional reports of ground-sloth sightings in Amazonia and elsewhere in South America.

The confrontation between Clovis Man and the giant ground sloth suggests a moral for our time. The sloths were large, they were placid, they were vegetarian, they were part of the known landscape. And then they were confronted by something radically new— something ravenous and extremely dangerous. Adaptability was not their long suit; and now they are gone. (Or are they?)

Netting It Out

We have examined the major developments that have shaped the evolution of business, and we have seen how and why the Internet presents itself as the culmination of that evolution. Its revolutionary nature tends to obscure a momentous fact, which is that—in crucial respects—the Internet is potentially very similar to other complex networks that figure in the lives of consumers and businesses alike. Whether revolutionary or taken for granted, the Internet is here to stay.

I have discussed business practices that the Internet will change forever, reviewed a number of businesses that provide models for the e-transformation, and surveyed a broad range of enterprises that share the mission of enabling their customers to conduct electronic business. Moreover, I have repeatedly pointed to the storm clouds being driven by the winds of the Web toward some of the world's leading corporations. Now it is time to reel in my net.

First, a few perspectives on the present and the near future.

- The supremacy of PCs and PC software is over. We have entered the Internet Age. The Internet is its central organism, and Internet enablers will be the flagships of the new online business model. The devices by which we will access the Internet are proliferating rapidly not only in number but in type; they already include PCs, NCs, PDAs, wireline and wireless telephones, and set-top boxes.

- The pace of change in business is breathtaking, particularly in Silicon Valley, where the acceleration is perhaps most obvious. Once it was mainframes; then PCs; then client/server; then the Internet, dot-coms, business-to-consumer, business-to-business, exchanges. . . .

The advent of the Internet has precipitated a crisis in the business world, which prompts two philological observations: First, as others have observed, the Chinese ideogram for *crisis* unites the characters for *opportunity* and *danger*. Second, the English word *crisis* derives from Greek *krinein*, "to separate." We need not await the Second Coming for a judgment between the quick and the dead.

- Many industries (entertainment/media is an example) have been changed little or not at all by the Internet—so far.

- The Internet will render some industries (high-end management consulting is an example) irrelevant, if not meaningless.

- Wild enthusiasm for AnyBusiness.com, already a thing of the past, has led to large numbers of Internet enterprises that can never be justified in financial terms. Dog food is not a great business idea; dog food over the Internet is a rotten one. Such businesses are among the leading turn-of-the-century fads and follies, the current equivalent of the hula hoop. The winds that will sweep them away are already rising.

- Current B2C leaders will evolve in many cases into B2B leaders. Amazon will provide a model for fulfillment; eBay will muscle into the exchange arena opened up by Ariba and Commerce One.

- The winds of change will drive one company to the fore in market capitalization. Microsoft is already flagging; the new pacesetter will be one of these four: GE, representing the "old economy", or Cisco, IBM, or Oracle.

- We call it *e-business* in 2000; in 2003, we'll call it *business*.

Why E-Business?

Information Week for June 7, 1999, carried the results of a survey of 375 IT and other business executives. Asked "Which business goals were highly significant in your decision to deploy E-business applications?" they cited eighteen goals, listed below from most-cited to least-cited. The proportion citing a given goal declined fairly evenly, from about 90 percent for the first goal to about 32 percent for the eighteenth.

- Creating or maintaining competitive edge
- Improving customer satisfaction
- Keeping pace with the competition
- Reducing operational costs
- Improving employee communications and satisfaction

- Establishing or expanding brand awareness
- Finding new markets for products or services
- Generating new sources of revenue
- Improving relationships with partners
- Improving time to market
- Creating new distribution channels
- Expanding product or service lines
- Becoming more entrepreneurial
- Improving supply-chain management
- Improving relationships with suppliers
- Empowering customers to configure products or services
- Creating new e-business units
- Improving inventory management

The extent to which companies can expect to accomplish these tasks by moving business processes online is suggested by estimates of the growth of the Internet itself, of the viewer population, and of electronic business. Forrester Research estimates that the total number of computers connected to the Internet will reach 250 million during the year 2000. International Data Corporation projects that the number of Web users will rise from roughly 50 million in mid-1999 to nearly 175 million by 2001. Forrester forecasts business-to-consumer e-commerce totaling $108 billion by 2003, and business-to-business exchanges of goods amounting by then to $1.3 trillion.

Any company transforming itself into an electronic business probably has what it takes to attain some of these eighteen goals on its own, but many will want to seek help from firms that specialize in e-business enablement.

Amazon as a Verb

Some companies will be driven out of business ("amazoned") by the Internet. Once they're out of business, it may not matter to them whether they went belly-up because they refused to establish an

Internet presence, because they established one too late, or because—although they moved smartly and promptly to exploit the promise of the Web—something else went fatally wrong. But it *will* matter to those who hope to learn the lessons they exemplify, and it will matter also to the validity of books like this one that take e-business as their subject.

Although e-business is only a few years old, it already has some conventions. One of these is to compare some company that made its debut as a Web presence with another company, already established in the world of brick and mortar, that is perceived as reluctant, or merely slow, to use an Internet site to augment its traditional sales channels. The table below provides data to support several such comparisons.

In the summer of 1998, it seemed easy to predict how some of these face-offs would turn out. The Internet seemed then (as it still does) the overwhelming new fact in the world of business, and many investors acted as if the sky was the limit for many Internet-based companies. But recent events and opinions appear to demonstrate once more that Yogi Berra—it *was* Yogi, wasn't it?—had a point about predictions.

For instance, many supposed that Amazon would sweep Barnes & Noble into the dustbin of history. Amazon's share price[25] exploded from $15.75 in 1997 to a high of $142.50 on July 16, 1999; during the same period Barnes & Noble's sank from $48 at the end of 1998 to a low of $20.06 on August 4, 1999. But meanwhile, Barnes & Noble was making a determined effort to reshape itself as a major Web presence. What has happened since summer of 1999 looks suspiciously as if it may be the direct result of Barnes & Noble's effort: by August 31, 2000, Amazon's share price had fallen by 71 percent, while Barnes & Noble's was down by "only" 14 percent. My interpretation, conditioned by Amazon's perceived dominance, is that Amazon has deeply injured Barnes & Noble but may be about to destroy itself.

Indeed, in mid-2000 there was widespread skepticism as to whether Amazon would ever turn a profit. The company is continuing to burn huge wads of cash, with net outflow in the second quarter of $317 million (though net operating loss was "only" $89 million, the rest being expenses related to acquisitions). And Amazon's cumulative deficit is about $2.5 billion. News came on July

Company	Employee Count[23]	Market Cap. ($ millions) (4/30/2000)	Years in Business	Annual Income ($ millions)	Serves...[24]
Amazon.com	2,100	19,300	4.5	-1,014	20,000,000 account holders; 15,217,000 unique visitors per month
Wal-Mart	910,000	246,000	38	5,563	
Ask Jeeves	200	1,060	3	-102	12,269,000 unique visitors per month
Encyclopedia Britannica	400	N/A	231	N/A	
autobytel.com	177	119	5	-30	5,000,000 unique visitors per quarter; 50,000 car buyers per month
conventional car dealers	N/A	N/A	N/A	N/A	N/A
drugstore.com	245	406	.2	-162	1,000,000 customers
Walgreen	107,000	28,400	98	687	
eBay	138	20,700	4	13	2,000,000 unique buyers and sellers per day; 11,155,000 unique visitors per month
Sotheby's	1,921	976	255	33	
eToys	306	965	3	-218	1,900,000 account holders
Toys "R" Us	70,000	3,430	51	256	
E*TRADE	1,735	6,220	7	-95	1,551,000 account holders
Merrill Lynch	63,800	39,100	85	2,724	clients with assets of more than $1.5 trillion
NetBank	42	311	4	4	78,000 account holders
Citigroup	173,700	199,000	188	10,750	
Yahoo!	803	70,800	5	125	48,336,000 unique visitors per month
Disney	117,000	90,300	77	1,014	

25, 2000, that Amazon's president and COO was leaving to become CEO at VerticalNet, and investors reacted with dismay: the company lost 20 percent of its market cap in four trading days. By mid-August the stock had recovered from that loss, and many analysts continued to defend Amazon. But it has become thinkable that this company, in many ways the outstanding pioneer of business on the Internet, is walking its last mile.

Meanwhile, most of the top ten companies of the *Fortune* 500— General Motors, Ford, IBM, Citigroup, GE, Boeing, Exxon, and AT&T—have developed sophisticated Net presences, defending themselves against Internet upstarts or merely raising the entry barriers that would-be competitors must hurdle. Even Philip Morris has at last made an appearance.

Analysts suggest many reasons why the tide that recently was flowing so strongly in favor of Internet-based companies seems now to have weakened:

- Traditional companies are usually much older than their Internet counterparts; many have secured customer loyalties over the years and have brand names the value of which reflects their greater age.

- Companies must have distribution systems if the goods they stock are ever to reach the customer. Established companies have established systems, as well as accumulated expertise in how to manage them.

- Some traditional companies hung back from the Internet because of the daunting challenge of integrating their existing IT systems with all the technical infrastructure required to support a Web site; but mounting pressure to establish a presence online has compelled most of them to bite the bullet and go live on the Net.

- Customers like to experience products physically before they buy them. Although some will check out the products "in the flesh" and then log on to the Net to make their purchases, they need to develop some resistance in order to do so: resistance to the blandishments of the salespeople in the conventional marketplace, and resistance to the temptation to buy the product at once and thus escape having to wait for the shipment to arrive. Many people seem still to regard the Internet as a fine place to gather information and to compare prices—but in order to be more fully informed when they go out to the store.

- A customer can more reliably avoid being dissatisfied by purchasing an item from a traditional store, and, if the merchandise nevertheless proves to be a disappointment, it can often be returned to such a store more easily than it could be shipped back to some distant warehouse.

- An extended brick-and-mortar presence provides meaningful synergies for an Internet-enabled company. Each medium can be used to promote the other, and each can be used in the ways that the enterprise considers most cost-effective. Internet startups have no obvious way to secure such advantages other than to ally themselves with traditional companies or to buy them—or be bought out by them.

Yet all these considerations have been overridden in some cases, and probably will be in many more. An example is Egghead, founded in 1984 as a chain of small retail stores selling mostly PCs and related products. The chain grew to as many as 280 stores, but then a variety of competitors began to erode its revenues, and Egghead was compelled to close its stores down in large numbers. At length, in February 1998, Egghead closed all its remaining stores, rechristened itself Egghead.com, and moved its entire business onto the Internet.

This strategy immediately boosted cash flow, and for a time it appeared to be the salvation of the company. The stock, which was trading about $27 when the store closing was announced, rose as high as $108 in late 1998. Since then, however, it has declined gradually, but fairly regularly, to a low in December 2000 of 78 cents. Company executives predict that Egghead will regain profitability by late 2001, but every statement and tactical move has been ineffective in stemming the relentless decline in the share price. Egghead's changes of strategy and of fortune make it a microcosm for the unpredictability of Internet commerce.

Vanquishing Consumer Resistance

The following chart, which encapsulates a theory of viewer behavior on the Internet, reflects nothing that can be called a fact. Also, to avert ridicule, it deliberately avoids showing a scale for either axis. Yet the theory is intuitively obvious: viewers, although they will always be

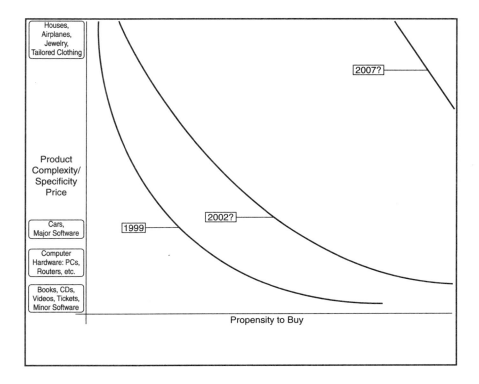

more hesitant to use the Internet to buy goods and services that are very complex, very personalized, or very expensive, will gradually grow more comfortable with the Web as a medium for shopping.

Even though the chart pertains only to Internet users, not to the general public, the tastes and inclinations of its subjects will vary greatly. Some people will never buy shoes over the Internet. Some will prefer to handle books or to test-drive cars before they commit to buy; but even some of these, once reassured by physical experience, will return to the Web to execute their purchases. Brick-and-mortar enterprises will constantly have to seek ways to differentiate themselves from their Internet competitors; as an instance, physical bookstores seem to be striving increasingly to enhance their "stickiness," luring and retaining shoppers by providing food and drink and by encouraging browsing.

The advent of promotional tools and techniques including guided selling, advanced pricing, collaboration software, and software for configuration is driving Internet sales of relatively complex and expensive products.

Survival of the Fittest

In all markets, competition enforces selection, and selection implies contraction. This process has played out, and continues to play out, in two related market segments, those known today as ERP and CRM. ERP comprises procurement, manufacturing, distribution, financials, and human-resource management; CRM comprises marketing, sales, service, call centers, mobile field agents, sell-side e-commerce, self-service customer care, and partner relationship management. Informally, these market spaces are referred to as "back office" and "front office" respectively. The big winners in e-business enablement are likely to be the companies that can bring forth application suites that integrate the two areas. For each, let's take a brief look at how the drama has unfolded.

Enterprise Resource Planning

Before the 1990s, ERP applications lent themselves more obviously to automation than did CRM applications; they were also perceived as having more direct impact on the corporate bottom line. The result is that the market is more firmly established and more mature than that for CRM. It has experienced four generations of contestants.

The first generation was a single company, McCormick & Dodge. Its ERP product was designed for mainframes; it never made the transition to client/server configurations, and today it is forgotten. McCormick & Dodge was bought by Dun & Bradstreet in the late 1980s, and then merged with MSA (Management Science America) as D&B Software; that was sold, in turn, to Geac Computer Corporation in 1996.

ERP has a big functional footprint, and the second generation saw an explosion of ERP vendors. The advent of client/server computing led to a profusion of development tools and a multitude of affordable solutions; companies of every size could find serviceable products. The vendor population grew to exceed 100, the leaders being Baan, J. D. Edwards, MSA, Oracle, PeopleSoft, Ross Systems, SAP, and Walker Interactive.

The third generation witnessed the start of major attrition in the ERP market segment. Companies that survived the shakeout were those that offered a broad suite of ERP applications (Oracle, SAP), those that specialized in one area (as did PeopleSoft in HR), and those that aimed at a specific range of customers (J. D. Edwards with small-to-medium enterprises). Together with Baan, these four were the major competitors left standing.

The fourth generation was shaped by the year 1999. Baan, unable to make the turn from client/server to the Internet, reported seven consecutive quarters of losses; its stock fell from an all-time high of $55.50, in April 1998, to $1.125 on May 23, 2000. At the end of May, the company agreed to be taken over by the English firm Invensys plc.

PeopleSoft has fared somewhat better. From an April 1998 high of $57.44, its stock dropped 80 percent in one year, then went nowhere over the next year. At one point, its net income was down 92 percent year on year. However, the company had acquired Vantive Corporation, a CRM-software manufacturer, and exploited Vantive know-how in producing a Web-enabled suite of e-business applications called PeopleSoft 8, which was released in July 2000. Meanwhile the stock was recovering from $12 in May to almost $25 by mid-August 2000.

New competitors are making a splash in niche ERP markets— witness Ariba and Commerce One in business-to-business procurement. These two now join Oracle, SAP, and PeopleSoft as the strongest players in the ERP space—and these five could easily dwindle to two or three.

There are few lessons to be drawn from this synopsis. First-mover advantage will often suffice for market dominance, but it can be trumped by technology shifts: McCormick & Dodge is dead and buried. Niche players can survive and prosper, but the dominant software companies will—*must*—produce integrated application suites or see their competitive advantage gradually destroyed.

Customer Relationship Management

CRM, to which automation came later, is now entering its third generation. The first consisted principally of Astea, a vendor of automation for customer care and field service, and Brock International (now Firstwave Technologies), selling automation for marketing and sales. Each company was a leader in its field, executed a high-profile IPO, and—for a while—maintained a high market capitalization.

Each, however, failed to react promptly to CRM market demands. Customers were looking for one or more vendors that could span sales and service applications; they also wanted vendors that addressed multiple channels of customer interaction, and particularly call centers and mobile applications. Brock and Astea both peaked in early 1996; since then their share values have fallen, respectively, from $11 to $2.50 and from $29.75 to 94 cents.

These plunges marked the start of the second CRM generation, which proved to be dominated by sales and service vendors. (Vendors of marketing automation, although they did appear, did not come into their own until later.) The four firms dominant in this period were Clarify, Scopus, Siebel, and Vantive; a late arrival on the scene was Oracle. The four leaders shared one strategic vision, foreseeing an integration of sales and service functionality for mobile professionals and for call-center operations. But each took its own path: Clarify focused on service and on vertical markets; Scopus on customer care and call centers; Siebel on sales; and Vantive on service and mobile applications.

The second generation ended in 1998-1999, with several of the leaders swallowed by larger enterprises. Clarify was acquired by Nortel, Scopus by Siebel, and Vantive by PeopleSoft. Meanwhile the landscape was transfigured by a general recognition of the centrality of the Internet. By designing its CRM suite for the Internet from the start, Oracle managed to capitalize on its late entry; Siebel seems to be making a successful transition from the client/server universe. A whole new class of vendors has emerged, including Agillion, BroadVision, eGain, and Kana. The market segment is also being invaded by a number of nontraditional participants offering point solutions. The most important of these is Cisco, with its acquisitions of GeoTel, a vendor for call-center middleware and routing applications; of WebLine, an e-mail interaction-management vendor; and of Selsius, an IP-telephony vendor.

The dominant medium is now the Internet; the dominant applications continue to be for marketing, sales, and service; the dominant targets are call centers and mobile agents. And the dominant vendors . . . will be those that can develop integrated suites that address as broad a range as possible of these targets and applications. This message underlies the urgency of recent attempts to consolidate and articulate CRM offerings, as exemplified by E.piphany's purchase of Octane and Kana's purchase of Silknet.

Parallels

The cultivation of the CRM arena appears to be repeating the patterns set in ERP. In both cases, the market was opened up by one or two pioneers, whose ability to compete was at length outrun by evolving technology. These were followed by a large number of competitors, each with offerings that were limited in scope. The third generation in each case saw a rapid contraction of the vendor set, though in CRM the vendors of point solutions continue to proliferate. The fourth generation in the ERP arena nets out as a struggle of titans, with a few smaller competitors snapping at their ankles; and it seems increasingly likely that the game in CRM will play out along the same lines.

Here are the lessons, in summary:

- The first-mover advantage is important, but in the long run it is neither necessary nor sufficient.
- Shifts in technology prove to be pitfalls for companies that are slow to adapt.
- Early crowds of vendors are ruthlessly shaken out, leaving a few leaders.
- The key to market dominance is to combine breadth, depth, and integration of functionality.
- Point solutions will continue to emerge and to thrive.
- The next wave will be software consolidation, as Web enterprises increasingly recognize that an integrated whole—an e-business suite—can be more valuable than the sum of many developers' parts.

Statistics

The following table summarizes changes over the last few years in the market capitalizations of companies in several industries, but especially in high tech. Patterns that it reveals form the basis for elements of the discussion following the table.

Various Companies Ranked by Market Capitalization

Company	Ticker Symbol	Market Capitalization (in $ Billions) at Month-End										percent Growth (annualized)
		6/98	9/98	12/98	3/99	6/99	9/99	12/99	3/00	6/00	9/00	
GE	GE	291.3	256.8	330.3	359.5	367.3	387.7	507.3	511.7	522.8	**572.3**	35.0
Cisco	CSCO	107.7	108.5	162.9	192.3	226.2	240.7	376.0	542.7	446.2	**387.9**	76.7
Microsoft	MSFT	285.0	289.5	364.7	471.4	474.4	476.4	614.1	558.9	420.8	**323.3**	5.8
Exxon Mobil	XOM	243.0	240.4	248.9	240.2	262.6	260.0	277.3	270.0	273.2	**310.1**	11.4
Intel	INTC	123.8	143.2	198.1	198.8	199.1	248.7	275.6	441.9	447.9	**278.9**	43.5
CitiGroup	C	133.9	82.8	109.7	141.5	158.3	147.1	186.7	201.3	203.0	**243.3**	30.4
Oracle	ORCL	23.3	27.6	40.8	37.5	52.7	64.6	159.1	221.7	238.7	**221.3**	172.0
Wal-Mart	WMT	134.3	120.9	180.5	204.5	214.3	211.5	307.6	251.7	257.0	**215.1**	23.3
IBM	IBM	156.0	227.7	213.4	190.5	209.3	193.9	190.5	209.3	193.9	**198.2**	11.2
Nokia	NOK	41.9	45.0	69.3	90.2	106.1	104.1	221.3	258.1	234.8	**191.3**	96.4
Sun Microsystems	SUNW	17.3	19.8	34.0	49.7	54.8	73.9	123.1	149.0	144.6	**188.0**	188.7
Coca-Cola	KO	207.5	140.2	163.3	150.0	151.9	118.5	143.5	116.0	142.4	**136.7**	-16.9
AOL	AOL	30.2	32.1	89.2	169.1	126.5	129.7	174.5	154.7	121.6	**124.5**	87.7
AT&T	T	117.6	120.3	156.0	164.3	172.4	135.0	158.4	176.2	100.2	**109.0**	- 3.3
HP	HWP	45.9	40.7	52.7	52.4	77.8	70.4	88.3	103.0	124.5	**95.9**	38.7
Lucent	LU	135.2	112.6	178.8	175.8	219.6	211.3	244.3	202.1	190.1	**95.5**	-14.3
Procter & Gamble	PG	116.1	91.0	117.3	126.1	113.8	121.5	142.5	74.0	74.3	**87.8**	-11.7
Dell	DELL	60.1	85.1	94.8	105.9	95.8	108.3	132.1	139.7	127.7	**80.7**	14.0
SAP	SAP		85.1	78.8	57.5	76.0	82.8	114.2	131.1	102.6	**77.5**	- 4.6
Motorola	MOT	37.2	30.4	43.5	52.2	67.6	62.9	105.3	104.5	65.2	**63.1**	26.5
Boeing	BA	39.8	30.6	29.1	30.3	39.4	38.3	37.3	34.2	37.9	**57.9**	18.1
Qualcomm	QCOM	5.1	4.4	4.8	11.5	26.6	35.0	130.5	110.6	44.5	**53.1**	183.3
Yahoo!	YHOO	10.7	17.6	32.2	45.7	46.8	48.8	117.5	93.1	67.3	**50.0**	98.4
Charles Schwab	SCH	9.1	11.0	23.5	40.3	45.7	28.1	32.1	47.9	42.4	48.9	111.1

Company	Ticker											
Ford	F	64.0	51.4	64.7	63.0	63.2	56.7	60.8	52.9	52.0	**48.2**	-11.8
Compaq	CPQ	47.9	53.5	71.0	53.6	40.1	38.8	45.9	45.4	43.5	**47.3**	- 0.6
Siebel	SEBL	3.2	2.9	3.4	4.7	6.6	6.6	16.8	23.8	32.6	**46.4**	228.2
GM	GM	32.5	26.9	35.4	43.2	39.9	38.3	44.6	51.1	36.1	**34.9**	3.2
Ariba	ARBA					(5.7)	8.5	20.9	24.7	23.1	**34.5**	311.3
Safeway	SWY	20.2	22.9	30.2	25.5	24.6	18.9	17.7	22.5	22.4	**23.2**	6.3
Kroger	KR	17.7	20.6	25.0	24.7	23.1	18.2	15.6	14.5	18.2	**18.6**	2.2
Commerce One	CMRC	5.8	6.5	18.8	30.3	(0.5)	2.5	15.3	11.6	7.1	**14.9**	1407.5
Amazon	AMZN					22.0	28.1	26.8	23.6	12.8	**13.7**	46.5
Phone.com	PHCM					(2.2)	6.0	9.1	12.8	5.1	**9.4**	219.2
Apple	AAPL	4.7	6.2	6.7	5.8	7.5	10.3	16.7	22.1	17.0	**8.4**	29.4
BroadVision	BVSN	0.7	0.3	0.9	1.7	2.0	3.7	14.2	11.2	12.7	**6.9**	176.5
E*TRADE	EGRP	1.7	1.4	3.4	8.5	11.6	6.9	7.6	8.8	4.8	**4.9**	60.1
Liberate	LBRT						(1.9)	11.6	5.7	2.6	**3.0**	47.4
Kana	KANA						(2.2)	9.2	6.1	5.6	**2.1**	- 4.4
Webvan	WBVN							(5.4)	2.5	2.4	**0.8**	-87.9
eToys	ETYS					(5.0)	8.1	3.2	1.1	0.8	**0.7**	-76.3

* From 5/31/98 or IPO date through 8/31/00. (For SAP, from 8/31/98 through 8/31/00.) If figure is parenthesized, date and starting price used for growth calculation are those of the IPO.

The preceding table contains many brief but telling synopses of business history over the last few years . . . the boom years:

- The market capitalization of eToys has gone from nothing through $7.3 billion to $500 million.

- The market capitalization of Webvan has gone from nothing through $8.1 billion to $1.3 billion.

- The market capitalization of Kana has gone from nothing through $9.2 billion to $2.8 billion.

- The market capitalization of BroadVision has gone from $400 million through $21 billion to $9.2 billion.

- Amazon has experienced a dramatic rise and fall comparable to BroadVision's. (Other Web startups, not shown in the chart, have failed completely, like living.com. Still others have burned through millions of dollars and are now trading at pennies per share, like PlanetRX, which was valued at almost $2 billion on the day of its IPO and had dropped to $32 million by early September 2000.)

- Meanwhile, Ford has dropped from $58 to $46 billion, having failed to capitalize on several opportunities presented by the Internet. Ford has *not* implemented build-to-order systems, has *not* implemented direct sales, and has been slow to automate its dealer network.

- Procter & Gamble has dropped from $106 to $81 billion, missing its own Internet opportunities: it could have used its existing shipping base to offer fulfillment services to Internet companies; it could have implemented direct B2B sales of its products across the Web.

- Microsoft, which the Justice Department has quarantined in a class by itself, rose from $223 billion to a peak (at the end of 1999—not shown in the chart) of $630 billion, the greatest valuation ever placed on a business enterprise, and then dropped precipitously to $367 billion.

- Yahoo! continues to reign as king of the Internet hill.

- Safeway's market cap has risen from $18 to $24 billion while the company has become the main supplier to Peapod and Webvan.

- CitiGroup has risen from $135 to $263 billion, largely on the strength of a major bet on Internet transactions.

- Intel has extended its steady rise in market value, unperturbed by Andy Grove's stepping down as CEO in 1998.

- Cisco has risen from $88 to $482 billion. Except for the danger of losing router market share to Juniper Networks, Cisco wins in every Internet scenario.

- Siebel has risen from $2 billion to $41 billion.

- Sun also has risen dramatically, from $16 to $202 billion.

- IBM has risen from $103 to $234 billion—on the strength of services, not that of software.

- Oracle has risen from $22 to $256 billion—and the engines are still humming.

- GE, during this period, has never stumbled. Having more than doubled its market capitalization over these 27 months, it is by several lengths the most valuable company in the world.

The following table, taken from the *DLJ Internet Report* for July 2000, categorizes retail sales.

In 1998, the leading "e-tailing" categories were nonbusiness travel, computer hardware, books, apparel, and software. By 2000, apparel ranks higher, and consumer electronics has surpassed software; meanwhile, music, health and beauty, and foods and beverages have grown enormously in importance.

By 2004, if the figures shown are correct, 7 percent to 8 percent of *all* retail sales will take place over the Internet. The top five categories will be nonbusiness travel, apparel, foods and beverages, automobiles, and computer hardware, accounting together for 60 percent of the e-commerce covered by the chart. I expect that a disproportionate amount of this activity will be conducted by repeat buyers, who will already understand issues of size, style, color, and configuration, who will know how to use their browsers to compare products from various suppliers, and who will exploit the Web as a convenient, low-pressure order-entry system.

Retail Sales Categorized

Online Retailing Categories (in the U.S.)	All figures in millions of dollars							CAGR (%)	Percentage of Total 2004 Retail
	1998	1999	2000	2001	2002	2003	2004		
Apparel[26]	530	1620	3607	6581	14710	20181	27128	93	9
Automobiles	n/a	n/a	400	1800	4500	12220	16567	154	4
Books	1202	1960	2744	3520	5788	7839	9407	41	9
Computer Hardware	1800	1964	3471	5737	9154	11424	12541	38	40
Consumer Electronics	50	1205	2315	3974	6163	8728	11670	148	10
Gifts[27]	225	301	448	787	1288	1772	2187	46	21
Health & Beauty	20	509	1189	2108	3833	6294	10355	183	5
Housewares[28]	n/a	446	1000	1574	2584	4113	5908	68	6
Foods & Beverages	235	513	1132	2459	5009	10836	16863	104	3
Flowers	212	354	550	1000	1565	2151	2472	51	13
Music	175	848	1386	2067	3213	3946	4286	70	25
Software	500	1240	1898	2472	2964	3168	3290	37	50
Sporting Goods	56	165	586	1162	1949	3068	4220	106	8
Tickets to Events	122	300	669	1208	1926	2917	3929	78	14
Tools & Gardening	n/a	177	944	1930	3273	5184	7156	110	5
Toys & Video Games	68	253	610	1098	1739	2991	3663	94	10
Travel (non-business)	2800	7798	13950	20732	26042	29447	32097	50	12
Videos	145	326	463	705	1190	1601	1743	51	15
Totals	>8140	>19979	37362	60914	96890	137880	175482	~67	7.2

7

The Shape of Things to Come

The Old Order Passeth

The centralization of complexity will foster new enterprises and threaten many that are now household names. While one could marshal examples in dozens—perhaps hundreds—of business arenas, I confine my remarks to three:

- Hardware and operating systems
- Billing
- Telephones and telephony

Hardware and Operating Systems

Home computing today is tedious, error-prone, and expensive. A typical home system includes a CPU, memory, a chassis, a monitor, a keyboard, a mouse, a printer, a hard drive, a CD-ROM drive, a floppy drive, speakers, and perhaps a scanner. Equipment breaks or grows obsolete; disk space is exhausted; programs are replaced by larger programs until memory is filled to the last byte. Some say that your machine is obsolete the moment you power it on.

Many of these expenses, constraints, and annoyances could be vanquished by putting the computing power onto the network. Then you could simply plug your monitor into the wall, compute as you wish, and get billed monthly for disk and CPU use, just as you are billed now for electricity, gas, water, or satellite TV. You would be left, in effect, with the Network Computer. Never again would you have to buy a computer; never again would you run out of disk space.

Here is a riddle: why must you be computer-literate to use a PC? How much does the typical TV user understand about TV technology? What does the average light-bulb user know about electricity generation, or the national power grid?

Over the next 3 to 5 years, the Internet will gradually erode the level of sophistication needed to sit down in front of a PC and do what you want to do. It will do so by providing network services to replace the products now being offered by computer hardware and OS manufacturers. Some maintain that concerns for security and reliability will prevent this outcome, but those who are skeptical about the networked future might as well be mounting windmills on their roofs to generate electricity.

Natural sponsors for such network services are large telecommunications firms: British Telecom, BellSouth, et al. The Web-based infrastructure required would include large DASD farms and a network operating system (UNIX would work) or the Oracle Internet File System. Much of the software that will be used by subscribers is already in place on the Net: spreadsheets from Tidestone, word processing from Netscape, Quicken's TurboTax, and so on.

- Companies threatened in this arena: Compaq, Dell, Microsoft, Toshiba . . .

- Companies empowered: Apple, Cisco, EMC, HP, Oracle . . .

Billing

In theory, billing is simple. Give each billable event a price or a rate; wait for the event to take place; use the price or rate to calculate an amount due; cut the bill. Indeed, billing usually *was* simple, before and during the PC era: events were easily recognized and rates were typically straightforward—for electricity consumption, water use, or telephone-call duration.

In the Internet Age, billing is increasingly complex. No one vendor can meet all the billing needs of the new economy—every billing solution will be customized. Many of the large utility providers and telecommunications firms have their own billing systems; many consulting organizations (AMS, Andersen Consulting, IBM) provide solutions configured to the needs of specific customers; and packaged solutions are provided by companies including CBIS, LHS, Lucent's Kenan Systems, Portal, and Saville.

No solution available today is suitable for e-business. Today's billers bill according to the client/server model; they do not bill for e-business events and conditions, which call for a new billing model for the new millennium. Such events and conditions include:

- Service orders, from first contact to provisioning
- Complex network routings
- DASD and CPU usage by network computers
- Convergent services (long distance, local, cellular, Web phone, bill presentment and payment)
- Access rates and bandwidth consumptions
- Application hosting
- URL sharing
- Purchases in online stores
- Click-through ad streams
- Auctioning

In most cases, such services will be hosted by telecommunications companies—British Telecom, BellSouth, perhaps Qwest. It makes sense for any such hosting company to double as the settlement agent. British Telecom, for example, has 30 million subscribers, and it is familiar with their credit profiles. Understanding the risk-management issues as well, BT could profitably serve as the net settlement agency between merchant and consumer, between business and business.

- Companies threatened in this arena: CBIS, LHS, Lucent's Kenan Systems, Portal, Saville, and many mid-sized banks . . .
- Companies empowered: BellSouth, British Telecom, Qwest . . .

Telephones and Telephony

Call centers are typically large—sometimes gargantuan—operations, involving major expenses for hardware and for staffing. The impact on these operations of the Internet (addressed at greater length earlier) will be formidable.

Although charges for telephone service in the United States have gradually fallen over the last 30 years, bandwidth has risen faster than charges have fallen—especially over the last few years, during which huge amounts of fiber-optic cable have been laid and the technology to drive up transmission capacity over such cable has advanced at breathtaking speed. Most consumers are still being charged much more for a typical call than that call costs the service provider.

Charges for voice calls have resisted reduction partly because every voice call has traditionally required a fixed line—that is, a continuous physical connection between the telephone of the caller and that of the person called. The next few years will see the end of this tradition, as Voice-over-IP (VoIP) telephony gradually displaces the service to which we have become accustomed. VoIP, by definition, uses packet-switching technology—your sentences must be disassembled into packets, routed to your listener's location, and reassembled. Shortfalls in the technology have been holding down the quality of such connections, but the problems are being solved, and the industry consensus is that, by the end of 2001, VoIP quality will be essentially the same as that of conventional service.

At that point, even the most exacting callers will be able to call New Zealand for the (reduced?) cost of a local call. Phone service will not be free: consumers will still be paying Internet access charges, and they may need to own IP telephones; but the communications bandwidth available will so dwarf their needs that the "supply side" will drive its cost to zero. Besides, the telephone companies may cease to care, because voice traffic is expected by 2004 to constitute less than 1 percent of all traffic across the Internet.

Internet Protocol Telephony will further allow the displacement onto the Internet of all the functionality now provided by automatic call distributors (ACDs) and interactive voice response units (IVRUs), which represent the major capital outlays for the traditional call center. Voice and data traffic will share a single wire; middleware for CTI (Computer Telephony Integration) will continue to interface with applications as it does today, but will do so via Internet routers. The Lucent Definity Series, the Nortel Meridians, all the major application-specific hardware, will cease to exist.

VoIP use of a router instead of complex and expensive ACD and IVRU hardware means that setting up a contact center to rely exclusively on VoIP communication could cost 50 percent less for hardware and 30 to 40 percent less for software than implementation of a traditional call center. Operational expenses for the center would also be reduced, because use of VoIP would reduce the cost of each call made, whether incoming or outgoing.

Meanwhile cellular phones are converging on the Internet. There has been no logical obstacle to using cell phones to manage accounts or to review contacts or stock quotations through the Internet; now you can do so, and can call up a Web browser on your cell phone, thanks to Nokia and Phone.com.

- Companies threatened in this arena: Alcatel, Aspect, Ericsson, Fujitsu, Hitachi, Lucent, Nortel, Oki, Rockwell, Siemens, Toshiba . . .

- Companies empowered: Cisco, Nokia, Oracle, Phone.com.

The Major Consultants

These firms figure in this story because they traditionally manage IT system implementations. The major consulting firms include Arthur Andersen, Andersen Consulting (which split off from Arthur Andersen in 1989), Deloitte & Touche, Cap Gemini,[29] KPMG, and PricewaterhouseCoopers. Some would add Grant Thornton. Other large consulting organizations exist within certain major corporations, including IBM, Oracle, and SAP, but excluding Microsoft. (I omit consultants—McKinsey, Booz Allen, and other consultants—that do not manage implementations.)

Implementations performed by the major consulting firms have traditionally been large, protracted, and expensive. Contracts often specified multiple-year efforts and ran to sums of $30 to $50 million. The same contracts typically called for the consultant firm, if it missed its target date or deliverable specification, to pay a penalty to the customer; but this was frequently cold comfort to a customer whose continuation in business could easily be imperiled by failure on so grand a scale.

Such implementations have also traditionally (and logically enough) involved software originating with multiple development companies. A typical implementation by Andersen Consulting might include:

- BroadVision for storefront
- Commerce One for procurement
- E.piphany for marketing
- i2 for supply chain
- Kana for e-mail
- PeopleSoft for HR
- SAP for financials
- Siebel for sales
- Silknet for service
- Vignette for content

Such gallimaufries may once have been justifiable—strictly from hunger. But they will be compelled to give way, over time, to solutions that have been planned and developed as e-business suites, a principal point of which is exactly to obviate implementations that take years and cost tens of millions of dollars.

PC Manufacturers

The Internet threatens the operating systems that enable PCs, and it challenges the manufacturers of those PCs—Apple, Compaq, Dell, Toshiba, and all the rest. It is true that PCs already have become very inexpensive, but this is a two-edged blade for their makers. Now we must ask whether the PC is even necessary.

Consider the message "Out of disk space." If you're using a competent Internet service provider (ISP) whose services include hardware, you may expect to see this message never again. The PC itself is likely to vanish, having been replaced by a smart terminal with a keyboard and a modem—in short, a true appliance. Consumers will subscribe to an Internet operating system (which may reside in a database, like Oracle's Internet File System), to DASD, and to online applications (word processors, spreadsheets, and others). Software will be upgraded automatically. Imagine an ad from Dell: "PC = Previous Century. NC = New Century. Swing into the third millennium! Don't buy our product, just subscribe!"

These changes again exemplify the trend toward centralization. They mean that traditional PC manufacturers will be driven out of the PC business into either Network-Computer manufacture, into the provision of online hardware services, or into extinction. Companies that will thrive in the e-millennium include manufacturers of network routers, of terminal displays, and of disk storage; providers of databases; and, of course, one or two of the current PC vendors that transform their businesses first.

Important Newcomers

Since the Internet was first commercialized, thousands and thousands of enterprises have sprung to life online. Five of these have introduced concepts and paradigms of such importance that every major company, to succeed in e-commerce, must adopt one or more of them.[30] The five enterprises are:

- Amazon
- eBay
- NetLedger
- Priceline
- Yahoo!

Amazon

A graphical user interface has four components: appearance, data presentation, interaction, and navigation. When the appearance is simple, the data presentation crisp and logical, the interaction intuitive, and the navigation easy, then the GUI that results will set a standard.

Amazon was the pioneer in defining the GUI characteristics that have become standard for Internet e-commerce. Central among these characteristics is the use of tabs to organize data and to direct navigation. By now, virtually every major e-business uses tabs to present the taxonomy of its site. Amazon further distinguishes its layout by judicious use of color-coded header bars to facilitate navigation within the site. By setting the GUI standard, Amazon has had perhaps the most pervasive influence on e-business.

Amazon is also notable for its logical, straightforward, and comprehensive *n*-step order management, comprising the use of a shopping cart, the provision of account status, the storage of credit-card numbers for follow-on purchases, and the recording of multiple ship-to addresses. A notable subset of this process illustrates Amazon's use of "click-wrapping," whereby the viewer is presented the terms and conditions of the business agreement with "I accept" buttons appearing at the top, in the middle, and at the end of the text. The text is wrapped with buttons that the viewer can click to wrap the contract.

Amazon's influence has been extended further by the introduction of *1-click* ordering, a process that the company has patented. Having made one or more selections, a customer who follows the traditional transaction sequence on Amazon must enter a password, enter or confirm a shipping address, enter or confirm a shipping method, and enter or confirm a payment method. The customer then verifies and places the order. But customers who choose to can implement 1-click ordering by setting defaults for all the selections in the extended process. Then, as long as the defaults apply for the merchandise chosen, the order can be placed—well, not with one click, but with two, the second required merely to confirm the first.[31]

After making these fundamental contributions to Web culture, it is not clear that Amazon has any others up its sleeve. The company seems to have moved past its innovative stage and to have entered a quantitative one in which it seeks to maximize its future revenues simply by extending its reach into every plausible market segment.

eBay

eBay pioneered the online customer-to-customer auction, and it did so using a business model that made eBay almost at once a profitable enterprise—a very unusual achievement for an Internet-only business. (eBay was also one of the earliest such businesses to recognize that it needed a pied-à-terre in the material world, which it acquired by its 1999 purchase of Butterfields, a San Francisco auctioneer dating from 1865.) Both its pioneering and its profits ensure that eBay will be a major presence on the Web for as far as the eye can see.

However, eBay seems to have ignored, or disdained, the implications of its auction model for business-to-business commerce. As we have seen, these implications are seismic; and eBay's noninvolvement in the B2B exchanges that are now developing confines it to its current role and cuts it off from revenues that might at length have eclipsed its current success.

NetLedger

NetLedger is the first site to enable online accounting for small- and medium-sized businesses. In the past few decades, such businesses would have bought a software package to keep their accounts, administer expense reporting and payroll, generate reports, and so on. Now all this functionality is available as an online service, and of course available 24*7 from anywhere in the world. Having set the bar for such an application, NetLedger must now try to keep raising that bar; if it can do so with conviction, it has the potential to become one of the most important companies on the Internet.

Priceline

Priceline's innovation was to enable you, the would-be customer, to "name your own price" and then await a favorable response from a participating dealer in the commodity you want to buy. Jay Walker, Priceline's founder, calls his business model a "demand collection system"—and so it is, providing a site through which demand can be funneled to would-be suppliers. Of course the demand in question is a subset of total demand, being limited to those who are willing to take the trouble to try to pay less than the standard price.

The service, which Walker has patented, clearly offers value to consumers, though at the risk of some delay and frustration. Suppliers, though many are uneasy about doing business this way, stand to gain as well: they can sell what they might otherwise not be able to, and they can assess the demand for their goods that would arise if the standard price were reduced.

In most cases, Priceline consummates the transaction by buying the commodity from the supplier and selling it to the consumer—which, incidentally, has the accounting impact of maximizing Priceline's gross-revenue figures. The company began by accepting bids for airline seats, but it rapidly expanded into bids to buy or rent cars, to reserve hotel rooms, and to take out home loans. Its range of potential markets is vast; the company recently expanded into gasoline, enabling any driver to bid on a lot of up to 50 gallons and to be put in touch with nearby filling stations willing to accept the bid. So far, the patent has deterred potential competitors, and Priceline's size and importance are likely to grow significantly.

Yahoo!

Yahoo! was, of course, the first major Internet directory service. As such, it has been a consistent leader in search mechanisms and technology. The technique of embedding its URL on the sites of affiliates, allowing viewers to click through to its own site, is another Yahoo! innovation. The company has distinguished itself in many respects that, taken together, make it a formidable contender for Internet commerce, into which it has begun to move. These are:

- Usability
- Personalization
- Performance
- Scalability

Though some readers may regard these considerations as unexciting, they are the keys to primacy on the Net.

- **Usability.** The Yahoo! user interface was among the first to establish the Internet standard—that, no matter how robust and extensive the service, the user should find it so easy to exploit that no manual will be required and that online help can be held to a reasonable minimum. Yahoo! offers more than fifty enumerable services, including e-mail, news, maps, stock quotations, weather data, personal ads, and calendaring, yet no manual is offered—or needed.

- **Personalization.** The company introduced My Yahoo! in 1994, taking the lead in enabling users to configure online services to their specific needs and tastes. One can set up multiple personalized pages, choosing one or more localities for weather reports, tracking a stock portfolio, selecting categories of news items, including an editable calendar, and specifying one or more search facilities—among many other options.

Among the benefits conferred by the Internet, the ability to personalize is crucial. The notion "My URL" has multiplied so wildly as to have become one of the clichés of the Internet, even providing the conceptual foundation for entire companies. An example is myCFO, which offers a spectrum of coordinated financial services expressly tailored to the distinct concerns of users.

- **Performance.** Yahoo! has made speed of response the focus of its service. To do so it has instituted formal rules for content. All displayed views are static—that is, they have been generated and cached in advance of any viewer request for them. Each view is limited in terms of amount of memory, CPU time, and number of disk accesses required.

  In this respect, Yahoo! has done only what might be learned from standard texts on software engineering. But it has done so with a relentless thoroughness that has dissected every component between the browser and the disk, analyzed it in detail, and reassembled the totality in the form most conducive to optimizing throughput. It is almost ironic that, in an age where memory, disk space, and processing power are growing cheaper every day, Yahoo! has concentrated intently on improving its service by tightening all technical constraints.

- **Scalability.** The scalability of Yahoo! derives from its exacting standards for performance. Ranking high in every survey of most-visited sites,[32] Yahoo! has long had a choice: relax and count the revenues, or bear down and use its favored position as a springboard into broader fields of service. The company has correctly calculated that the latter course calls for it to husband its network resources with care in order to maximize the return they can yield.

  Yahoo! has already entered into services for small businesses: auctions, bill payment and presentment, calendaring, contacts, scheduling. It is no stretch to imagine that it will move into customer care, financials, HR, marketing, order management, and sales automation. If it continues to lead the world in Internet innovation and to manage its technology with the vigilance it has shown to date, Yahoo! has the potential to become the GE of the Internet . . . and possibly the most important company in the world.

The Computer Colossi

Let us examine the implications of electronic business for the leading computer hardware and software suppliers.

Cisco

For Cisco, the vision and the road to its realization are clear. The company needs simply to maintain its supremacy in routers and associated hardware; if it can do so, it will continue to grow in proportion to the growth of the Internet. Cisco figures as the hardware favorite in all the major Internet arenas: Web sites, dot-coms, ASPs, private networks; IP telephony, online banking, e-commerce, and so on. However, there are signs of trouble: Juniper Networks has secured 24 percent of the core router market, eating into the Cisco share, and Nortel has established a clear supremacy in optical networking. On September 15, 2000, Cisco stock closed at a price it had first reached on February 8; during the same period, Nortel's stock was up 25 percent and Juniper's 138 percent, eroding Cisco's competitive advantage in acquiring smaller companies with needed technology.

Recent moves by Cisco help to clarify its strategy for the next century. It has acquired WebLine, an e-mail interaction-management vendor, and Selsius, an IP-telephony vendor. It has also taken a billion-dollar stake in KPMG, the U.S. unit of KPMG LLP, third among the big five accounting firms. KPMG will use the money to develop Internet-based data, voice, and video services, and to deliver them to its clients. Cisco continues to work toward a transformation of call centers and of telecommunications in the new millennium.

IBM

IBM's role for the next century will be defined in part by its record of consistent failure as a software developer. Its Lotus Division is unproven, and its compilers and word processors have never performed well. OS/2 has lost the operating system war to Windows; as a tool for performance monitoring and measurement, Tivoli (acquired in 1996) seems destined to succumb to Oracle Enterprise Manager and perhaps to HP's OpenView. IBM's partnership with BlueGill in a fledgling EBPP solution appears to be outclassed by Netscape, and Corepoint (once Software Artistry), IBM's bid to compete in CRM with Siebel and Oracle, was quietly put down in 1999, just after its first birthday. DB2, IBM's relational database management system (RDBMS), remains viable but does not present serious competition to Microsoft, or, especially, to Oracle, in the database market. Of the top ten business-to-consumer sites on the Internet, ten use Oracle databases; of the top ten business-to-business sites, only one—IBM—does not. (My attempt to balance this paragraph with an outstanding software success story for IBM has drawn a blank.)

IBM coined the term *e-business*; yet, ironically, it neither owns the URL www.ebusiness.com nor offers an effective product portfolio to manage a customer's e-transformation. But the company retains two strengths that will sustain it as a major presence in the twenty-first century. The first is its dominance in "big iron" (large and mid-range mainframe computers), now commanding more respect with the trend back to centralized computing. The second is its professional-services business, which continues to provide effective, if expensive, customer solutions—even custom software.

Microsoft

*"Success is a lousy teacher. It seduces
smart people into thinking they can't
lose."*
                                        Bill Gates, Jr.

As the Internet Age advances, Microsoft is doomed to shrink in revenues and in importance. By concentrating its efforts on defending its operating system treasure, the Redmond giant has squandered its opportunity to convert its market position into a commanding presence on the Net. What effort it *could* expend on the Net focused on browser development at the expense of a broader and potentially more lucrative Web strategy, and led directly to Judge Thomas Penfield Jackson's ruling on April 3, 2000, that Microsoft was guilty of violating Section 2 of the Sherman Antitrust Act.

The significance of any penalty to be imposed in this case is rapidly evaporating. The debilitation of Microsoft, which the Department of Justice has thus far failed to accomplish, the Internet is bringing about. Unless the government actually fragments Microsoft, there will be no dramatic conclusion to this process. Instead the company faces a future like that of fourth-century Constantinople—a drawn-out chronicle of alternating expansions and contractions leading at last to irrelevance and perhaps to final demise—which, if it happens, will have an importance more symbolic than actual.

Microsoft Revenues

The *Microsoft 1999 Annual Report* states revenues as follows:

Business Division	Revenues ($ billion)		
	1997	1998	1999
Windows Platforms	4.92	6.28	8.50
Productivity Applications and Developer	5.62	7.04	8.82
Consumer, Commerce, and Other	1.40	1.94	2.43

What is the prognosis for these lines of business?

Windows Platforms

Major retailers of personal computers have conventionally treated Microsoft operating systems, whether Windows or NT, as default offerings for desktop PCs, with which one or another such system is typically bundled. Selling an operating system as a feature of the PC has usually made sound business sense, because the PC has generally been of little use without one.

Compaq and Dell, which lead in the retailing of PCs across the Internet, provide Microsoft operating systems as defaults. As for retail stores, a survey conducted in 1997 by NetAction (www.netaction.org) found that "consumers in Silicon Valley cannot purchase an IBM-compatible personal computer off the shelf from a retail outlet without the Windows operating system." The survey covered retail stores belonging to eight major chains: Circuit City, CompUSA, Fry's, Good

Guys, Office Depot, Office Max, Radio Shack, and Sears. "Although the survey was conducted on Apple Computer's home turf, NetAction found surprisingly few Apple computers for sale at the retail outlets surveyed. Neither of the chain office supply stores sold any Apple computers. Moreover, the stores that sold Apple computers had a very limited selection to choose from."

NetAction further reported that "the top three ISPs serving the U.S. consumer market—America Online, CompuServe, and Internet MCI—all bundle Microsoft's Internet Explorer into their start-up software, and all three have agreements with Microsoft that specify IE as the browser customers receive. Only one of the three top ISPs tells consumers they have the option of downloading Netscape Navigator as an alternative to IE."

The scale of this sales channel is reflected by the *Microsoft 1999 Annual Report* (page 11):

> Microsoft distributes its products primarily through OEM licenses, organizational licenses, and retail packaged products. OEM channel revenue represents license fees from original equipment manufacturers who preinstall Microsoft products, primarily on PCs. Microsoft has three major geographic sales and marketing organizations: the South Pacific and Americas Region; the Europe, Middle East, and Africa Region; and the Asia Region. Sales of organizational licenses and packaged products via these channels are primarily to and through distributors and resellers.
>
> OEM channel revenue was $3.49 billion in 1997, $4.72 billion in 1998, and $6.40 billion in 1999. The primary source of OEM revenue is the licensing of desktop operating systems, and OEM revenue is highly dependent on PC shipment volume. Growth was also enhanced by increased penetration of higher-value Windows NT Workstation licenses.
>
> Revenue in the South Pacific and Americas Region was $4.39 billion, $5.57 billion, and $7.25 billion in 1997, 1998, and 1999. Revenue in the Europe, Middle East, and Africa Region was $2.77 billion, $3.50 billion, and $4.33 billion for the three years. Growth rates have been lower in Europe than in other geographic areas due to higher existing market shares and a faster shift to licensing programs. Asia Region revenue was $1.29 billion in 1997, $1.48 billion in 1998, and $1.78 billion in 1999.

(Revenues reported in this passage of course derive from all three major lines of Microsoft business.)

Retailers will continue to offer Microsoft operating systems, but consumers will come to recognize the decreased utility of these systems in the context of the Internet and will develop a resistance to the systems' prices and complexities. In fact, the company has revealed that, in compliance with customer wishes, it is developing an Internet-based version of Microsoft Office. Microsoft says that it is examining pricing models that would be "more Internet friendly," but which the company would presumably find less lucrative. Meanwhile, alternative operating systems, most notably Linux, are gaining prominence.

Productivity Applications and Developer

The products that constitute this line of business are primarily desktop applications (notably Microsoft Office), server applications, and tools for software development. The annual report does not show how revenues are distributed across these constituents, but Microsoft Office probably generates by far the greater portion of revenues for this line of business.

The Internet-based version of Microsoft Office that the company has announced will relieve casual users of the need to license the application suite, just as it will relieve them of the need even to think about an underlying operating system. Users who would once have bought Microsoft Office will now have no sunk cost and will be free to compare the suite with rival products that are also available for rent; some users will defect.

More importantly, the ability to rent applications over the Web will open up a new market for products competitive with the Microsoft Office applications, products that Microsoft has deliberately locked out of the market for years with its bundling practices. Each of these developments means a net loss of Microsoft revenue from this line of business. The company will of course have the option of raising license fees in hopes of recouping its losses; but access to competitive products, made suddenly easy by the Internet, makes this tactic risky in a way that Microsoft never had to ponder in its monopoly heyday. The long-term effect will be to drive down revenues from this line of business, probably more and more as the years go by; but how fast and how far those revenues will sink remain to be quantified.

Consumer, Commerce, and Other

To quote again from the annual report,

> This category of product revenue includes learning and entertainment software; PC input devices; training and certification fees; consulting; and the online services. The Company's Internet services include the MSN portal, MSN access, WebTV®, and vertical properties such as MSN Hotmail Web-based e-mail service, Expedia.com™ travel site, CarPoint car buying site, and MoneyCentral personal finance site.
>
> Learning and entertainment revenue was relatively flat in all three years. Mouse, gaming device, and keyboard sales increased in 1997 and 1998, but were steady in 1999. Training and certification fees from system integrators, along with consulting services to large enterprise customers and technology solution providers, increased strongly in all three years. Revenue from MSN Internet access fees and WebTV services increased due to higher subscriber levels. Advertising revenue, although relatively small in amount, increased exceptionally well in 1999 for the online portal and vertical properties.

In this area Microsoft's revenues will continue to grow as the company morphs into a provider of infotainment, thus solving its two outstanding corporate problems: (a) its weakness in technical innovation; and (b) the prospect of declining revenues from the other two lines of business. Because the company is not viewed as possessing monopoly power in this area, it is once more oiling up and rolling out its trusty monopolizing stratagems.

As an example, consider the Xbox, the gaming machine announced by Bill Gates in March 2000. The machine is supported by DirectX, which its Web page describes as "a group of technologies . . . for running and displaying applications rich in multimedia elements such as full-color graphics, video, 3-D animation, and surround sound." To be explicit, DirectX is a technological infrastructure for computer games.

Microsoft's strategy is to incorporate DirectX into Windows and to strike agreements with hardware and games companies to build DirectX or support for it into their products as well. Programmers who use DirectX to develop games for the Xbox will find that those games can readily be ported to any machine that runs Windows, whether at home or in the office—and also to any gaming console with DirectX in its infrastructure. The economics of scale will make

DirectX-compatible games potentially very lucrative—and will have the effect of driving all other games out of the market. The plan is that ultimately every box running a game will have generated revenue for Microsoft, whether because it was bought from the company or because it uses Microsoft-licensed technology. Once this stranglehold has been established, we may expect to see the prices of games go up.

I'm still looking for information as to the current size of the world games market. Given that its size in 1996 was estimated by *The Economist* at $8.4 billion, Microsoft's plans for the market segment are ambitious, even when weighed against the company's current gross revenues. Notably, those plans have nothing to do with producing outstanding games, a task for which Microsoft has shown little talent. As with Internet Explorer, they have everything to do with manipulating the company's operating system monopoly—to influence people to promote and buy games originating with Microsoft and its partners, and to choke off the lifeline to its competitors.

The Internet, Business at the Speed of Thought, and You

In his second book, *Business @ the Speed of Thought,*[33] Bill Gates begins by setting forth twelve key steps "to make digital information flow an intrinsic part of your company." The numbered steps appear below, quoted and categorized as they appear in the book. The comment following each step is my own.

For *knowledge work:*

> 1. Insist that communication flow through the organization over e-mail so that you can act on news with reflexlike speed.

I agree. IMAP, the leading technology enabling e-mail, is free. Your browser, which enables writing, editing, viewing, sending, categorizing, and filing e-mail, is also (currently) free. Moreover, a number of companies (including eGain, Kana, Oracle, and Cisco) offer products that take advantage of e-mail and optimize its processing in support of self-service customer care. Microsoft offers no solution here other than a free browser.

> 2. Study sales data online to find patterns and share insights easily. Understand overall trends and personalize service for individual customers.

I agree. These processes are known as data mining, business intelligence, and sales automation. The leading companies providing solutions in this market segment are Siebel and Oracle. Microsoft has not addressed these processes.

> 3. Use PCs for business analysis, and shift knowledge workers into high-level thinking work about products, services, and profitability.

I agree in part. Once financial, HR, manufacturing, marketing, sales, service, and supply-chain data have been centralized, business analysis applications from vendors including Oracle, SAP, and Siebel will indeed come into their own. But they will not rely on PCs. I agree that the basically clerical tasks that now occupy many knowledge workers must give way to work that carries more value for the enterprise, or else those workers must be radically redeployed. However, Microsoft offers support neither for business analysis nor for upward redeployment of knowledge workers.

> 4. Use digital tools to create cross-departmental virtual teams that can share knowledge and build on each other's ideas in real time, worldwide. Use digital systems to capture corporate history for use by anyone.

Again, I agree in part. Clearly, the Internet enables worldwide access to and sharing of corporate data. But the heart of the process by which corporate data are converted into information and knowledge is the database that enables the centralization and organization of those data. Here Microsoft does offer a product, MS SQL Server, of which Version 7 sells for as little as $100/user; this gives it respectable price/performance figures even though it is far slower than its major competitors. Larger enterprises must turn to databases with higher performance levels and with greater reliability and scalability; challenged to choose among IBM's DB2, Informix, Microsoft, Oracle, SAP's Adabas, and Sybase, an overwhelming majority select Oracle.

> 5. Convert every paper process to a digital process, eliminating administrative bottlenecks and freeing knowledge workers for more important tasks.

Once more, I agree in part. For decades now the paperless office has been a holy grail for businesses all over the world. Does the realization of that vision entail the conversion of every paper process to a digital process? No, of course not. For e-businesses in particular, the transfiguration of commerce by the Internet means that many traditional business processes become irrelevant overnight, and that many others must be revised—re-envisioned—if they are to contribute cost-effectively in the new environment. Most enterprises will find that some of their paper processes must be automated without (other) major changes, but that the advent of the Internet provides them with a once-in-a-lifetime opportunity to transform or to deep-six many of the others. Microsoft offers no product that supports drawing the needed distinctions or making the needed changes—except for a free browser which is, of course, valuable during and following the automating to be done.

For *business operations:*

> 6. Use digital tools to eliminate single-task jobs or change them into value-added jobs that use the skills of a knowledge worker.

This item basically repeats the pieties of items 3 and 5, and I have no objection to those pieties. But Microsoft offers no product that advances them.

> 7. Create a digital feedback loop to improve the efficiency of physical processes and improve the quality of the products and services created. Every employee should be able to easily track all the key metrics.

I agree; compare my response to item 3 above. Once the business data have been centralized and integrated, the value of the database created is greater than the sum of the preexisting—scattered—parts. (This is Ellison's Law.) That value is realized by the transformation of the data into business intelligence. No Microsoft product supports this transformation.

> 8. Use digital systems to route customer complaints immediately to the people who can improve a product or service.

I agree. Companies leading the charge in this field of business include eGain, Kana, Octane, Oracle, Siebel, and Silknet. Beyond its free browser, Microsoft has made no contribution to a solution in this area.

9. Use digital communications to redefine the nature of your business and the boundaries around your business. Become larger and more substantial or smaller and more intimate as the customer situation warrants.

This item perhaps hedges its bets to some extent. Any company that fully achieves the flexibility recommended here will be able to take a globally integrated view, when that is called for, yet still be able to interact with customers in one-to-one fashion in order to serve the needs of the customer and the business. I have addressed global integration in discussing earlier items. As for personal engagement with customers, the leaders in one-to-one interaction are BroadVision, Net Perceptions, and Vignette. Microsoft offers no support for such flexibility other than its free browser.

For *commerce:*

10. Trade information for time. Decrease cycle time by using digital transactions with all suppliers and partners, and transform every business process into just-in-time delivery.

I agree absolutely. The process described here is electronic procurement, and the de facto standard for this arena has been set by Ariba, Commerce One, and Oracle. Microsoft offers no solution here.

11. Use digital delivery of sales and service to eliminate the middleman from customer transactions. If you're a middleman, use digital tools to add value to transactions.

I agree. Consumers that traditionally have bought from retailers will increasingly turn directly to manufacturers to effect purchases or to secure support. For instance, somebody who buys a Sony stereo from *the good guys!* will be able to go directly to the Sony site to buy additional products or to get services. Companies leading in this market are the CRM standard-setters, Oracle and Siebel. Microsoft does nothing to enable consumers in this context other than to provide a browser.

12. Use digital tools to help customers solve problems for themselves, and reserve personal contact to respond to complex, high-value customer needs.

I agree. This item relates to many of the preceding ones, perhaps especially to item 11. Companies leading in developing the relevant technology include Clarify, Kana, and Oracle. Again, Microsoft does nothing to enable the behavior recommended.

What is the moral of this twelve-part tale? The tale is told by the CEO of Microsoft, and it is reasonable to assume that his company has taken these twelve steps already or that it is seriously engaged in doing so. But Microsoft is doing little or nothing to enable other companies to bring about the self-transformations that Bill Gates identifies as crucial for the new century. The moral is "Microsoft not required."

On this analysis, Marc Andreessen's vision of Microsoft reduced to a set of mundane, hastily tested device drivers appears to be at hand. But not so fast! While it is clearly the case that the road to e-business does not run through Redmond, it is also clear that Microsoft— whether as one company, two, or three—will continue for a long time to market its operating systems, its applications, and its tools in one form or another, though with decreasing profitability. The words of the (waning) profits are written on the corporate walls.

But Microsoft has read those words, and has gradually swung its enormous resources, as one might swing a battleship, in a new direction—one inspired by a tardy and incomplete understanding of the potential of the Internet. It is now intent on establishing itself as a power in communications, information, electronic games, and entertainment—fields generally expected to be revolutionized by the advent of "smart" connected devices, for which more compact operating systems are being developed (see *Windows CE,* the next section in this chapter).

Microsoft will continue to make money through e-commerce, and it will provide (in addition to Internet Explorer) some tools that other companies can use to promote their Web efforts; MS Visual Java++ is an example. But this is a far cry from its position—in the previous generation—as the supplier of the underlying operating system and the suite of office applications used almost universally by major corporations. To quote Scott McNealy of Sun Microsystems, "Microsoft is now a severely overpriced personal productivity tools applications vendor with an OS business that is no longer able to 'captivate' the end user by being the only platform to run desired applications." The self-trumpeted champion of technical innovation has conceded its own sterility and seeks to survive by buying potential rivals when it can, co-opting their ideas when they cannot be bought, and marching resolutely toward the technological rear echelon.

Windows CE

When, about 1993, Microsoft began work toward enabling devices other than PCs, its strategy was to develop an operating system that was a much-reduced version of Windows. This approach had several attractions for Microsoft: it reduced the need for innovation, it held the promise of development that could benefit both the larger and the smaller operating systems, and it meant that the company could leverage the Windows expertise of its existing programming staff. There was also an obvious benefit for prospective users—that what they knew about working with Windows would help them in working with the smaller system.

Windows CE was released in September 1996. After 4 years in the field, the operating system can be seen to have failed, together with the strategy on which it was based. It is not evident that more innovation was a prerequisite to success, but Microsoft's principal competitor—Palm Computing—has innovated more radically and has succeeded.[34] Windows CE has undergone three rounds of revisions in response to the concerns of customers and retailers, but it has never been able to catch up. For the first half of 1999, handheld computers from Palm accounted for 70.4 percent of sales worldwide and 79.1 percent of sales in the United States. In the subcategory of palm-sized devices, products based on the Palm OS outsold Windows-CE-based products by 83.5 percent to 9.7 percent.[35] In January 2000, Microsoft produced yet another version of its operating system, now renamed "Pocket PC" in a tacit admission that Windows CE had been judged and found wanting (and might get farther in disguise).

Microsoft (as IBM had done earlier) had committed the classic mistake of the company highly successful in one generation and trying to extend its success to the next big thing: It had failed to cut the umbilical cord linking its new efforts to its prior success. Though Windows could be scaled down for palm devices, it carried a lot of irrelevant baggage. The conventions of the UI required an inconveniently large amount of screen space on the new devices. Functions much needed on full-scale PCs were retained even though nobody ever found much use for them on handhelds, and Windows CE's storage requirements bottomed out at about 12 megabytes, compared to 2 megabytes or less for competing products. Conventions that were well-suited to full-scale PCs, which are relatively homogeneous in design, were shoehorned into smaller and more disparate machines over the design of which Microsoft had no control. Finally, in an ironic twist, many users were alienated by finding that functions with which they were familiar from full-scale Microsoft Office worked differently, not at all, or—frustratingly—not beyond a point that could be identified only by trying to get past it.

Watching this market being carried away by the current, Microsoft grew increasingly desperate to win over major partners. In May 1999, it invested $5 billion in AT&T, securing a deal that guaranteed the use of Windows CE in 5 million set-top boxes that will enable Internet access via TV screens. But AT&T kept open its option to use other operating systems for that application, and, indeed, the telecom giant had already acquired TCI—and, with it, millions of set-top boxes that use Sun Microsystem's Java technology. In earlier years, Microsoft might have used its monopoly powers and the cash it had derived from them to pressure potential partners; today, in consequence of the ruling that it has abused those powers—and awaiting court-ordered remedial action to follow—it is less eager than before to throw its weight around.

The world will need to accustom itself to an Internet on which Microsoft is one of many sideshows.

SAP

SAP is the world's largest applications provider. The Morgan Stanley Group has estimated SAP's annual license revenue at $2.35 billion at the end of calendar year 1999;[36] this compares (adjusting for fiscal-year boundaries) to about $1 billion for Oracle, SAP's nearest rival.

SAP has codified many client/server business practices into its monolithic applications offering. The company is deep into dozens of verticals, and its suite comprises applications for HR, manufacturing, supply chain, and financials. Not yet a CRM vendor, SAP is executing a strategy to enter this market space via partnerships with other companies.

SAP faces four challenges:

- To move from local and regional systems to single-instance computing
- To move from a client/server architecture to one based on the Internet
- To extend its expertise and dominance in the ERP market space into CRM
- To codify Internet-based business practices into its offering, augmenting or replacing client/server practices.

Having begun trading on the NYSE in 1998, at $60, SAP shares were driven down steeply during 1999 by anticipated Y2K troubles and by the perception that the company was slow to extend its application offerings beyond ERP and into the CRM space. The stock struck a low of $23.60 in late March. It then began a slow recovery, accelerating to a peak at $85.70 at the height of the Internet mania of early March 2000. Shares then dropped to a low of $40.65 in April, partly on perceptions that SAPMarkets, SAP's Internet subsidiary, was falling behind competitors.

In June, SAP announced that it had struck a deal with Commerce One to develop a common architecture enabling companies participating in exchanges built by Commerce One to integrate their exchange activities with SAP-developed supply-chain, inventory management, and other back-office systems. The alliance has won contracts to support consortia for the metals and electricity industries and is reported to have several additional deals in the pipeline. The effect has been to foster the view that SAP can successfully turn the corner into the Internet Age, and the stocks of both companies have risen in consequence. (SAP's closed August 2000 at $64.19.)

Nevertheless, SAP appears to be turning into another version of Computer Associates. Large and noninnovative, the company appears stretched out like a weary dragon on the hoard of its maintenance revenues. Once notoriously disdainful of partnerships, SAP now has entered into several, perhaps acknowledging implicitly the limits of its abilities to prevail on its own.

But this Frankenstein strategy for e-business—stitching onto the SAP torso a face from Siebel, legs from Nortel, and arms from Commerce One—is dangerous. Galvanize this ragbag and it *may* spring into spasmodic action, but at what price? SAP offers not a *suite* but a *kit*, including no instructions, requiring costly teams of consultants, imposing protracted deployment cycles, and enabling a seriously emaciated body of e-business practices.

Sun Microsystems

Sun continues to rise and shine. No other "big UNIX" company rivals Sun today, and Sun's Solaris Operating Environment reigns as the de facto standard for dot-coms, ISPs, and ASPs. Most of the major software companies regard Sun as the development standard for building, performance testing, certification, and production environments.

The popularity of Java continues to grow, and its adoption by companies including IBM and Microsoft constitutes a major testimonial, although some dissent has broken out in relation to Java 2 Enterprise Edition. In 1998, Sun followed up with Jini Technology, which potentially enables any devices containing microchips to communicate over a network by using a protocol that allows each to recognize the others. Jini is in use by Canon, Cisco, Kodak, Motorola, Sony, Toshiba, Xerox, and many others.

Oracle

Traditionally, Oracle has functioned as a single business entity that has spread its efforts across several technical areas: database, tools, consulting, services,[37] ERP, and (most recently) CRM. These areas will continue to constitute a single business entity because each heavily relies on and must coordinate its work with each of the others.

With the advent of the Internet, Oracle has moved into a new business world. Continuing to pursue its mission to maximize return to its shareholders, it has found a way to do so that simultaneously suits the new environment and gives it a corporate style distinct from that of many of its rivals. Where the Microsoft style could be characterized as "karate" (Webster: "a Japanese art of self-defense in which kicks and openhanded blows are delivered esp. to vulnerable parts of the body"), Oracle is developing instead a "judo" style (Webster again: "a modern refined form of jujitsu utilizing special applications of movement, balance, and leverage").

Oracle has embarked on a course of developing and spinning off a large number of subsidiary companies in each of which it retains part ownership, a majority interest, or full control. These include auto-xchange, e-Travel.com, Liberate, Oracle Exchange, OracleMobile, RetailersMarketXchange.com, and a number of analogous ventures to follow—not to mention Oracle Japan. Through this process Oracle is evolving into a corporate ecosystem, with successive offspring branching out to colonize business niches that are not yet fully exploited.

This strategy is feasible only when the spin-offs are not deeply interdependent; for this reason it cannot be applied to the traditional constituents of the parent company. But, when it works, it confers enormous business advantages both on Oracle and on its descendants. By granting full visibility to the transcorporate enterprise, it enables would-be developers, executives, investors, and business partners to target their efforts and resources with much greater discrimination than would otherwise be possible. In this respect, the Oracle strategy exploits possibilities of movement, balance, and leverage within the competitive environment. Meanwhile the distinct corporations retain their fraternal bonds and an inclination to direct their efforts symbiotically.

Early results of this strategy suggest that it has helped to drive the rapid ascent of Oracle stock. (In July 1999, Oracle ranked 122nd in the world in market capitalization. In July 2000, it ranked 13th.[38]) All indications are that the company will continue this trend, transforming itself gradually into its own corporate network.

The pace and quality of innovation at Oracle have been extraordinary. Results—over the last 2 years alone—include:

- The deployment of a global single instance of each internal application

- The implementation of the virtual private database (with server-enforced access restrictions) within Oracle 8i

- Business OnLine, the company's premier ASP program

- Rapid proliferation of Oracle-sponsored e-business exchanges

- e-Travel.com, a travel marketplace serving internal and external users

- Oracle's Internet Application Server—which, though based on the Apache server, Oracle has commercialized by providing fee-based support

- E-Business Network, Oracle's Web-based TV series for business

- Many online services, including OracleSalesOnline.com, OracleExchange.com, OracleMobile.com, and planetrights.com

- Oracle Parallel Server and iCache, which, respectively, distribute database accesses and accelerate responses for output in high demand

- The Oracle E-Business Suite

In May 2000, Oracle strengthened its competitive position with the release of Oracle E-Business Suite 11*i*, the first comprehensive and fully integrated suite of business applications for the Internet. Its competition consists of applications for CRM applications only, others for ERP applications only, and still others that address one or a few subsets of those broad ranges. None of these can offer a full-scale solution to any company's business needs without subjecting that company to a complex, expensive, and often painful process of integration.

Oracle's success with business applications has already slashed the substantial lead that SAP had won with its ERP products. As Oracle continues to exploit its position as the flagship enabler of e-commerce—as growing database sales, driven by the proliferation of e-businesses, help to drive application sales and vice versa—the company appears destined to grow vigorously for many years to come.

Trends

Here I'll bite the bullet and hazard a view as to where the priorities will lie for electronic business over the next few years. Businesses will transform themselves extensively, especially by broadening their horizons to meet the market needs in areas related to their current competencies; some, but relatively few, will develop suites of products or services that comprehensively address one or more major business areas. In most cases, such developments will be driven in part by acquisitions: the current ranks of competitors will be thinned by consolidation and, in some cases, by failure.

But the most important trend, now that many great—and thousands of not-so-great—business ideas have been realized, will be optimization, which will manifest itself along several important axes. This optimization, like the proliferation of e-businesses that we have already experienced, will take place with bewildering speed; and it will encompass five pivotal transitions:

- **Local to Global Commerce**. Any company that establishes an Internet presence is, by definition, global. But the barriers to conducting actual business across national boundaries are substantial. Over the next 5 years, Internet enablers will dedicate a great deal of effort to lowering those barriers, and e-businesses will be intent on vaulting them. Companies will increasingly conduct business in multiple languages and currencies, employing global price books and using license and renewal contracts that may vary from one country to the next in order to accommodate varying national law codes. Companies with physical presences in multiple countries will increasingly develop payroll policies and sales-compensation plans that will be global in reach but sensitive to regional differences.

   This transition will forcefully impact entire national economies. The increased difficulties of doing business internationally mean that the efficiencies of domestic business will, in varying degrees, be sacrificed—not a desirable outcome for either the companies or the consumers they serve. And, as a company from country X pushes its way into country Y, it will encounter increasing resistance from homegrown competitors—not a desirable outcome for the invading company, but probably a plus for consumers.

- **Duality to Community**. In the past, it was hard enough to arrange two-way business interactions, and a company would typically deal with only one of its customers, or one of its employees, or one of its partners, or one of its suppliers, at any one time. The physical constraints yielded in some degree to airplane flights and conference calls, but it remained unusual to convene stakeholders from even three different categories. Now it is possible for everybody involved with a business to interact with everybody else in a single forum: the electronic business can bring together customers, employees, partners, and representatives from both its demand and its supply chains. To convene them simultaneously, though still problematic, is much easier than it used to be; to convene them virtually, by providing a Web site that all can access at any time of the week to register comments or execute transactions, is now standard operating procedure.

The manifestations of this change include mechanisms for collaboration in product design, in demos, and in selling. But the ultimate in collaborative environments are the countless online exchanges that are springing into existence. While most of these will continue to be forums for procurement, new varieties will emerge, including demand and customer exchanges. New laws will be created and challenged as this form of business continues to evolve. The entrepreneurial opportunities that will bubble up in this environment, where every business idea can be evaluated at once by everybody who would be affected by it, will prove innumerable.

- **Batch to Real-Time Processing**. Once virtually all computerized business practices used batch processing, because machine power was inadequate to respond satisfactorily in real time. Batch processing continues to figure importantly in contemporary business applications, whether for client/server systems or for e-businesses. But the transition to real-time processing, already well advanced, will continue, and eventually applications such as sales credits, order processing, order status, support renewals, and customer care and support will be conducted almost exclusively in real time.

- **Physical to Virtual Inventory**. Businesses will increasingly deal in virtual inventory. Where the standard model today is buy-sell-ship, the standard model tomorrow will be sell-buy-ship. Real-time inventory systems enable this change, and growing consumer selectivity necessitates it. Retailers will gradually phase out their warehouses, and what warehousing business survives will consolidate in the hands of companies that do nothing else; and these, to stay competitive, will have to develop very high-tech operations.

- **Nascent to Mature Order Automation**. Order entry was first automated only a few years ago. Since then, the progress in this arena of automation has been breathtaking, with the technology sequentially embracing teleplacement of orders, Web stores, product configuration, Web auctions, and Web exchanges. Now the front-line action addresses the available-to-promise model, in which order placement is answered in real time by automatic confirmation of the availability of the goods ordered, and the build-to-order model, in which automatic support is provided for configuring ordered items to the exact specifications of the order (so that a consumer may be assured delivery of an item different from anything ever before produced).

This process is advancing toward its culmination in the capable-to-promise model, in which the item ordered, if it already exists, is selected at once, and stock automatically replenished; if the item does not exist, its manufacture is automatically initiated.

A Concluding Caveat

There is some danger that this book, or parts of it, will sound more authoritative than it can be in fact. Be careful to make allowances as you think appropriate, especially in regard to predictions. Let's remember what Yogi Berra said, back at the start of Chapter 1; and let's give him the last word too:

"It ain't over till it's over."

Glossary

.com: see *dot-com*

ACD: *n* automated call distributor

ARPA: *n* Advanced Research Projects Agency

ASP: *n* application services provider

B2B: *adj* business-to-business

B2C: *adj* business-to-consumer

BI: *n* business intelligence

BIS: *n* business-intelligence system(s)

BOM: *n* bill of material

brick-and-click: *adj* comprising channels that include both traditional physical outlets and the Internet; example, Barnes & Noble

brick-and-mortar: *adj* consisting of physical outlets to the exclusion, or effective exclusion, of the Internet; example, Philip Morris

CAGR: *n* compound annual growth rate

CD: *n* compact disk

CD-ROM: *n* compact disk–read-only memory

CE: *?* (in Microsoft's "Windows-CE") Microsoft says that "CE" is not an acronym

CEM: *n* contract electronics manufacturer

CEO: *n* chief executive officer

CFO: *n* chief financial officer

click-through: *n* the process by which a viewer accesses a desired URL by clicking on a link or an icon (as, for instance, a banner ad)

click-wrapped: *adj* the condition of an order once the viewer has clicked on a link or an icon that represents approval of the order's details

COO: *n* chief operating officer

CPU: *n* central processing unit

CRM: *n* customer-relationship management

CSR: *n* customer service representative

CTI: *n* computer-telephony integration

DASD: *n* direct-access storage device

DBA: *n* database administrator

DES: *n* Data Encryption Standard

DoC: *n* Department of Commerce

DoD: *n* Department of "Defense"

DoJ: *n* Department of Justice

dot-com: *n* a company that does business primarily or exclusively across the Internet; for example, Amazon

DW: *n* data warehouse

EBPP: *n* electronic bill presentment and payment

e-business: *n* (abstract) business conducted in ways that exploit or rely on electronic media—and, more specifically, on the Internet

n (concrete) an enterprise that depends wholly or largely on the Internet for commercial interactions of various kinds and particularly for financial transactions

EC: *n* European Commission

ECML: *n* Electronic Commerce Modeling Language

EDI: *n* Electronic Data Interchange

EFT: *n* electronic funds transfer

ENIAC: *n* Electronic Numerical Integrator and Calculator

ERP: *n* enterprise resource planning

e-transformation: *n* the process by which a company full-fledged before 1995 (or so) becomes enabled for business over the Internet, not necessarily to the exclusion of its longer-established business patterns

EU: *n* European Union

extranet: *n* a set of Web sites and associated functionality that a corporation makes accessible to one or more business partners and possibly to some subset of its employees; access to an extranet is normally protected by logon provisions

FAQ: *n* frequently asked question

FTC: *n* Federal Trade Commission

GMT: *n* Greenwich Mean Time

GNX: *n* GlobalNetXchange

GUI: *n* graphical user interface

HR: *n* human resources

HTML: *n* HyperText Markup Language

HTTP: *n* HyperText Transfer Protocol

HVAC: *n* Heating, Ventilating, and Air Conditioning (companies)

I/O: *n, adj* input/output

iBOM: *n* Internet bill of material

IDC: *n* Internet Data Center

IE: *n* (Microsoft's) Internet Explorer

IMAP: *n* Internet Message Access Protocol

INS: *n* Immigration and Naturalization Service

Internet time: *n* the time experienced by Bud Abbott and Lou Costello when you run *The Time of their Lives* on "Fast Forward" on your VCR

IP: *n* Internet Protocol

IPO: *n* initial public offering

ISP: *n* Internet service provider

IT: *n, adj* information technology

ITFA: *n* Internet Tax Freedom Act

JTAPI: *n* Java telephony API

LAN: *n* local-area network

LLP: *n* Limited-Liability Partnership

MSN: *n* Microsoft Network

NASA: *n* National Aeronautics and Space Administration

NC: *n* network computer (a device that displaces onto the Internet much of the hardware and software traditionally found at the location of the PC)

NCSA: *n* National Center for Supercomputing Applications

NT: *adj* (in Microsoft's "Windows NT") New Technology

NTE: *n* National Transportation Exchange

NYSE: *n* New York Stock Exchange

OECD: *n* Organization for Economic Cooperation and Development

OEM: *n* original equipment manufacturer

OLE: *n* Object Linking and Embedding

one-to-one: *adj* addressing or responding to a viewer, across the Internet, in a way conditioned by information specific to that viewer

OS: *n* operating system

PC: *n, adj* personal computer

PDA: *n* personal digital assistant

PGP: *n* (Phil Zimmermann's) Pretty Good Privacy (encryption/decryption program)

PRM: *n* partner-relationship management

PSTN: *n* public switched telephone network

QA: *n* quality assurance

RAM: *n* random-access memory

RDBMS: *n* relational database management system

RFP: *n* request for proposal

RFQ: *n* request for quotation

ROI: *n* return on investment

SFA: *n* sales-force automation

spiff: *n* a special often informal end-of-day award to an employee in recognition of some notable achievement

SQL: *n* Structured Query Language

SSL: *n* Secure Sockets Layer

SSR: *n* Support Service Representative

TAPI: *n* telephony API

TCP/IP: *n* Transmission Control Protocol/Internet Protocol

TRADIC: *n* Transistorized Digital Computer

TSAPI: *n* telephony-server API

UCLA: *n* University of California at Los Angeles

UI: *n* user interface

UK: *n* United Kingdom

URL: *n* Uniform Resource Locator

URL-sharing: *n* a technique (using Java applets) by which an agent can direct a caller's browser to an Internet page that appears simultaneously on the agent's screen; a more sophisticated level of URL-sharing enables the agent to fill in data on one screen and have it appear simultaneously on both screens

USPS: *n* United States Postal Service

VAT: *n* value-added tax

VoIP: *n, adj* voice over IP

WAN: *n* wide area network

Webtone: *n* fully provisioned access across the Internet to one or more services; this comprises the provision to the user (typically a subscriber) of a URL and of Internet access mediated exclusively by the provider of the ultimate service, masking from the user all issues relating to telephony and to generic access to the Internet

whiteboarding: *n* a form of URL-sharing that enables the agent to paint or draw on the caller's and the agent's screens simultaneously

WTO: *n* World Trade Organization

WWW: *n* World Wide Web

XML: *n* Extensible Markup Language

End Notes

[1] This possibility is explored by John McPhee in his fascinating book *The Deltoid Pumpkin Seed* (Farrar Straus & Giroux, 1973).

[2] Exchange of goods does take place between animals of other species; for example, masked boobies in the Galapagos exchange nesting twigs during courtship. But such exchanges probably grew out of their symbolic value and do not reflect an expectation by each bird of material profit by the transaction. Yet this criterion is essential to our understanding of barter.

[3] Amber's strong electrostatic properties made it important to early research in electricity. In fact, the words *electric* and *electronic* derive from *elektron*, the Greek word for amber.

[4] This issue is treated in *Money Unmade: Barter and the Fate of Russian Capitalism*, by David M. Woodruff, Cornell University Press, 1999.

[5] What follows here summarizes, in very cursory fashion, "The Information Age and the Printing Press," by James A. Dewar (http://www.rand.org/publications/P/P8014/). Dewar, in turn, draws heavily on Elizabeth L. Eisenstein, *The Printing Press as an Agent of Change*, Cambridge University Press, New York (1979).

[6] Dewar, *op. cit.*

[7] Larry Ellison of Oracle helped to popularize this phrase, using it as the title of the Oracle Annual Report for 1998.

[8] Oracle had more than 2,000 servers in Europe alone, counting *only* servers with four or more CPUs each! In Canada and the United States, there were too many servers to count. At one point, the company removed servers to free up floor space; if nobody complained when a server went away, it would stay decommissioned.

[9] Oracle is moving to consolidate all its call centers into only three: one for the Americas, one for Asia and the Pacific, and one for EMEA.

[10] Translation requirements mean that this event cannot be instantaneous.

[11] The full text of this work appears at multiple places on the Internet—for instance, at http://www.bibliomania.com/NonFiction/Smith/Wealth/index.html.

[12] This paragraph draws on a survey of the world economy in *The Economist*, September 25, 1999.

[13] The DoC's position on PGP raises the specter of a Kafkaesque future in which governments all over the world would be stalking foreign nationals whose actions have been inconsistent with their laws. A visitor to Iran might find himself in court, listening to a judge declaiming (in Farsi) that ignorance of the law is no excuse.

[14] See http://www.ilr.cornell.edu/trianglefire/.

[15] Harry M. Caudill, *Night Comes to the Cumberlands*, Boston: Little Brown & Co., 1974.

[16] Rachel Carson, *Silent Spring*, New York: Houghton Mifflin, 1994.

[17] All implicit comparisons here are to conditions in the United States.

[18] www.netmarketmakers.com

[19] Owens Corning, for instance, is reported to have saved about $20 million on $200 million worth of goods purchased through FreeMarkets. However, FreeMarkets estimates its cumulative savings for customers at almost 20%.

[20] The B2B Market Maker Book, #5078, 3 February 2000.

[21] Thus far, most such exchanges have been oriented toward or even confined to U.S. businesses. However, a European venture was announced in January 2000 by SAP and Statoil of Norway, which combined to develop an exchange for equipment and services for the oil and gas industry. March 2000 saw the announcement of a collaboration between Cable & Wireless HKT and Oracle to set up an exchange for Chinese businesses across several industries.

[22] Major finds at Monte Verde, in Chile, beginning in 1977, have pushed back by about 1300 years (to about 11,000 B.C.E.) the earliest accepted presence of *Homo sapiens sapiens* in the New World.

[23] Employee counts taken from *The Standard* (http://www.thestandard.com/companies/), but updated in some cases from company Web sites.

[24] For pre-Internet companies, meaningful figures for this column may be unknowable.

[25] All prices quoted here have been adjusted for splits.

[26] Includes accessories and footwear.

[27] Includes specialty gifts and greeting cards.

[28] Includes appliances and furniture.

[29] In 2000, Cap Gemini acquired Ernst & Young's consulting organization for about $11 billion.

[30] In some cases, the concepts in question are protected by patents—which will delay their general adoption on the Web.

[31] Despite the mismatch between the process and its name, Amazon has successfully prosecuted competitors (including Barnes & Noble) for infringing its patent.

[32] On August 31, 2000, Nielsen/NetRatings reported that, for the month of July, Yahoo! ranked first in the world with 66 million unique visitors.

[33] *Business @ the Speed of Thought*, Bill Gates, New York: Warner Books, 1999.

[34] Emerging competitors include Apple, Sony, Symbian Ltd., and possibly manufacturers using Linux.

[35] Figures are derived from a study by International Data Corporation

[36] As a German company, SAP is exempt from the FTC's reporting standards and does not disclose its license revenues; hence the estimate.

[37] Oracle Services include the company's technical-education organization, which is the largest such commercial enterprise in the world.

[38] According to *Business Week*, July 10, 2000.

Index